FOREWORD BY JIMMY WHITE

JOHN VIRGO

Say Goodnight, JV

MY AUTOBIOGRAPHY

WITH DOUGLAS WIGHT

JOHN BLAKE

Published by John Blake Publishing,
2.25 The Plaza
535 Kings Road
Chelsea Harbour
London SW10 0SZ

www.johnblakebooks.com

www.facebook.com/johnblakebooks 🔲
twitter.com/jblakebooks 🔲

First published in hardback in 2017
Paperback edition first published in 2019

ISBN 978-1-78606-975-7

British Library Cataloguing-in-Publication Data:

A catalogue record for this book is available from the British Library.

Design by www.envydesign.co.uk

Printed and bound in Great Britain by Clays Ltd, Elcograf S.p.A.

1 3 5 7 9 10 8 6 4 2

Papers used by John Blake Publishing are natural, recyclable products made
from wood grown in sustainable forests. The manufacturing processes
conform to the environmental regulations of the country of origin.

Every reasonable effort has been made to trace copyright-holders of material
reproduced in this book, but if any have been inadvertently overlooked, the
publishers would be glad to hear from them.

John Blake Publishing is an imprint of Bonnier Books UK
www.bonnierbooks.co.uk

To the late Ted Lowe, MBE, my inspiration
in the commentary box.

CONTENTS

ACKNOWLEDGEMEMNTS

Richard Johnson – my friend and CEO of Bonnier Publishing without whom this book would never have happened.

Douglas Wight – for lending a patient ear to all my life stories. You make the whole experience a sheer pleasure.

Toby Buchan – editor extraordinaire; kind, patient and the best I have ever worked with. It was an honour...

John Blake, Rosie Virgo, Lizzie Dorney Kingdom, Graeme Andrew and all the team. Thank you for your hard work and enthusiasm.

Geoff Lomas – my great friend and confidant of forty-five years.

Des Ashley, who drove me everywhere in my amateur days and would never take a penny towards petrol – couldn't have done it without him.

Rocky Taylor – life would have been mundane without the moments we have shared.

Rodney Hutton – for introducing me to golf... not sure if it was a good thing!

Jim Davidson – for making the transition from snooker player to television that much easier, and for the philosophy 'If it's funny it's funny.'

Jimmy White, Ronnie O'Sullivan and the late Alex Higgins – for taking snooker to the limit and beyond.

Jason Francis – for giving me another lease of life touring with Snooker Legends and the laughs along the way.

Stan Holden – for his interest in me and getting me started.

Ray Reardon, MBE – the ultimate professional and the ultimate gentleman.

The BBC – for giving me opportunities I could only have dreamed of.

My sister Marjorie – thank you for all your help locating my childhood photographs, and for all the wonderful memories.

FOREWORD
by
JIMMY WHITE, MBE

It seems I've known JV all my life – particularly since winning the Amateur Championship in Cornwall in 1979, when I was sixteen. JV came along with our then manager, Henry West. It turned out to be a memorable year for me as I went on to win the World Amateur Championship in Tasmania as well, and it also happened to be the year that JV got to the semi-final of the World Snooker Championship and then, later that year, won the UK Championship. So you could say it was a special year in both of our lives.

We've always had a great friendship, although it was was nearly spoilt on a trip to Australia a few years later. It happened after a heavy night on the town in Sydney, where we had spent long hours in a bar drinking – I'm not sure how much but I am certain it was a lot! When we got back to the hotel, in my drunken wisdom, I decided to try and shock JV by appearing at his hotel bedroom window. The problem was that we were seven storeys up. But I was fearless and determined, so I climbed out from my balcony onto the ledge and made way next door to JV's balcony, and hammered on the window. I have never seen anyone look so shocked and horrified! He opened the window and hauled me in, where I landed in a heap on the floor – all the while he screamed 'What the hell do you think you are doing? You could have f***ing killed yourself.' He then went on to give me the biggest dressing down of my life. I've never forgotten it...

Apart from that incident we've never had a wrong word. When we were overseas in tournaments we never, ever dreamed of going out to dinner without him ringing me or me ringing him to ask what he was doing. Invariably we would go out for meals and laugh like lunatics.

Snooker on the road can be a very lonely life and nowadays when we do exhibitions together it's always good to know you are going to have a good time. When the *Snooker Legends* tour was launched, originally devised as a vehicle for myself and Alex Higgins, I told the promoter that the magic ingredient would be to have JV on board. We've now done over 200 shows – I've definitely called that one right!

Some people in the past have perceived JV as a bit grumpy, but – as people who know him will tell you – he's a very funny man and, as far as I am concerned, a friend for life.

I'm pleased to have been asked to write this foreword, and really look forward to reading his full story.

JIMMY WHITE, MBE

PROLOGUE:
THE BEST AND WORST
DAY OF MY LIFE

I woke early. My day of destiny had arrived.

Three years into my professional snooker career, just seven months after losing in the semifinal of the World Championship, here I was in the final of the game's second-most prestigious tournament – the UK Championship.

My opponent was the reigning world champion, Terry Griffiths, in a best-of-twenty-seven-frame final, the first to fourteen, played over three sessions. After two sessions yesterday, the final session would begin this afternoon, televised live on the BBC's flagship sports programme *Grandstand*.

When I had got back to my hotel on the Friday night I was feeling pleased with myself. I was playing some of the best snooker of my life and was leading 11–7 – just three frames away from my first major title.

My manager, Henry West, had suggested we stay in the hotel at the M6 services, ten miles away from Preston, to save money. Most of the other players were staying two minutes away from the Guild Hall, which hosted the tournament. Being removed from the action must have helped me.

Throughout the tournament the afternoon sessions had begun at 1.45 p.m., so my plan was try to relax and time it so I wasn't at the venue too early. There were no practice tables and I didn't want to be hanging about, getting anxious. At the same time I didn't want to be rushing for what was the most important day of my snooker career so far.

I had a shower and looked out my evening suit.

At 11.50 a.m. the phone in my room rang. It was the tournament director, Peter Hatherell. 'John, where are you?'

I told him I was at the hotel.

'We start at twelve noon,' he said.

'What?' I was horrified.

I hadn't checked the start time for the final session. I hadn't even thought to check that it might be different from every other afternoon session of the tournament.

Panic set in.

Fortunately, I'd showered but I threw my clothes on and raced from the hotel. So much for my calm preparations. I spent the twenty-minute, ten-mile journey fretting that I was late. We arrived in the town centre to find it busy with the usual Saturday-afternoon traffic. I reached the municipal car park at 12.25 p.m. and ran through to the venue.

When I reached the Guild Hall, ashen-faced and breathless, the first person I saw was the promoter, Mike Watterson.

'I regret to inform you, John, that you have to forfeit two frames for your late arrival,' he said.

I couldn't believe it. Somewhere deep in the snooker rulebook it states that the penalty for being late in a tournament is one frame for the first twenty minutes and then another frame for every ten minutes after that. It was a rule that had never been enforced – until today.

'No one told me,' I said, shaking.

'Leave this to me,' Henry said, and stormed upstairs.

Instead of being 11–7 in front, without hitting a ball, I was only leading 11–9. My day of destiny was turning into a nightmare.

When we eventually went into the arena to start that final session, I was introduced to widespread booing from the audience. I could understand their frustration at having to wait, but surely they could understand I hadn't done it on purpose.

To play under those circumstances was nearly impossible. Still shaking, I lost the first two frames. Now, as we headed into the interval, it was all-square.

Back in the dressing room it was mayhem. Henry West was threatening to sue everybody in the game. My head was in bits. So many negative thoughts I could do without.

Amid the chaos, Terry Griffiths came in, looking sympathetic. 'I don't want to win like this,' he said. 'Do you want to split the money?'

That was the last straw.

I wasn't there for the money. I was there for the title. He had his. I knew Terry's offer was genuine but I replied, 'You've not won this yet.'

After the interval I somehow managed to win a scrappy frame to at least put me on the board for the day. I now led 12–11.

During the next frame a strange thing happened. The television cameras were still in their position but there were no operators behind them. They looked like still Daleks in a scene from *Doctor Who*. After that frame, which Griffiths won to tie the match once more, we were told the BBC had gone on strike. I couldn't help but wonder whether, if I had arrived on time, the match would have been over by now.

I was thinking a million things. Why was I late? Why hadn't I checked the time? It was the first time anyone had been docked frames and it had to be me. My head swirled with all the consequences of losing from that winning position.

Griffiths won the next frame to lead 13–12, just one away from victory. With everything that was going on around me I was convinced I was beat. I thought of my dad. Thanks to him and a snooker table he bought me when I was eight years old I'd fallen in love with the game. He'd then banned me from playing in the snooker clubs, convinced they were dens of iniquity and rat pens that attracted the worst kind of people. He'd been quietly proud when I won the Boys' Championship and then the Youth title. Sadly, he'd died before I turned professional but, a day earlier, when I'd raced into that commanding lead, I'd wondered what he would have thought of my winning a major honour. And now, as I stared defeat in the face, I could only think that at least he'd been spared witnessing this humiliation.

I don't know whether being resigned to defeat relaxed me but when the balls were racked for the next frame I felt calmer. I somehow managed to complete a break of fifty. I can't recall how I managed to pot the balls. It was as if I were operating from memory. I won the frame to take the match into a decider.

This was it. Do or die. Redemption or confirmation that I'd blown my biggest chance of glory. The frame was a blur. How I managed to stay composed to strike the cue properly I'll never know.

I can remember the emotions as I lined up each pot. One

red down. That was for my old boss, who never thought I'd amount to anything. Another red. I recalled the anger I felt when I was written off in the Boys' final as a teenager. The gap between Terry and me was widening. As the balls went in his chances of a comeback were dwindling.

There was no record break, no spectacular clearance. However, each time I came to the table I managed to build on my lead.

Finally I was on frame ball. The moment the cue ball connected I knew it was in.

I had done it! I was the 1979 UK snooker champion!

I've never known such elation. It was like waking up from a bad dream. I unashamedly started crying and ran around the table like a headless chicken.

When I was presented with the trophy, for a moment I felt a tinge of regret. Not only was my father not able to witness his son's triumph, but also the BBC strike meant that no one was watching those final moments on television. There would be no clip to show my mother or son, or any future grandchildren. A British sporting occasion lost in time.

I lifted the trophy and those thoughts disappeared. I just felt relief.

It was the best and worst day of my life.

★ ★ ★

After our battle in the UK Championship, Terry and I were booked to do a tour of universities in Britain. With the two of us holding major titles, we played to packed venues. When we played a couple of shows in Wales, Terry kindly invited me to stay at his house in Llanelli. His wife, Annette, made me feel very welcome. Terry also had a snooker room in his house, and we would practise together. As I have told many people when they ask how I get on with other players, I reply that we have lived a life together and get on fine.

That was proved when I was staying at Terry's house: I woke up in the morning and there he was washing my car.

His reason for this, he explained, was that, since he won the World Championship, the local bus would stop outside the house and the driver would announce, 'This is the house of Terry Griffiths.' My dirty car on the drive would not look good. I have to say he did an excellent job.

CHAPTER 1

THE BLACK HORSE

SALFORD, 1946

Whenever I say I come from Salford, the response is nearly always the same. 'Ah, yes, Manchester.' No, I say, not Manchester. Salford is its own city, with its own identity, its own heartbeat and rhythm. And it's where, on 4 March 1946, I was born, in the front room of Number 3 Robertson Street, Salford 5.

The timing was significant. I arrived almost exactly ten months after VE Day, the end of World War Two. The elation at the cessation of five long years of fighting must have reached this little terraced house – the type you'd see on *Coronation Street* – because I was something of a surprise. For William and Florence Virgo to have a child at their age – my father was forty-four, my mother in her late thirties – was practically unheard of. I can only imagine the war was over and they got carried away.

When I was born my brother Bill was eighteen. His wife

would give birth to my nephew, John, just a year after I came along. I also had three sisters, Marjorie, Barbara and Dorothy. My mother had given birth to a fourth daughter, Joan, before I was born but, tragically, she died when she was only three years old. My mother said to my sisters she couldn't believe she was pregnant, but she used to say that, once she saw my beautiful little face, she knew what a pleasant surprise I'd been.

It wasn't as if we had room for another mouth to feed. My brother might have been all grown up but from my birth until the age of seven I slept with my parents. My sisters shared the one other bedroom. Downstairs we had three rooms – a parlour, kitchen and scullery. There was no bathroom. The toilet was outside, with cut-up newspaper on a piece of string attached to a nail for loo roll. The tin bath was kept on a hook in the backyard and there was no hot and cold running water. If you wanted to use the toilet you took a bucket of water with you.

This was a time when rationing was still very much in force. It would be another two years before the first restrictions on bread would be relaxed and a further eight years before rationing would end for good.

I don't know how my mother did it. She didn't have access to half the luxuries we take for granted today, yet she always seemed to have a smile on her face. She was simply the loveliest woman I have ever known, quick to laugh and utterly devoted to her family.

Her relatives all hailed from the Salford area and her brothers were all singers, so some of my earliest memories are of music and laughter in the house. You made your own entertainment in those days. We didn't have a television – not many people did – but we did have a radio and I remember huddling around it to listen to Radio Luxembourg, the first station to play popular music. Our claim to fame was that the first record David Jacobs played on his show was one my sister Barbara had requested – a tune by Eddie Fisher, the singer who went on to marry Debbie Reynolds and became the father of the late *Star Wars* actress Carrie Fisher. I don't think it was Barbara's choice – it was probably my father's – but she had her name read out on air. The family were very excited.

The other time we crowded round the radio was when my brother was on *Opportunity Knocks*, which was a big hit on the radio before it found its way onto television. The winner was decided on a 'clapometer' and he finished runner-up to two comedians. My dad said the only reason they beat him was that they'd done a song at the end by Flanagan and Allen, the comic duo who'd become popular during the war.

All my mother's brothers were singers and they used to get paid by pubs to go in and sing there at the weekend. My brother did the same and he even used to take his own pianist with him sometimes.

Every Sunday we had two papers delivered, the *Sunday People* and the *News of the World*. During the week we had the paper delivered and with it a comic, such as the *Dandy* and the *Beano* or later the *Topper*. I was raised on Dennis the Menace and Desperate Dan. My sisters used to get *Girl*. When I think back, it's amazing that we could afford them – these were our luxuries.

The only house in the street to have a television in those early days was Mrs London's. She put it in the parlour window. It was round about 4.30 p.m. and my friends and I would gather outside and peer in to watch *The Cisco Kid*, with his trusty sidekick Pancho. That was until Mrs London would catch us staring in and crossly close the curtains.

In those postwar years, money was still tight, but my

parents found ways to get by. Mum would always go to the corner shop next door. The one disadvantage to living so close to a convenience store was that we invariably had mice coming through. We were always putting mousetraps down. Mum would go out at six o'clock and be in there until eight o'clock at night before coming back with two cardboard boxes. We didn't have a fridge or anything, so it amazes me how we managed in those days. One of the things that astound me today is when you hear people complaining that they're struggling, yet they seem to find the money to shower children with the latest mobile phones and gadgets. Items that were considered luxuries in my day, such as televisions and fridges, it took us years to attain. We were always among the last in the street to get them. Back then, maybe people lived more within their means. Otherwise, you wouldn't have survived.

How my mother managed to feed us and have a hot meal every day of the week is beyond me. After rationing ended, we had a roast on a Saturday and all the family would come round for another roast on the Sunday. I could tell you every meal we had every night of the week. It was always fish on a Friday. There was no waste. If you had a ham shank one day you made soup from the leftovers. My mother seemed like a miracle worker.

We may not have had a television then, but my brother did. We would go round to his house in Croydon Street on a Saturday afternoon and watch it. When the street parties were held across the nation for the Queen's coronation, the cameras came to Robertson Street. There was a clip of me standing against the wall by the parlour window, posing like a little James Dean. It was only a fleeting glance but I was pointing excitedly: 'There I am.' It was the first time I'd seen myself on TV.

My father was born in Hereford but his family were from Newport in South Wales. They must have moved for work and Salford Docks, where my father was a crane driver, was a place with guaranteed work. I'm often asked where the name Virgo comes from. I've traced my family tree but the exact origins are unclear. My wife Rosie's mother is convinced it's Portuguese, and certainly a lot came over to Britain in years gone by, so some must have landed in Wales.

My father earned £9.50 a week and that money had to go a long way, put food on the table, clothe us and pay for the bills. It meant there wasn't a lot left over. He didn't go to the pub. His life was his wife and his children and supporting them with everything he had. If they handed out medals for that he would have had a chest full.

Two of my father's passions, however, were football and horseracing, and you didn't have to go far from our front door to experience the best of both sports. Within a two-minute walk you were on Eccles New Road, which led to the crossroads of Trafford Road, Regent Road and Cross Lane. Stowell Memorial Church, where I was christened, was on the corner. All that's left now is a spire. Going down Trafford Road, over the swing bridge, turning right and a next left would take you to Warwick Road, now Sir Matt Busby Way, and the home of Manchester United, the team my father would introduce me to and the club I've supported since before I can remember. Take the Number 71 bus up Cross Lane, do a left, at the top turn right at Pendleton Church and you were just a couple of stops from Manchester Racecourse, again an arena that would give this young child a glimpse of another world.

Notice everything is prefixed Manchester? It's no wonder Salford has always had a bit of an identity problem.

There have been a few people from Salford of whom you may have heard: Albert Finney, the world-renowned actor who bought a betting shop for his father; *Lovejoy* star Ian McShane, whose father once played for Manchester United, had a newsagent's next to the tripe shop on Eccles New Road, near Cross Lane; and my favourite folk singer, Ewan MacColl, not just because he came from Salford, but because he wrote classics such as 'Manchester Rambler', 'Dirty Old Town' and perhaps his most famous, 'The First Time Ever I Saw Your Face', the song my wife Rosie and I had played at our wedding.

It was an incredible area in which to grow up. Salford Docks was a target for the German Luftwaffe during the war and the streets near our house bore the scars of those bombing raids. Where the building had been demolished, the rubble was cleared to create a 'croft' or rough patch of ground where my friends and I would play football, cricket and even rugby. That said, although we much preferred the proper rugby league code – not the southern union version – all we could play was touch rugby as no one fancied tackling on hard ground.

On the outskirts of Manchester was Belle Vue, a zoo and funfair, where every year a circus was held. It was a special place for young kids and another early memory was when we all went there and, amazingly, they were offering children the chance to have a ride on an elephant. I remember pulling at my father, asking, 'Have you got any money left? I want a ride on the elephant.' It was probably threepence a ride – just over a penny in decimal money. There was a big saddle, with children stacked up on both sides. I was the last one on, so the keeper let me sit on the neck of the elephant. Can you imagine that happening today? I loved it.

THE BLACK HORSE

★ ★ ★

The first school I went to was Stowell Memorial Infant School, and then to Trafford Road Boys School, down the road from the docks, which were only ten minutes from our house.

I would never stay at school for lunch. My mother would always cook a meal for my father, so a choice between school dinners and her cooking? No contest.

After lunch my mother would sometimes say, 'Your dad's left this.' She'd give me a folded piece of paper, which I knew contained money, usually four shilling pieces (20 pence), for his little wager for the day – his best three doubles and a shilling treble.

I knew what I had to do. On my way back to school I made a detour, down a lane, in an opened backyard door, towards a small shed on the left-hand side.

I never saw the face of the man inside. A hand would appear; he'd take the bet. There was no receipt, no bookie's slip, just an understanding a bet had been placed.

Then it was off to school as usual. I'd run off, pretending to be riding one of the great horses of the day.

If Dad's horse won, I never collected the winnings. The only sign I got that his luck was in was when my mother said, 'We're going to Manchester Saturday morning. You need a new jacket.'

One day I was in class in the afternoon dreaming of what treat might be in store should my father's horse come in when I slipped my hand into my pocket. My blood ran cold. I didn't need to pull it out. I could feel the money wrapped in paper. I had forgotten to put the bet on.

My first instinct was to run out of class and back to the bookies. But, when I looked around at all my classmates opening their books and the teacher starting to scribble something on the blackboard, I knew I couldn't.

Just thinking about the consequences made me shiver. What happens if they all win? He will kill me. It just built up and up. It could be the biggest win he'd ever had, I thought.

After the longest afternoon of my life I trudged home slowly, not running as I usually did. I did the only thing I could: I told my mother immediately.

'Let's hope they don't win,' she said, with an air of resignation. But she added, trying to smile, 'They don't often.'

When father came home I hid in the kitchen. I listened as he put the radio on to hear the results. I couldn't bear the tension. As soon as they'd finished my mother said, 'Any luck?'

This wasn't the norm but clearly she couldn't stand the agony either.

'No luck,' my father said.

Overjoyed, I ran in all excited and gave him the piece of paper with the money in it. 'Well you didn't lose.'

I thought he would be pleased. Not a bit of it. He gave me a right rollicking. He couldn't tell me anything with regard to what would have happened if they had all won. I'd spent the afternoon in class working that one out. But the main lesson was that, if you are given a job to do, even though you are only six years old, then do it.

I never forgot again.

★ ★ ★

My father wasn't a compulsive gambler. He didn't bet beyond his means. He was just hoping that his bet would come up and give us a bit of extra cash – the means to buy his children new shoes, jackets and trousers.

It was the working-class mentality, I believe. Would you rather go out to the pub being able to afford only a couple of pints, or have that money on a bet? If it won you could have a good night out. If it lost, you stayed in. What was the difference?

Gambling is a recreation that is frowned upon by a lot of people. My father was able to restrain himself, but living in this environment encourages a culture of chance.

It was into this culture that I was brought up. And, even if you resist, it can suck you in. As I was about to realise when one day, out of the blue, Dad informed me that on the forthcoming Saturday we would be going to Manchester Racecourse, or Castle Irwell at it was also known. I was about to enter the real world.

I could sense the excitement the moment we stepped aboard the Number 71 bus. Everybody, it seemed, was reading the *Sporting Chronicle*, the only racing paper at the time. 'Kettledrum' was the pseudonym of Quintin Gilbey, the feature writer, and my father said he was a good judge, so whatever his headline tip was had to be respected.

The conductor, trying to walk down the aisle shouting, 'Fares, please', could hardly move for the broadsheets fanned out from the seats. The jingle of money, the rustle of papers, the chattering of opinions – the excitement was starting to build. When we arrived at the course the atmosphere was electric. It seemed that everybody was letting on to my father. He had never mentioned it before but he had done some clerking for one of the bookmakers some years before and a number of his pals from the docks were there. Perhaps taking me was an excuse to start going again.

Apart from the donkeys at Blackpool sands and the one pulling the rag and bone man's cart, the only horses I had seen were at the cinema. Going to the racecourse didn't bring the horses much closer mind you. Not at first. We couldn't afford to go into the Tattersalls enclosure, the largest section with some good views of the finishing post, so our place was in the silver ring, which stopped about a furlong from the winning post.

Back then the course had a commentary over the Tannoy but, when the horses got to the last fifty yards, it stopped, and then, a minute later, the result would be announced.

This strange idea was to show me the dark side of gambling.

My first experience came and went in a flash, but after that initial taste I couldn't wait to go again.

To say I pestered my dad was an understatement. Eventually, one Sunday, he told me that there was a meeting on the following Saturday and, weather permitting, we would go. 'Weather permitting' was always a proviso at Manchester Racecourse. This was because it ran so close to the River Irwell. Even on the best of days you could have mist that put racing in jeopardy.

Even though it was a week away, it was so exciting. In the *Sunday People* there was a tipster called 'Pegasus' and every week he'd name his best tip for the coming days. I couldn't believe he could pick a potential winner that far in advance but, to my further amazement, that morning his tip of the week was for Manchester the coming Saturday. It was called The Black Horse. I showed the paper to my father: 'Have you seen this, Dad? Pegasus fancies The Black Horse for Saturday.'

My father glanced at the paper and raised an eyebrow, nodded and said he would check it out.

Needless to say, every night at teatime (we never called it dinner) I would mention The Black Horse and ask my father, 'Are you going to back The Black Horse, then?' Just to keep me

16

quiet, he said he would. If he said he would then I believed him.

Come the day of the races I was up very early, looking out my window to see if it was clear. It was! We were off for a day at the races. It was going to be only my second time, but I remember everything.

As had happened on the first visit, friends of my father were chatting to him about what they fancied. Side-of-the-mouth Sids, they were, because they sidled up and whispered out of the corner of their mouths. One guy said he fancied a horse called Dingo. My father agreed. To my horror, when I looked at the race card I saw that it was running in the same race as The Black Horse.

'Dad, Dad,' I said, agitated. 'Dingo's in the same race as The Black Horse. I thought you said you were going to back that one.'

He sighed, looked at the card.

'It's OK,' he said. 'Don't worry. We'll still back your horse.'

For me to get a good view of the race my dad put an outstretched arm on the top railing and I sat on it so I could see the horses. I couldn't wait for the race to start. We could hear from the commentary that The Black Horse was running well. When they passed with a furlong to go The Black Horse was about a length in front, but Dingo was challenging on its outside.

I could hear the commentary: 'As they come towards the last fifty yards Dingo's taken it up and gone a length clear . . .'

Silence.

The commentary, as was the custom, stopped before the finish. Who had won?

I looked at my father. His face told me the answer.

'What am I doing listening to a seven-year-old?' he spat, real anger in his voice. 'I don't know.' He shook his head. 'That was the horse I fancied and I didn't back it because of you. What am I doing listening to you? What do you know about horses? Well, it serves me right.'

He had shouted at me before but this was different. Money was involved. I felt dreadful.

Suddenly the Tannoy sparked back into life.

'Here is the result. First: The Black Horse.'

It was as though the world stopped revolving. How could this be? Dingo had passed him with only fifty yards to go.

Both of us were so stunned we didn't listen to the second and third. If we had done, then we would have realised that Dingo wasn't even in the first three. Word soon came back that he had broken down with just twenty-five yards to go and that allowed The Black Horse to get back up.

I don't know what happened to poor old Dingo. I don't remember any announcement, but why would there be?

In that ten-to-fifteen-second delay I saw a completely different side to my father. I saw how gambling could affect people. I should have realised then how easy it was for the darker side to reveal itself. Instead, I left the racecourse believing my first experience of a bet at the races was brilliant. Although my dad probably had only a small wager on The Black Horse, it had won! It wasn't the money that mattered: it was backing a winner. My heart was jumping. What a feeling!

Something inside me had stirred. Racing would become a passion that brought me unbelievable highs – and spirit-crushing lows.

What I didn't know at the time was that my father would introduce me to two other sports that would shape my life in ways I daren't think possible.

CHAPTER 2

THE DEN OF INIQUITY

Christmas Morning 1954 was a big day. Obviously, I had no idea how significant a moment it would be, but that was the day I came downstairs to find my first and very own snooker table.

My interest in the sport had been sparked previously by a broken cue my mother used to unfasten an airing rack that hung from the ceiling. My father had played the game and I was curious to know how to play it. Now I was going to find out.

It was six foot by three foot and didn't have legs of its own. It lay over the dining table. We put bits of cardboard underneath. From the moment I started playing, I loved it – the feel of the green baize, the click of the balls. As it was winter, my father would bring a shovel of coal and dump it in the fireplace in the parlour whenever he wanted a game. Every Friday, my brother came round and we would knock about and play some frames together. I was so happy, hanging out with the two of them.

All of a sudden, one Friday night, I racked up the balls as usual and asked my father, 'What time's our Bill coming round?'

'Oh,' he said, 'I don't think he'll be coming round now.'

'Why not?' I couldn't understand it. I thought we were all having fun.

It turned out Bill had ordered the table out of one of his wife's catalogues, paying it off at half a crown (12.5 pence) a week. After a few weeks, my father had paid him the money for it, so, once it was all paid up, there was no need for my brother to come round any more. I was absolutely gutted. Friday night had been my big night. I used to ask Dad for a game but, more often than not, I had to play by myself and invent some player, and I'd take on Joe Davis, the most famous snooker player in the world at the time and the man who had won the first fifteen World Championships from 1927 to 1946. He was no match for me, however. I beat Joe Davis more times on that table than you'd believe!

Just as a kid's imagination runs away, I remember dreaming about playing in the big tournaments and tried to picture what it would be like to win a major title.

Another exciting day came a few months later when we finally got our first television, from Radio Rentals. It had the worst picture in the world, all grainy and in black and white, but it gave us something different from crowding around a radio, and, if we weren't able to make the racing at Manchester, now we could watch some on the TV.

My father's interest in snooker may have been erratic but his loyalty to Manchester United was unwavering. I was desperate for him to take me to Old Trafford so I could finally sample the atmosphere for myself and in 1955 my dreams came true.

He was taking me to my first match.

It was 1 October and the visitors were Luton Town, newly promoted from the Second Division. I knew the names of most of the players but, funnily enough, the ones I always remembered were the goalkeepers. That's because I used to get *Charles Buchan's Football Monthly*, the magazine edited by the former Sunderland player. The only players he seemed to have photos of were the goalies. I don't know if it was because they provided the best action shots, but that's why I can remember distinctly the Luton goalkeeper was Ron Baynham.

We got there early and my father positioned us right on the railing. The crowd that day was over thirty-four thousand, nothing like the crowds today at Old Trafford, but it could be dangerous when people pushed forward. It was only just a picket fence in those days before health-and-safety concerns became a big issue.

It was amazing to see the players I idolised in the flesh. United ran out 3–1 winners, thanks to two goals from star striker Tommy Taylor, on their way to winning the title that year. It was the start of the famous Busby Babes, the team of young players moulded by Matt Busby who lit up English football.

As there was no racing on television at the time, or very little, Saturday afternoons watching Manchester United were special. Like all young lads, you know your team, but there was something about that United team that seemed to roll off the tongue: Wood, Foulkes, Byrne, Colman, Jones, Edwards, Berry, Whelan, Taylor, Viollet, Pegg. To this day it still sounds like the perfect team.

After that first game I was allowed to go to matches on my own, even though I was still only nine years old. These days you wouldn't dream about it. Two years after my first game, in 1957, they erected floodlights at Old Trafford. Stepping outside our house, you could see the lights from the stadium. Prior to that you could just see the big buildings at the docks. You could even hear the big roar when they scored, and, when you realise it's a couple of miles away, it's amazing that noise travels that far.

Not only did Manchester United take the title in 1956, but they followed it up with another a year later. They were aiming for three in a row and were in the semifinals of the European Cup when in February 1958 the plane returning them from a match in Belgrade crashed on take-off following a refuelling stop in Munich. Eight players died in the tragedy, including Tommy Taylor, whose heroics I'd witnessed for the first time just two years earlier. The aftermath of the disaster was a bleak time for the club and it took a long time for the team and the city to recover.

That was all in the years to come, however. Although I was honing my skills on the snooker table at home, my two big passions were watching the horseracing and Manchester United. And they both clashed on a day that would go down in history in April 1956.

The stage was set some months before, on a damp and murky autumn day at Manchester Racecourse. On this particular Saturday the big race was a three-mile steeplechase. My father's fancy was a horse called Sundew. He thought it would win but accepted that the distance might be a bit short for it. Dad was already backing it for the Grand National in the coming spring, as it was one of the best jumpers he had ever seen.

That day Sundew was ridden by Fred Winter. His main rival was a horse called ESB, ridden by Dave Dick. The two horses set off in the lead, jumping every fence stride for stride. They were still level as they jumped the last, but ESB had a little more speed on the run in than Sundew. Although, as per usual, we didn't get the commentary for the last fifty yards, it was obvious which horse was going to win. My father had backed a loser but he was philosophical about it.

'Not far enough,' he said, 'but he will beat that horse at Aintree.'

The home of the Grand National was owned and run by Mrs Mirabel Topham, who even I knew back then was a law unto herself and refused to have the race televised. As I wasn't able to watch the race – to see if my father's faith in Sundew was going to be rewarded – I went to Old Trafford. My dad stayed at home to listen to the race on the radio, but that wasn't for me.

Even while I was at the game, however, my mind was wandering to the events at Aintree. There were few transistor radios in those days, so nobody around me would come up with the result. Halfway through the match, as the players were making their way to the tunnel, I heard the click of the Tannoy.

'Here is the result of the Grand National,' the announcer said. 'First, ESB, second was Gental Moya, third was Royal Tan.'

Sundew wasn't mentioned. Before the players came out for the second half I was halfway down Trafford Road on my way home. I just had to know what happened to my dad's horse.

My father was surprised when I walked through the door. He knew the match hadn't finished but, before he had time to ask I got in first. 'What happened in the National?'

'It was unbelievable,' he said. 'The Queen Mother's horse, Devon Loch, was well clear on the run-in and fell.'

I wasn't really listening properly. 'But what happened to Sundew?' I said.

'He fell at Beechers,' Dad said, I think now realising that I wasn't interested in the demise of the Queen Mother's horse. Then he asked me about the football.

It had been one of the defining moments in Grand National history – Devon Loch inexplicably collapsing while well clear, ridden by Dick Francis, who would go on to become a best-selling author – and I had missed it.

The next day all the headlines were about this horse that had jumped every fence, had the race at his mercy and sprawled to the ground one hundred yards from the finish. Theory has it that he saw the water jump on the other side of the rail and tried to jump it, causing him to finish up flat on his tummy. As the Queen Mother herself said afterwards, that's racing. Apart from all the sad pictures of Devon Loch, ESB had won the race, the horse that had just beaten Sundew at Manchester. Surely, if he had stood up he would have won the race.

A year later, the Grand National was run on a Friday, because, my father said, Mrs Topham wanted to put the television companies in their place.

'Let's hope Fred Winter can stay on him this time,' my father said. He was backing Sundew once more.

I was so desperate to hear what happened, I convinced my mother I was too unwell to go to school. Listening to the Grand National on the radio wasn't perfect but I needn't have worried. Sundew jumped like a stag. He was one of the few horses to have led all the way and won the Grand National.

Later that year, after a fall at a water jump at Nottingham, he had to be put down. Ironically, he had jumped all the big fences round Aintree, yet one of the smallest caught him out, a bit like Devon Loch. Both horses went into the history books, although the Queen Mother's horse is remembered more than Sundew.

Not in our family, however. My dad backed him at 20–1. I got treated and he certainly lit up our lives for a time. Most of all, my dad was right – he was a great jumper and would win a National. Good judge, my old man.

Aside from these big days, however, there were regular reminders that money was tight. When I was around eleven years old my school organised a trip to Westward Ho! seaside village near Bideford, in Devon. The trip cost £3.50. The teacher said we needed to have the money in by a certain date but I wanted to have it in immediately. I went home and said to my dad, 'Can I have the three pound, ten shillings, please?'

His face fell. 'Oh, OK,' he said, then he added, 'I haven't got it.'

'What do you mean you haven't got it?' I was concerned I wasn't going to be able to go.

'Listen,' he said, 'if I have to carry you there on my back you're going. But just give me some time.'

It was a lot of money. I assumed he would have it but he didn't. It was the first time I realised you couldn't just go out and buy something.

I had only one pair of trousers a year, one pair of shoes. A man called Freddie Westbrook used to come round on a Friday night. I thought he was my uncle at first but he was the guy who collected the money for the clothing company.

By this time I'd sat the eleven-plus exam but none of us took it seriously. We had it drummed into us that you left school at fifteen so you could start contributing to the household. While I was at Old Trafford School, people would smoke in the back row of the class. That was one of the great dares. I never smoked then, but the other kids were sneaking one behind a book. Even when I started attending Ordsall Secondary Modern, there was no real push for us to achieve any qualifications. Exams were considered a bit of a joke.

* * *

One evening when I was thirteen I went out to the croft to see who was about for a game of football or cricket. There was nobody there. I went round and knocked on the door of a friend called Alan Hayward, or Chinner, as we all knew him.

'Oh,' his mother said, 'he's gone to the billiard hall.' I knew the place she was talking about. It was on Small Street. Nobody called them snooker clubs back then.

The next day I saw Chinner and asked him what it was like. He said it was great, but you had to be a member. It was seven and a half pence in today's money, not a lot but still more than I had. To get the money I tried the same way I would if I wanted to go to the pictures: I asked my mum. She shook her head. 'Your father doesn't want you setting foot in that place. He thinks it's a den of iniquity.'

I knew it must be serious because my dad never used words like that. I didn't even know what 'den of iniquity', meant but it must be bad.

Anyway, after a couple of nights of my coming straight home from school and moping round the house because none of my friends were around to play, she relented and gave me some bottles to take back to the off-licence. They weren't alcohol but any bottle had a refund on it. At two pence a bottle, taking four bottles back meant I could become a member.

The snooker clubs sprang up around the time of the general

strike in 1926. They were originally called Temperance Billiard Halls. You couldn't serve alcohol in them but they were places to keep the unemployed happy. It was a bit like giving them a leisure centre and there were quite a few around the Greater Manchester area, of which the Riley billiard hall in Small Street was one.

Although I had enough to become a member, I didn't have any left over to play an actual game. I didn't care, though. I was just desperate to see inside one of these clubs.

It didn't disappoint. I can still remember the feeling today. It felt as though I were entering another world. The dim lighting over the tables, which seemed huge compared with the little one I played on back home. Everything was bigger – the balls, the cues. The sound of the balls clicking on the sixteen tables was hypnotic. I fell in love with the place immediately.

That first night I met up with my friends but, as I had no money, I just sat and watched them play, drinking it all in. After each game I would watch them pay each other out, only half a crown (or twelve and a half pence). If ever I was going to play in this club I needed money. In the meantime I would play with my pals. We could afford to play for only half an hour. But whoever lost would have to pay for the lights. At the time I never really noticed but I didn't have to pay for the lights that many times. I was itching to play some of the better players but to do so I needed some money.

My chance came one Saturday afternoon when I was studying the racing pages in the paper and spotted a horse I was sure was worth a bet. The horse was called Aggressor, ridden by Jimmy Lindley, running in the King George VI and Queen Elizabeth Stakes at Ascot. It was 25–1, but the reason he was such a big price was that the favourite, Petite Etoile, was ridden by Lester Piggott. Before the race, Lester described the filly as 'the best I have ever ridden'. My father had already gone to place his bet, so I told my mother. Aggressor pulled off the race of his life – and my mother and I had a sixpence-each-way winner. I couldn't wait to get to the billiard hall with my winnings.

One of the most popular games on the tables in Small Street was golf, where four people could play. The rules of the game were simple: you had two balls, a white and a red. If you can imagine looking down the table from the 'D', the top left pocket was the first hole, top right the second, the middle pocket on your right the third hole, the bottom pocket on your right the fourth, on your left the fifth and middle left the sixth and final hole. You had to go around the six pockets on the table. If you made a foul you would go back a hole. Whoever potted their ball in that pocket first was the winner. Apart from the fact that four people could play at the same time, it was also a gambling game. It was over a lot quicker than a frame of snooker and you were getting 3–1 on your money.

I went in that night, my pockets bulging – well, for me anyway. I sat and watched the others play. Eventually, one of the players dropped out. Nervously, I asked if I could make the four up, quickly adding that I had money. Aggressor's great victory over Petite Etoile and the elation I'd felt with my mother was soon a distant memory when, after about twenty minutes, all my money had gone. Nerves had got the better of me. My pals had all been watching, most wondering where I had got the money from to play with the big boys. I wasn't that upset: I had played in the big school and, but for missing a couple of easy shots, might have stayed in the game a bit

longer. It wasn't playing for the money that made me miss –
just the opposite. It was money that made it possible.

From then on I was in the billiard hall every night. There
was no more playing on the croft. I had found a sport that was
filling my senses like no other, even horseracing.

I had been going into the billiard hall for about nine months.
My father wasn't an idiot. I am sure he knew but he never said
anything. I wasn't really doing anything wrong. I was going to
school, was home for tea and came back home no later than
nine o'clock. Those were the unwritten rules, whether I had
been going to play snooker or any other pastime.

I was introduced to a number of characters in those first few
months. One of them was Alf Knight. His claim to fame was
that he had never done a day's work in his life. I later found
out that he would make his money tipping at the horses or the
dogs. His tactic was simple on the dogs: he gave six people
one name each. The hard part was remembering whom he had
given the winning name to – and then hoping the lucky punter
slipped him some of his winnings for his trouble. He once
found a tomato that was the exact same shape and colour as a
red snooker ball. When he set the balls up he put the tomato in
among them and for all the world it looked like a regular ball
until someone hit it and it went splat, all over the table. That
little stunt earned him a ban for two months.

That was the only downside to the place. The manager,
Mark, was a giant of a man who always wore a trilby. He
laid down the rules – no whistling, no playing without the
lights and no running about. Not to follow those rules and any
other he might have forgotten to mention meant immediate
expulsion.

Another character was Jack Scholes. Being so young, I didn't have a lot in common with most of the men who went to the club. Jack Scholes was an exception. Sometimes if you didn't have much money he would be happy to have a social game, one with no bet.

One night, however, he challenged six of us to play him one game each. If any one of us could beat him he would pay for the lights; if not, then we would pay. I was improving but Jack was one of the better players in the club. Despite this, we convinced ourselves that one of us could beat him.

Snooker was a bit different in those days. Hundred breaks were very rarely made. Six frames of snooker took quite a long time. One by one my friends lost their matches. I was up last. I put up a decent fight but, although I came closest to winning, we had to pay up.

When I looked at the clock I couldn't believe it. It was 10.20 p.m. The time had flown by. I ran home all the way but, as soon as I arrived, panting, I knew I was in trouble. The smack round the side of my head confirmed that. My father had never hit me before. 'Don't you ever go in there again,' he scolded.

I remember catching a glimpse of my mother. I know she didn't want him to hit and shout at me but he was teaching me a lesson. They were just worried where a schoolboy could be at that time. And he knew the sorts of characters who frequented these clubs. They were usually the unemployed, the chancers, people on the make.

It was a harsh lesson. I was barred from ever going to the club again.

My snooker dreams looked finished for ever.

CHAPTER 3

BRIGHT LIGHTS, BIG CITY

Crawling through the grass leopard style, we were trying to keep out of sight of enemy fighters. As we edged forward I felt something snag. I was stuck. It was my belt. It was caught in the long grass. If I could just get up to free it . . .

Ra-ta-tat-tat, ra-ta-tat-tat!

I guess I wouldn't have been very good in the army. The rattling signified a Bren light machine gun. I'd have been a goner. In reality, it was two cups rattled together to mimic the sound. But my participation in this mock battle, staged in a field near Rhyl in North Wales, was as good as over.

After being barred from the billiard hall, I needed to find somewhere else to go. So I joined the army cadets, who were based further up Cross Lane.

It was great, walking out of the house looking like an actual soldier, proudly wearing the black beret with the yellow hackle, which signified the Lancashire Fusiliers. The regiment was famous for 'Six VCs before breakfast', which was how the newspapers had reported its heroics during World War One, when half a dozen soldiers were awarded the Victoria Cross for their bravery.

The first time I ever properly stayed away from home was when I went with the cadets to the Isle of Man on a week's camp. When I went to the adjutant, he said, 'We've got your uniform. What size shoes are you?'

'Ten,' I said.

He looked down. 'Nah, you don't take a size ten.'

So he gave me a pair of nines. They pinched a bit, which I just had to put up with. After one day's route march on the Isle of Man I ended up with blisters all over my feet. I was excused boots for the rest of the week. I had to stay in a tent on duckboards, like those they had in the trenches in World War One. They didn't even have sleeping bags in those days. We just had to make do with rough army blankets. While everyone was going out playing soldier games, I was stuck in the tent with blisters on my heels. That was not much fun.

The following year, however, was when we went away to Wales and camped in a field near Rhyl. By this time, I had managed to persuade them that my feet were a size ten. So I was able to join in the leopard crawl through the long grass during our mock battle – before I got shot, of course, for standing up to fix my belt.

I was in the cadets for two years and I had a great time. It taught me a bit of discipline and, if I'm being honest, I wasn't missing the snooker. I used to have to shine my toecaps so I could see my face in them. You had to heat a spoon to get the dimples off the leather.

They were great times. Going away from home was very exciting. I learned how to shoot a rifle, receiving a certificate for shooting a .22 from twenty-five yards and getting all five pellets in the bullseye – a sixpenny group they called it.

We learned to march and travelled to Chester to take part in marching competitions, visiting a proper army barracks. There was a snooker table there and, while we were there, a few people were knocking around on it. When I had a go, somebody said, 'Oh, you're a good player.'

'I used to play,' I said.

It didn't really bother me then that I wasn't able to play more frequently, though. I knew it was off-limits. We played five-a-side football too and it was a great way of learning skills, getting some exercise and getting out of the house.

I was even promoted to corporal, so I was able to tell a few people what to do.

This was a time when National Service was coming to an end. The government started to phase it out in 1957 for people born during or after World War Two.

At one stage I almost considered going into the army when I left school. My father wasn't for it, though. 'What do you want to join the army for?' he said. 'It was bad enough when you *had* to go in.'

So I never had any encouragement on that front. As I entered my teenage years, however, I had to start thinking about finding a job somewhere. It was expected that I would leave school at fifteen and start contributing. The only advice I got from my father was, 'Get a white-collar job. You don't want to be working in the pits or down the docks.'

I didn't realise at the time that you would probably earn more down the pits or the docks than you would in most office jobs.

My first job came around the time that I joined the cadets

and was still at school. I helped out a local window cleaner called Arthur Valentine during the summer holidays to earn some extra money. There wasn't a lot of free money floating about in those days. Nobody was any different, so it didn't really bother me. It didn't feel as though I was any worse off than anyone else, but having some coins in your pocket made a bit of a difference.

These were the days when most likely I would have gone about with cardboard socks in my shoes. If they had a hole you couldn't just go out and buy a new pair or have them resoled. It was the done thing just to slip some cardboard inside and get on with it.

I was on a pound a day for the window-cleaning and Arthur paid me an extra ten bob – or fifty pence – for collecting the money. He had a thirty-foot ladder and the funny thing about him was that he was scared of heights. Not ideal for a window cleaner! He used to clean the big CWS building near Salford Docks. He would hold the ladder and I'd be the one up there. I'd be looking in these office windows and you'd see people staring, probably thinking, How's he got up there?

Whenever I looked down I used to think, What am I doing up here? But it was a way to earn some pennies.

Before I left school and tried to find a job, we all had meetings with a careers officer. He said to me, 'When you leave school have you got any idea what you want to do?'

I was a big fan of Sherlock Holmes. The collection of stories by Arthur Conan Doyle was probably the first book I ever read. I told the man I wanted to be a detective.

'Well,' he said, 'you know, to be a detective you've got to be a policeman first and you've got to pass exams.'

That was a bit late for my class. Many of us thought the GCE was an electrical appliance, rather than the General Certificate of Education (the predecessor to the current GCSE).

'Anything else?' he asked.

'I wouldn't mind being a bus conductor,' I said. I didn't have high aspirations and I used to see the conductors hanging off the backs of their buses and thought it looked an all-right job. The careers adviser just lowered his head.

One lad who went in after me, when asked what he wanted, said, 'A trade.'

'What sort of trade?'

'A trade,' he repeated. All he'd heard was people telling him he needed to get a trade, that he couldn't fail with a trade. He just didn't have a clue what it was.

Without any qualifications, I left school at fifteen. My first job was with structural steel stockholders called Banister Walton & Co., whose office was in Trafford Park. My job title was 'invoice clerk' but really I was a runner, going upstairs, getting the drawings from the draughtsman and giving them to the proper invoice clerks. For this they paid me £3 10s a week, of which I gave £3 to my mother and kept ten shillings.

Trafford Park was over Trafford Road Bridge, past Manchester United's ground and straight on. The bus was always packed, so what I used to do was catch a bus to Trafford Road Bridge, walk over the bridge, turn right and catch one of the buses coming from Manchester. There would be a queue of people and, when the bus came into view, they'd all be lining themselves up, like at the start of a marathon. The bus would come round the corner, slowing down, and everyone would jump on. When it got twenty yards down the road the bus stopped because it was full, and another twenty people would jump on. It was a case of get on when you could.

Later, I got a bike I used to ride to work. The only trouble with that was the old tramlines on the road. Believe me, if you got your front wheel stuck in a tramline you were in trouble.

Banister Walton's great claim to fame was that they had built every Woolworth's store in the country. They even used to say that if there were a Woolworth's store on the moon, Banister Walton would have built it.

Not long after I started working there one of the guys asked me if I fancied playing hockey for the YMCA in Manchester. At the time I still loved playing all kinds of sport. I went down there with him. While we were there I noticed they had a big snooker hall, with about twelve tables. He saw me eyeing up the tables. 'Can you play snooker?'

'Yes, a bit.'

We racked them up and played four frames. I beat him 4–0. I still had that feel for the game.

Around the same time, towards the end of 1961, people at the company asked me what I wanted to be in the long term. I hadn't a clue. There were opportunities to become a structural engineer but for that I had to have a degree – an S1 Struct E. I didn't really know what I was doing or what such a course would entail, but I followed their advice and went to enrol. The first question I was asked was how many qualifications I had. None, I had to admit. I couldn't do the course, then, without maths and English GCE. So I enrolled in those. To get one I had to pass a certain number of exams, and to do that I needed to enrol at night school.

I was very good at maths, so I thought I could take that, plus English. I enrolled at night school and filled in a form. The classes were to start the following week. I walked out unsure of what to do. It was too early to go home and I was reluctant to do so. I wasn't sure what I would say about the course. I suppose I felt inadequate – all those years at school with nothing to show for it.

I wasn't far from Small Street. I hadn't set foot inside the billiard hall for the best part of two years. It seemed to be calling me, though. Plus, playing recently had reminded me that snooker was something I was quite good at. And, now I was paying my own way at home, it surely wasn't still the same big deal.

★ ★ ★

Stepping inside those doors once again in many ways changed my life for ever.

The club had gone through some changes. The old manager, Mark, had left and a new one had taken over. His name was Stan Holden, from Bolton, one of the top amateurs in the area, and he was to have a profound influence on me. From the moment I got back among the balls on the table and started potting again, I was hooked.

Small Street was just around the corner from where I caught the bus, so it was far too tempting just to pop in.

My pals and I had been to see *The Hustler*, a film about American pool starring Paul Newman. When we called into the billiard hall, after watching the movie, Stan was practising on his own. We started asking him about certain shots: how do you draw a ball back, that sort of thing? Every shot he showed me I played it right first time. He asked me how old I was. Being tall, I suppose I looked older. He was surprised when I told him I was fifteen.

'You're a good player,' he said.

It was funny to hear someone say that. I had no idea if I was any good or not.

From that moment on he took an interest in me. For free table time I would work behind the bar a couple of nights a week. It was Stan who gave me my first proper cue. I had one that I played with but he came up to me one day and said, 'I've found this. I think it'll be better for you.'

Albert Rowbotham, the self-proclaimed secretary of the billiard hall, found out that an under-sixteen boys' snooker championship was being held in London in the coming April. To enter you had to be under sixteen on 1 January. I wouldn't be turning sixteen until March 1962, so I could enter.

It would mean going to the Burroughes and Watts hall, one of the most renowned snooker venues in the country, in Soho, London. I didn't think my father would allow it but I took Stan round to meet my parents to explain the tournament. I knew they would like him. Thankfully, they did, and they agreed to let me enter the tournament. The organisers of the tournament paid for the hotel, so, basically, it was like a school trip.

What I didn't know was that his pal Alan, known as Yogi Bear, had some other ideas about this trip to London.

Back then a road trip from Manchester to London was a bit different. There were no motorways. A Ford Cresta was our mode of transport. It was a lovely car, with a column-change gearbox. In fact, it was the car I always wanted, but, by the time I passed my test, Ford had stopped making them.

Once we had packed the car I noticed that there were a couple of transistor radios on the back seat. Radios weren't at their best then. When I wound down the window and stuck the aerial out to get a better reception all hell broke loose.

'Don't do that!' was the cry from both of them. 'We don't want anyone to see them.'

Little did I realise that there were another three-dozen in

the boot. Apart from selling radios Alan had already made enquiries as to where he could get some action in the snooker clubs. I quickly twigged that my attempt to become boys' champion was just a sideline, but I didn't mind. I was glad of the company.

It was my first time in London and I remember being struck by how many cars were on the roads. In Salford there wasn't a lot of traffic. If you saw one car parked in the street you'd all run around to have a look in, as if it were some extraterrestrial object that had landed from outer space. In London, and particularly around Shaftesbury Avenue and Piccadilly Circus, which already had the huge advertising displays, there was the hustle and bustle of a big city. Even Manchester didn't come close.

Everything to do with the tournament was run to military precision. The organiser herded us up two by two as if we were on a school trip and took us for lunch and our evening meals. Apart from the odd school-trip meal and being away with the cadets, my experience of food came exclusively from my mother. Here, we were taken to nice restaurants, offered food I'd never heard of before. When we went to the Tavistock restaurant in Shaftesbury Avenue it was grandeur to me. I'd never been in a restaurant like it.

On the first morning of the tournament a representative from Burroughes and Watts picked us up and escorted us to Soho Square. Although my snooker game was improving on a daily basis I had no idea if it would be good enough to beat any of the lads here.

Before my first match I was incredibly nervous. I had seen how nerves could affect my game in Small Street. I spent some time in the toilet trying to calm myself down.

Everyone was saying how tight the pockets were, but once I got out there I was pleasantly surprised. They were wider than I was used to at Small Street, which were all old billiard tables. Anyone who has ever played the game will tell you that a billiard table was not about potting balls: it was about canons and in-offs. So the pockets were tighter.

I came through it, though, and progressed to the next round. All the matches were played in the morning or afternoon and once I was free I met up with Stan and Yogi Bear and joined them looking for action. While I had been at Soho Square, Alan had been looking for somebody who would play Stan for money.

The place to go was the Windmill Snooker Club on Windmill Street, opposite the famous revue theatre of the same name. The opponent was a man called Cello, so called because he used to play that instrument in an orchestra some years before. Whatever he did, he didn't look like a snooker player. He looked more like my office manager in Trafford Park.

As soon as I stepped inside I could tell this wasn't like the billiard hall in Small Street. It had a more menacing feel about it. It didn't take long for Cello to realise he couldn't beat Stan. After a couple of games they stopped playing and for the next twenty minutes tried negotiating a handicap. Even with a handicap Stan was too good. It was obvious to everyone that backing their man wasn't a good bet.

I continued to make progress in the tournament but, although I was growing in confidence, I couldn't shake the pre-match nerves.

When my match was over, we went back to the Windmill Club. During the afternoon a row broke out between the manager and a customer. Before we knew it the customer was throwing snooker balls at the manager, who was crouching behind the bar. The balls were smashing bottles on the shelves. It was like witnessing a scene from a Western at the pictures. So *this* was what my dad had meant by a den of iniquity!

In these clubs there is always someone who spies a moneymaking opportunity. In the Windmill his name was Taffy. He saw how good Stan was and suggested there was a greyhound trainer in Leytonstone, east London, who liked a bet and had an inflated sense of his own ability. I was about to witness something I'd see many times in clubs over the years – decent players who thought they were a lot better than they were, rven on their own home table, in front of their own crowd.

While Taffy was setting up a money match between Dozy, the greyhound trainer, and Stan, I had my own matches to win. I continued to improve and reached the semifinal with a minimum of fuss. With each game my belief was growing.

We travelled to Leytonstone for Stan's match with Dozy. Taffy was in the club when we arrived. When the action finally started it was clear Dozy was a decent player. It took quite a long time for Stan to get to grips with him but, eventually, his superiority shone and he finished up with all the money Dozy had on him.

Meanwhile, back at my tournament, I won my semifinal and could scarcely believe I was in my first final.

Before the match I had nerves again – but this time they were worse than I'd ever experienced before. Stan kept telling me I could beat my opponent. I can't now remember hisis name, but he had been very impressive on his run-up to the final.

It was a best-of-seven final but the first few frames went by in a blur. Before I knew it I was 3–0 down and staring defeat in the face. Somehow, I managed to compose myself and slowly clawed my way back into it. I won the next frame, which gave me something to build on; then the next – it was 3–2 and I could start to see the first signs of doubt in John's eyes. I won the next to take the match into a decider. By now, though, the momentum was all with me and I closed out the frame to win. My first tournament, and I was the boys' champion of Great Britain!

Before I could really celebrate there was a big stewards' inquiry after the final frame. Suddenly, accusations were flying that I was too old to play in the tournament. Someone found out my birthday was on 4 March. I had to fight my corner and argue that the rules stated you had to be under sixteen on 1 January. It was eventually all cleared up and I got my hands on the trophy.

Looking back, I see there were signs even then that an unbelievable high could be tempered by events lurking around the corner. But at the time I was just delighted to win.

It had been a great week – I was boys' champion and Stan won a few quid too.

After winning the final we headed straight back home to Salford. In 1962 there were no mobile phones. My parents didn't even have a landline telephone. When I arrived home cradling the cup in my arms it was the first contact I'd had with them for seven days.

They were chuffed to bits. I didn't get a hug from my dad but I could see in his eyes how proud he was. Unbeknown to me, however, they had known the result of every match to the final. Our local paper, the *Salford Reporter*, had covered the tournament, so everybody in the street knew.

I relived the drama of the matches with them – omitting to

tell them where I'd been with Stan. I was looking forward to a lie-in on the Sunday morning, but Mum got me up bright and early. Some of the neighbours had already been knocking on the door wanting to hear all about it.

We perched the trophy on the dresser in the parlour. Then something surreal happened. It seemed that everybody in the street wanted to congratulate me and have a glance at the cup. They came in through the front door, shook my hand, looked at the cup, told me what an exciting week it had been and then left by the back door.

It was my first glimpse of fame. And from that day my future was written.

CHAPTER 4

DANGER MAN

Although I was boys' champion any thoughts that I could earn a living from snooker didn't even enter my head. The professional game did not exist in 1962. The game had been in decline for years and an official World Championship hadn't been played since 1957, when John Pulman won the first of his seven titles. The only player anyone had ever heard of was the legendary Joe Davis, and, apart from the occasional match on Saturday afternoon's *Grandstand*, there was no coverage.

Despite this, however, snooker was all I could think about. I'd finally found something I was half good at and my appetite to learn about the game knew no bounds. I continued my lessons with Stan, finding I could pick up easily any new shot he showed me. Given that I was working behind the bar I was spending more and more time in the snooker club. That said, working in the bar was counterproductive. I had hoped it meant I'd have more time to play snooker but the reality was that the opposite was true.

That changed one night when two guys walked into the club looking for some action. They asked me if there was anybody in the club who played for money. Unfortunately, the club was quiet and Stan had gone to the pictures. I explained that, normally, there was but not tonight. They decided to play one another. I kept an eye on them to see how good they were. I'd heard stories of hustlers going into clubs and pretending to play badly until they found a victim and suddenly their game improved dramatically. Eyeing them suspiciously, I figured this was a chance I was prepared to take.

The normal stake to play for was half a crown (twelve and a half pence in new money). I got one of my mates to cover for me behind the bar. I assured him that would beat these guys and give him something from my winnings. I went up to the table they were playing on. I said something about my relief arriving and I would play them. To say they were keen would be an understatement. For a moment I thought I'd made a wrong move, particularly because, if I were to lose, I would have to borrow the money from the till. Only one of them wanted to play. The bet was £5 a game. To protect against being knocked, or ripped off, we put our stake in the middle, in this case under a bottle on the shelf behind the bar.

The first game was close, too close for my money, probably because I was wondering who was hustling whom. But I won it on the brown. After that it was easy. We played eight games and I won them all. If Stan had been there he would probably have won more. The reason I say so is that, as you go through the games, you offer them a start, or play for more money.

Anyway, I was happy with £40 and my mate was delighted with the fiver I gave him for covering.

My routine of work and snooker suited me fine. As I was to find out, nothing lasts for ever.

I walked in one day to find everyone struck with a sense of shock.

'What's going on?' I said.

'Stan's been sacked,' someone said.

I couldn't believe it. Stan was really popular, not just with me but all the members. His problem was that he just wanted to play. Like me, he found it frustrating being stuck behind the bar, and his departure meant the end of my little stint as barman.

Life goes on, as they say. Stan was back in Bolton, which was closer to where he lived. I could still see him but it meant catching two buses from Salford to get there.

★ ★ ★

I had two weeks' annual holiday from work. For the most part I cleaned windows with Arthur Valentine but it began to make my arm ache. It was affecting my game to the extent that players I was beating easily were now getting closer.

On a Friday, with my cue in my hand, I decided to take a chance and go to Bolton. It was a temperance club like Small Street. When I arrived there was a game of golf on the main table. I was expecting Stan to turn up at any time. At about three o'clock the golf school broke as people prepared to go out for the night.

By about four o'clock the club was quieter than Small Street was at that time. The manager, Cyril Hampshire, was behind the bar. He looked less like a snooker player than anyone I have ever met. When he took a shot everything moved, but he was not to be underestimated. When there was no one else around for me to play, he offered me a game.

We started playing at about 4.30 p.m. and just kept going and going. If the club got busy I had to wait while he went behind the bar. In one comical moment I was left sitting for fifteen minutes between shots while he made sandwiches for a customer. We were still playing when the clock hit closing time at eleven o'clock.

By now the only light in the club was behind the bar and on our table. The only sound was the click of the balls.

As the night went on I gave him a start. The stakes were raised several times. I had been well in front for most of the session but with the handicap it was bringing us together. I never thought about the time. I would tell my parents that I stayed at Stan's, but I had never played for this long.

The first thing that started to ache was my thumb. I always had a very firm bridge, but my thumb was really beginning to ache every time I went into position.

By the end of the session I was £70 in front. Cyril wanted to play on. The problem when you give a start in snooker is that you have to play at your best if the handicap is right. Just because the start had been right halfway through the session, it didn't mean it was right now.

It was the longest time I ever played in one session. We finished at 6.30 a.m. I had a bacon sandwich, said goodbye to Cyril and left the club to head home.

It was about 8 a.m. when I got on the Number 8 bus from Bolton. The best way home was to get off the bus at the top of Cross Lane. The bus from Bolton terminated at Piccadilly, Manchester. My stop was Cross Lane, Salford. Sitting on the bus reflecting on what a great night I'd had, I was, as you can imagine, surprised when the bus conductor woke me up and informed me we had arrived at Piccadilly, some three miles further on than where I should have got off. No problem – he didn't charge me for the extra distance. I had to get on the Number 15 bus from Piccadilly to Salford, but I fell asleep again and woke up in Weaste, five stops after I should have got off. I was shattered but I didn't take another chance and so walked home from Weaste.

I didn't tell my parents what I had been doing. I said I had stayed at Stan's, but my dad had an inkling I had been up to something when I slept all day. I couldn't even stay awake long enough to watch the racing on this Saturday afternoon. I have always loved my racing on a Saturday afternoon.

★ ★ ★

The longer I spent in the billiard hall, the more I got to know the characters who hung out there. Times may have been harder back then but life had buoyancy, largely due to the personalities you encountered.

You could get anything in the club – usually the day after you'd bought it! There would always be someone who'd break it to you that they could have got the exact same type of record player you'd just bought, and for a fraction of the price.

I learned a bit about life in there, what you could and couldn't get away with. A lot of the conmen tried to make a living by doing something they shouldn't. In Salford the best way to get someone to do something was to treat him with a bit of respect. People weren't violent: they were more 'Charlie charm'. I remember one argument breaking out between two men and one of them tried to get away by hiding under the table.

The man after him picked up the table. Imagine picking up a snooker table! No wonder the other guy ducked underneath it. I've seen a few cues broken as tempers got heated. I was even barred once. I missed an easy pink and was so frustrated with myself I smashed the black and it went flying across the club. I stayed away for a few days, until it was safe enough to sneak back in, figuring they'd forgotten all about it.

There'd be arguments but the snooker club didn't really deserve the reputation it had. It was like the pool halls in Hollywood films. Whenever there was a detective on the hunt for someone, the first place they called was the pool hall for the word on the street. Similarly, with the billiard halls, if you were looking for a bad egg you might find them in there, but that didn't necessarily define the place.

My life was revolving around the club, my work and going to the races or the dog track at White City, which was just round the corner on Chester Road. The telephonist at Banister Walton was a lovely older lady called Sheila Pendleton. She used to ring up the racecourse for me to find out how the going was.

Sadly, Manchester Racecourse was on its last legs. Attempts to modernise the course had seemed to be a success with the construction of a new stand, the first to have private viewing boxes. But the course had been struggling financially and the cost of the new stand pushed the owners to breaking point. In 1963 the site was sold. The final race, held on 9 November, attracted twenty thousand spectators to watch Lester Piggott score his final victory there, but it was a case of too little too late. Most of the races moved to Haydock Park on Merseyside.

Without the horse racing, I spent more time at the dog track. Tony Hayhurst, whom I met in the club, loved a bet, and from the age of sixteen we had a routine of going to the track on Tuesday and Thursday nights. That interest grew to include Belle Vue dogs on a Wednesday and Saturday and we'd go to Salford dogs on Mondays and Fridays.

We would see a host of regulars. One was nicknamed Joe Soap. He had been happily married with two children. One day he had a yankee – a bet on four selections consisting of eleven separate bets: six doubles, four trebles and a fourfold accumulator. It came in and he won handsomely. His problem was that he thought he could do it every day. When we knew him he was running around the dog track trying to tip winners. Not surprisingly, he was divorced with not a penny in his pocket.

Hawaiian Eye was another wonderfully named character. He also used to tip winners on the dogs. He was one of those 'side-of-the-mouth Sids', the guys who came up and whispered information to you. He got the name because he had one eye that was a bit dodgy.

There were some great nicknames for characters. Bronchial Tony was so named in the snooker club because he was forever taking sickies from his work, citing a dicky chest.

My only system at the dogs was Trap 3. I loved Trap 3. If the dog got out fast it always had a chance, because it seemed to take the first bend quicker. Going to the dog track was good fun because it was live action and it was a night out as well. If we won a few quid we used to go to the Luxor club in Old Trafford. A converted cinema, the Luxor was a cabaret club and casino where Chubby Checker once played after the worldwide phenomenon that was his hit single 'The Twist'. When we used to go, there were invariably some blue comedians and a couple of strippers. The door charge was 2s 6d (12.5 pence) but that included a meat-and-potato-pie supper.

The snooker club felt like a private universe but in the outside world things were starting to change.

The football newspaper the *Pink* used to advertise what live music was on at the local coffee clubs, as the venues were in those days. 'Cellar clubs' they might be best described as now, but back then the cellar was where we kept the coal.

In February 1963 I looked in the *Pink* for the live shows that coming weekend. At the Oasis club, in Lloyd Street, Manchester, a band called the Beatles were playing on the Saturday night. I'd never heard of them, although at that time they'd had a minor hit with their debut single, 'Love Me Do'. On the Sunday night, Johnny Kidd and the Pirates were playing. I had heard of them because they'd had a No. 1 record with 'Shakin' All Over'. So my friends and I went along on the Sunday night to catch them.

Later that month the Beatles had their first official No. 1 with 'Please Please Me', but it wasn't long before they were back at the Oasis. I went along to see them and for the first time that I could remember there was a queue outside. It was only about twelve people long but even that was unusual. As we were standing there, two taxis pulled up and out got the Beatles. The only one I could recognise was John Lennon because he was married to Cynthia and I saw a woman with blonde hair with one of them.

You were lucky if you got more than eighty people in the Oasis, so everyone there was really seeing the Beatles at close quarters. From the moment they started playing you could tell they were a cut above everyone else. What a sound they produced! I know that, later, when they got to work with the legendary producer George Martin, there were a lot of different sounds; but back then, with just lead guitar, bass guitar, rhythm guitar and Ringo on the drums, it was a real earthy sound – the type of sound I used to love with the early Elvis music and Buddy Holly, who was one of my great favourites.

From growing up with my family and their passion for singing, I'd always been a fan of live music and to see the Beatles up close and personal like that was a great thrill. Prior to that, most of the music was coming from America.

A year after 'Please Please Me' they went on tour doing the Roy Orbison–Beatles show at the Odeon in Manchester. Roy Orbison started the tour top of the bill but, by the time they came to the North, the Beatles had claimed top billing. Also on with them were the fellow Liverpool outfit Gerry and the Pacemakers. It was then I realised how fortunate I had been to see the Beatles in the Oasis. When Roy Orbison came on you could hear a pin drop. It was wonderful to hear that voice. Orbison was once described as the 'opera singer of pop music' – and that wasn't wrong.

Then the Beatles came on – and all you could hear was screaming. You couldn't hear one word of what they sang. The only previous time I had seen any reaction similar was when I saw the movie *Rock Around the Clock* in the mid-1950s with my grandmother. People were getting up and dancing in the aisles. It was unheard of. Rock'n'roll music had sparked something and it was transforming people's attitudes.

I loved that whole rock'n'roll music scene. Listening to the early Beatles live you could tell what an influence people such as Little Richard were on Lennon and Paul McCartney. To me, Elvis was the king but when you hear Little Richard it's hard to argue that he was the greatest rock'n'roll singer of all time.

There was a real sense that something was in the air. We didn't know then that a cultural revolution was taking place and that we were at the forefront of it, but there was certainly a feeling that people could be bolder, live more freely.

★ ★ ★

At that age, seventeen and engrossed in snooker, I'd never had time for girls. I'd never had a serious relationship and I'd never taken a girl back home to meet my parents. That all changed when I fell for a girl who worked in the office.

Looking back, I see that it was just a fling, but we fell hard for each other. She was living with a guy but she told me it was all over between them and he'd moved out.

We went on a weekend away together to Blackpool, which most people did if they could afford the bus fair. We were walking along this line of B&Bs and, as soon as we found one that said 'vacancies', we went in. I remember putting my name down as 'John Drake', Patrick McGoohan's secret agent in the TV series *Danger Man*. In the morning I was looking at the bill and the man from the B&B says, 'Is that OK Mr Drake?' I was ignoring him because I thought he was talking to someone else!

After that weekend, she handed in her notice and said, 'I won't be in again.'

I hadn't a clue what was going on. 'That's a shame,' I said. 'Where are you going, then?'

'I'm coming with you,' she said.

She had it all planned. We were going to run away together and live in Nottingham. It was a bit of a surprise to me. I didn't even know where Nottingham was. In fact the only thing I knew about the place was Robin Hood.

One morning I left the house as normal as though going to work. It was the day my mother went to the wash house, so I snuck around the corner and waited until I saw her leave, and then I went back into the house. I was packing a suitcase and getting ready to leave when my mother's brother John, who came round about two or three times a year, just happened to be passing and popped in.

'What are you doing?' he said when he saw me packing my things.

I said, 'I've met this girl and we're going to run away together.'

He looked shocked. 'Have you not discussed this with your mother?' he said.

I said I hadn't because I didn't think my dad would like it.

'It'll break your mother's heart, John,' he said.

He kept me talking until my mother came home and of course they talked me out of it. I don't think my heart was really in it but for a moment it seemed exciting. I had to go to the phone box on the corner, ring her up and tell her I wasn't coming.

'Where are you?' she said.

'I can't do it,' I said. 'My mother's too upset.'

Now she was upset too. I thought I'd better go to her house to try to smooth things over. When I arrived the ex-boyfriend who'd moved out was there.

I just grunted.

'Oh, well,' he said. 'You can have her – you've got the big house and the car.'

I thought, Hang on, what's she told him? I haven't got anything. I haven't even got a driving licence.

'I live with my parents,' I said. 'I don't have anything.'

Then it got really heavy. Having been brought up in Salford, I wasn't a shrinking violet. I had gone round there prepared for anything, but I wasn't expecting what happened next.

The girl got really upset, ran into the kitchen, grabbed a knife and threatened to slit her wrists. He then ran in after her and the next thing was that they were arguing and he threw a glass against the wall. I stepped in and said, 'Cut that out!'

She ran into the bedroom and, when he went in to console her, I took the chance to get out of there. I'm not proud to say I legged it but what would any other seventeen-year-old do in the circumstances?

I never saw her again. She'd quit her job to start a new life and didn't come back to work. I was in bits for a week. I thought she was the love of my life. I've often wondered what would have happened had my uncle not walked in when he did. How would my life have ended up?

Thankfully, I had snooker to help take my mind off things.

★ ★ ★

Later in 1963 I entered the Youth Championship, which was open to players under nineteen. It was in London again but now that Stan didn't work at the snooker club I had no one to take me. One of the lads from the billiard hall knew a lorry driver who drove to London once a week. He agreed to give me a lift.

I must have looked a sight, standing at the junction of Cross Lane and Trafford Road with suitcase and cue in hand, and even more so when my lift arrived. It was an articulated lorry. My journey down wasn't as magical as that first trip in the Ford Cresta, but at least it didn't cost me anything.

Once I got to London the biggest change I noticed was the effect being on my own had on me. The nerves I'd experienced a year earlier were still there but this time I didn't have the antics of Stan and Yogi to take my mind off the tournament. Here, I was eating and sleeping the championship. I had no outlet.

Before every match I would spend even longer on the toilet. I managed to get through the early rounds but, although I progressed, I was never truly comfortable. I lost in the semifinal to a London lad called Joe Fisher. It was the first time I appreciated that I needed to get a handle on the pressure I felt playing big matches if I was going to achieve more in the game. I'd already experienced moments when I'd used that pressure to my advantage. Was there a way to control it, though?

I came back to Salford brooding over opportunities missed. I was still young, however, and vowed to come back a year later stronger in more ways than one.

CHAPTER 5

TAKING A GAMBLE

It was as if history was repeating itself. I was in the final of the Youth Championship – it was 1964, the year after I lost in the semifinal – but trailing 3–0 in a best-of-seven match.

My opponent was a young lad from Tottenham in London called John Hollis. Before the fourth frame I nipped into the washroom, tried to refocus and get back to the mindset that had got me this far. The door behind me swung open. I glanced round. It was one of the other players, one who had been knocked out in an earlier round.

'Never mind,' he said. 'You've done well to get to the final.'

I turned in a flash.

'He hasn't won it yet,' I snapped and stormed past him. The boy's words lit a fire inside me.

Unlike in 1963, this year I hadn't been on my own. I'd travelled down on the National Express bus, but between matches I relieved the tension by going to Herbert Holt's snooker club in Windmill Street. This one was of a somewhat better class than the other club I had been in with Stan a couple of years before. It was there that I met a guy called John Shepherd and I practised with him and his friend Derek Cox, who was also a pianist in many London clubs. On the day of the final John had to work, but Derek was there to give me his support. It would prove invaluable.

When I came out of the washroom, Derek was there. He took me to a quiet room for a cigarette. I told him what had happened and what I'd said.

'That's the attitude,' he said. 'Now, go back in there and remember how you play in the clubs.'

I went back in and won the next frame. Derek took me for another cigarette break. 'Keep it up,' he said.

I went back, won the next frame. Went for another ciggie.

And so it went. After each frame he allowed me to channel the anger I was feeling, made me focus, helped me switch off from everything else going on in my head.

I won four frames in a row and was crowned the youth champion of Great Britain.

Something happened in London that year. There I was, staring defeat in the face, yet I turned it around. I still believe that, if that lad hadn't said anything then, I probably would have lost. Hearing him write me off made me mad. As in the Boys' Championship two years previously, being one frame away from defeat seemed to release the pressure. I had nothing to lose.

Meeting John Shepherd was also an unexpected blessing. He was an excellent snooker player and the first person since Stan Holden to see potential in me. He gave me encouragement, worked on my flaws and helped me become a better player.

Although I was youth champion, the opportunities still

weren't there. I was able to apply to compete in the English Amateur Championship so that was my long-term focus. When I was next on leave from work I travelled back down South and met up with John. He lived in Ilford, Essex. We practised together every day. He took me to the Lucania Snooker Club in Romford. Years later it would become famous as the place from where Barry Hearn and Steve Davis emerged to take on the world. I was playing there before they had even heard of it.

My victory as a youth champion had some repercussions, however. In Small Street, a Christmas handicap was held every year. Jack Scholes – the man whose challenge kept me out late a few years earlier – was on the handicap committee. After I won the competition the year before, and then won the Youth, he was adamant I'd be so handicapped I wouldn't have a chance in the next one.

'Even Arkle couldn't win it this year,' he said, referring to that year's Cheltenham Gold Cup winner on its way to achieving legendary status.

It wasn't just I who was being hit hard with handicaps: I heard other people mutter 'dear me' when they saw how much of a start I had to give opponents. Even having to give people a start, I made it to the final without dropping a frame. In the final, I was up against another up-and-coming player called Paul Medati. I knew Paul well. He used to have a window-cleaning round and I sometimes went with him on a Saturday morning. Everyone assumed we had the same ability, yet I had to give him a twenty-one-point start. Some people were ridiculing my chances: 'There's no point you turning up: you've got no chance.'

I beat him 4–0 without breaking a sweat. That's when I realised my game was getting better. You need to test your game to see the progress you're making, and I was improving out of all proportion.

★ ★ ★

Increasingly, snooker was interfering with my work life. The billiard hall was where I came to life, where I was respected and appreciated. At Banister Walton, they docked me a penny a minute if I was late. That grinded a little. I was getting paid pennies as it was. I was losing interest. I would take days off if I'd had a late night. I couldn't drive, so relied on buses or lifts to get anywhere. If I missed the last bus from Bolton, I had no choice but to walk the five or six miles back to Manchester and catch a night bus to get home. If I called in sick on a Friday, I invariably took Monday off as well to make it look more believable that I'd picked up some sort of virus. Plus, people didn't expect me to be off when it was pay day, so it aroused less suspicion. Or so I thought.

Coming from the sort of environment and the family that we had, it was important I had a job, but I was a reluctant worker. I was making extra money working in the snooker club. Having a job seemed less important than it had when I'd left school.

My attitude didn't go unnoticed. Eventually, the office manager called me up to his desk and said, 'If you don't buck your ideas up, John, I can see you selling shoelaces in the park when you're twenty-five.'

It wasn't the greatest motivational speech I've ever had. I did think, Well, it would be better than working here.

It was a demanding place to work. My colleagues were hard-working people. You never saw them with their heads up. Two of the people I worked beside suffered strokes, yet, once they'd recovered enough, they came back and taught themselves how to write left-handed so they could keep going. I used to watch them struggle, but I didn't pity them. I respected them for refusing to let a setback stop them from working.

We cherished our lunch breaks in there. We were allowed half an hour and in that time we'd have a two-course meal and a game of cricket. As soon as that bell rang we ran for the canteen. One chap once fell over and everyone just ran over him and he was trampled in the stampede.

Another guy, Ernie Brophy, was nearing retirement age. He had a great way of disguising a mid-afternoon nap. He would sit at his desk, pretending to look at this piece of paper, with a pen poised, but he would be fast asleep. To anyone passing it would look as though he were writing. Whenever the door opened he'd wake up and resume his paperwork. He was a pipe smoker and loved a puff after lunch. He'd knock the end off it and put it on his desk. What caught him out one day was that, after he'd had his smoke and had fallen asleep as usual, we noticed flames licking out of his waste paper basket. We didn't want to wake him up to tell him.

My disaffection really came to a head when, after I'd been there for three years, a new lad started and I was asked to teach him my job because I was moving to start something else involving invoicing. I looked at his wage packet and saw he was on two pounds a week more than I was.

To say I was hacked off was putting it mildly. It was 1966 and my job prospects were looking bleak. Thankfully, events away from work helped to make life more bearable. In February, not long before my twentieth birthday, Manchester United defeated Benfica in Portugal in the quarterfinal of the European Cup. The match announced the arrival on the international stage of George Best, then just nineteen, who scored twice, earning him headlines pronouncing 'El Beatle' on his return home in a sombrero. The victory marked the first signs that United were assembling a new team of Busby Babes after nearly a decade recovering from the Munich Air Disaster. I looked upon George's early days with the excitement of any United fan, not realising our paths would cross many times in the years to come.

The Beatles had become a worldwide phenomenon since I'd seen them back in the Oasis club. Not only did I love their music but I was a fan of their films *A Hard Day's Night* and *Help!*, starring, among others Victor Spinetti, along with the band themselves. The Beatles' success was another boost for the North of England. There was something of a North–South divide between the Beatles and the Rolling Stones. Whenever the Stones hit No. 1, we felt like saying, 'Come on, Beatles, get another one – knock them off their perch.'

It was a great thing to be part of and it gave the North some credibility, while at the same time there was a feeling the country was getting smaller.

That divide was set to one side, of course, in the summer of 1966, when the World Cup united the country like nothing since the war. Not all of us got to enjoy every kick of the ball, however. I remember England were playing Mexico and I reminded my dad the game was on so he could change the channel.

'Your mother wants to watch *Coronation Street*,' he said. 'It's the only bit of enjoyment she gets.'

I was looking at my mother. She said, 'I don't mind; let him watch the football.'

Dad refused and so we missed Bobby Charlton's great goal

when he picked the ball up on the edge of the penalty area and went right through and scored. It was England's first goal in the tournament and, after an uninspiring opening 0–0 draw against Uruguay, it kick-started a campaign that ultimately ended in our winning the World Cup in the final against West Germany.

Looking back, I don't think my mother wanted to watch *Coronation Street* – my dad did!

Those events aside, I was twenty and my life was still a routine. By then it revolved around going to work, going home, having dinner – or tea, as we called it – and going to the snooker club, or the local pub for a game of cards. My local was the Station on Cross Lane. Our big game was 'nine-card don'.

They used to say that there were so many pubs on Cross Lane that, if you started with a thimble of beer in the first pub and doubled up in every pub you went to up the road, by the time you were in the last one at the top of the lane you'd be having to drink 360 pints.

If I wasn't out late playing snooker, I was up late drinking. Some nights we'd go to Plymouth Grove in Manchester to an Indian restaurant, which was open until 2 a.m. I'd get home and be stumbling up the stairs, going up one and falling down two. Although my parents never really frowned upon my behaviour, I had a nagging feeling that it was time to leave the nest.

There was a view of life that once you had a job, you'd get married, find a house and have children. Marriage wasn't something I was entertaining when I was a teenager. I'd meet a few girls but not that many, because I was so engrossed in snooker.

Occasionally, however, I did meet a girl in the billiard hall.

I remember one occasion when I took a fancy to a girl who worked on reception in Small Street. A gambling friend had gone out with her previously and, although she was married, she seemed to take a shine to me.

One night I ended up back at her place when there was a knock at the door. She said, 'He's back early.' I panicked but she said, 'When I open the front door you go out the back door.'

Well, it wasn't a back door, it was a side door, so as I snuck out I caught a glimpse of this chap standing at the front. I legged it. I jumped over the back gate but landed right in a throng of thistles. I had to fight my way through them.

The next day my mate said to me, 'Not only are you a good snooker player, you're a bloody good runner as well.' It wasn't the hubby at the door: it was him!

So I was having some fun with friends but slowly it became apparent that our number was dwindling. They were all getting married. I don't know if men have a clock ticking but it hit me one day when a mate said to me, 'I'm going to get married next year.'

'Oh, who are you going out with?' I said.

'I haven't met her yet,' he said, 'but I'm definitely going to get married next year. I've had enough of this living at home.'

I started to think maybe I should get married.

★ ★ ★

There were no phones in those days. Socialising came down to popping into your usual hangouts and seeing who was about. The more places you went into and the fewer friends to have a drink with, you began to think you might get left behind.

Some of the lads from Small Street put a football team

together and it was while playing with them that I met Susan, who knew one of the lads in the team. We ended up going out together. Her parents had recently split up and she had been living with her grandfather near Maine Road, close to where Manchester City's football ground was then, deep in the heart of Moss Side. When her grandfather died she was living in the house on her own.

We became serious quite quickly. Susan was the first girl I ever took home to meet my parents. They could tell how serious I was about her because I started to stay over with her on a Saturday night and missed Sunday lunch. My mother's Sunday roast was the highlight of my week, so to miss it was a big deal!

It never crossed our minds to live – as we called it in those days – over the brush, to live with someone before you were married. The natural scheme of things was that you got married.

Susan and I tied the knot in a register office two years later. It was a very small ceremony and we had a reception back at my parents' house. I heard her father saying to her, 'You could have done a lot better than this.' I'm not certain if he was referring to her choice of husband or the fact that we were having a low-key celebration. Perhaps it sounds sad to say but, to us, getting married was no big deal. For a start, we didn't have the money to make it a lavish occasion. It was a case of tying the knot so we could live together.

The biggest thing for me was moving out of the house for the first time. I knew nothing about running a home, as I'd demonstrate in years to come. We moved to a ground-floor bedsit in Cheetham Hill. We didn't have the money to buy a home. In fact it wasn't even a consideration then. My parents had never owned their home.

The bedsit had a communal toilet upstairs that we shared with an alcoholic. We heard him getting up in the middle of the night, wailing that he could see imaginary spiders and all sorts. We practically had to book in advance if we wanted to use the bathroom. It wasn't the ideal setting but moving out of the house was a good thing for me. I had been feeling a bit entrapped by my circumstances. Once I moved out I did feel I had my own independence at last, albeit with my wife.

Cheetham Hill had its own snooker club. I used to call in on my way home from work. Their best player was Dennis Hughes. He knew I'd come from Small Street and had a reputation as a bit of a player. Every night when I called in – not always to play, just to have a look – he'd say, 'How much do you want to play for, then?'

I kept refusing to play him, quite simply because I didn't have any money. All the money I earned went into the upkeep of our bedsit.

One morning, however, I got a letter through the post. It was from a racing expert, offering tips on the horses for free. I didn't realise it at the time but it was a bit of a scam. The idea is that they give you the first tips for free, then it's a fiver for three more. It's designed to entice you in and ultimately to make you spend more money.

I got in touch with Tony Hayhurst and told him about the tip. Well, the horse won. Then the next one. I think the first three or four all came in. That got us hooked. Every day I was going into the snooker club and they were asking, 'Have you got anything?'

Those tips got me involved with the racing to a degree I had never been previously. Now, I was supplementing my income in the billiard hall and in the betting shop. I was betting only small amounts but sometimes it meant I had a bit of extra cash in my pocket.

Soon I started to follow form and studied the top owners, trainers and jockeys. I quickly had a little system – if Eddie Hide was ever riding for Bill Whiteman, it was usually a good combination and worth a punt. Hide was the top Northern jockey – the 'cock of the North', they called him. One day I had a bet and the horse won, so I went into Cheetham Hill Snooker Club with about £20 in my pocket.

Dennis Hughes came up to me as usual. 'OK,' I said, 'I'll play you.'

After about three weeks he stopped asking me! He kept trying to find different games on the snooker table where he thought he could beat me, but after a while he just stopped asking.

The gambling was paying off. I was doing well in the clubs and was enjoying married life. I had it made, yes?

If only. I should have known that nothing lasts for ever.

CHAPTER 6

NEAR MISSES

It was a day like any other. I headed out to catch the bus. Either I was running a little late or the bus was early, but I saw it coming just at the point I was crossing the road. I saw my chance and was about to step off the kerb. I don't know what then made me stop but it was as though a hand grabbed hold of me as a car whizzed by right in front of my face. One step and I would have been dead.

It's funny, the moments on which your life turns. I often think about them – and how differently things might have turned out but for the slightest change in circumstances. It has often felt that little moments have big consequences. Similarly, there are the big decisions you take, hoping they will change your life for the better.

I had been at Banister Walton for eight years and, careerwise, I had hit a brick wall. I had been thinking about finding another job for a while, but what could I do without any qualifications?

Since 1960, and the legalisation of off-course gambling, betting shops had been opening up, effectively bringing an end to the backstreet bookies. I was getting more into horses and thought working in a betting shop might be the ideal job. This was at a time when I was struggling to find people to play me for money. My reputation was preceding me. I was earning more from horseracing than I was at the snooker table. I did apply for a job at the betting office but they told me they weren't hiring at that time. It was probably a blessing in disguise. The temptation to have a bet in every race might have been too much.

Whenever I applied for jobs I always felt at a bit of a disadvantage with my name. I visualised them putting the applicants in alphabetical order – if that were the case there wouldn't be much chance for me.

Soon the decision was taken out of my hands. My bosses at Banister Walton grew weary of the days I was taking off. Inevitably, I was asked to leave. For a brief moment, when I was enjoying a hot streak, it crossed my mind that I might be able to make a living backing horses, but I was making too little to give it serious consideration. Besides, my wife was adamant that I should have a nine-to-five job with a steady income.

I managed to land a job at Miles Druce Metals, another steel stockholding company also based at Trafford Park. I worked in the transport department and I enjoyed it more because I wasn't stuck in an office all day looking at sheets of paper. My role was to check off the lists of items on the wagon before they were shipped to different parts of the country. An unforeseen benefit was that it would help with my geography of Britain, when over the coming years I had to travel the country for snooker tournaments, exhibitions and money matches.

The transport manager lived in Rochdale and he knew a few people on the council. A new block of flats had just been built and he pulled a few strings to get us pushed up the housing list so we could get one. It was in Florence Way, which seemed like destiny, as that was my mother's name.

We moved into what was a two-bedroom flat. I still didn't have much of an idea when it came to setting up a home. When it came to ordering a carpet I looked for the cheapest we could find. I bought one with a foam-rubber backing, not appreciating that the flat had underfloor heating. Every time we had the heating on the whole flat reeked of rubber. It was unbelievable. I don't even think they sell that type of backing any more, for health reasons, but we had no choice; we just had to put up with it.

My transport manager would sometimes give me a lift to work. Otherwise, I caught the train. To get to Rochdale Station from the centre, there were a lot of steps. I used to run up there, a bit like we'd see Rocky do a few years later in the boxing films. The only difference was that I didn't throw my arms into the air when I got to the top – I was too busy running to the train.

Not long after I started at Miles Druce Metals, I had another near miss. I was working overtime on a Saturday doing some stock checking. I had to count a rack of huge metal sheets stacked on top of one another. These things weighed half a tonne. I turned and a sharp corner of metal caught me just at the side of my right eye. A centimetre to the other side and I might not have had much of a career to write about. Losing an eye would have finished me as a player.

As with the incident in the traffic, it's only when you look back that you realise how things could have changed your life.

Luck was on my side in other ways, too, even if it took me some time to appreciate it.

The Riley billiard hall in Small Street closed down. It was sad to see it go but it was a victim of changing trends. With no professional game to speak of, snooker was struggling. Some clubs tried to diversify by setting up card tables but soon all anyone wanted to do was play cards. The tables were nowhere near as busy as they had been.

I was still keen for a game and needed new players to test myself against so I started going to Chorlton-cum-Hardy, to the south of Old Trafford. It was a bit of a trek from Rochdale. I had to take two buses but I had been reading in the snooker magazines about players such as David Taylor, the world amateur champion known as the Silver Fox, and how many century breaks he was making. At Small Street it was nearly impossible to make a century – I came the closest – because of the tightness of the pockets. When I went to Chorlton snooker club I couldn't believe the size of the pockets. No wonder they were making all these hundred breaks. Almost instantly, my game stepped up another level. They say when one door closes another door opens. Small Street may have closed but Chorlton would open up new opportunities.

I was practising one day when I was vaguely aware of two young men watching me. I didn't really pay them much attention but when they left Tony Hayhurst said to me, 'Do you know who that was?'

'Who?'

'George Best.'

I had yet to see Manchester United's rising talent in the flesh, as I was spending so much time playing snooker that there didn't seem to be the time to go to Old Trafford. But soon after that I did. Bobby Charlton was my all-time United hero. His performances were fantastic. As one spectator once shouted, 'If we had eleven Bobby Charltons we would win every game.'

But, as soon as I saw George Best, I could see what all the fuss was about. You could tell he was a star. I got the same feeling watching a young Cristiano Ronaldo years later when he began to turn it on for the Red Devils.

It turned out that George liked to hang out at the Chorlton club after training. He liked watching the players potting balls. It was a place where he could come and relax away from the limelight.

Over time I got speaking to him and we became quite friendly. The George I saw was nothing like the playboy portrayed in the newspapers over the years. He was quiet, shy and thoughtful. I once asked George what he thought of my great hero Charlton. He agreed he was a great player, but revealed that they didn't really get on, because they were completely different people.

I think Bobby, like a lot of supporters, didn't think George put United first.

After United had won the final of the European Cup in 1968, George became the first rock-star footballer. The sad fact about George was that he was this incredible talent but was easily led. Mind you, to most people in his shoes that temptation of booze and women would be hard to resist.

I hoped that the improvement I got from playing on the tables at Chorlton would lead to more triumphs on a national level. For a while, though, that wasn't the case. My ambition had been to win the English Amateur Championship. There were still no aspirations to play professionally. For a start, the legends of the game, such as Joe Davis, had been operating a closed shop for years. Davis, considered by many the greatest to have ever played the game and the man who won fifteen World Championships from 1927 to 1946, did not like the idea of amateurs who played matches for money entering the professional arena.

So for the amateurs the English title seemed the pinnacle. For me, however, it was proving elusive, sometimes due to circumstances outside my control. I still couldn't drive, so not having my own transport presented problems. Often I relied on other people to give me a lift. One year my wife said she knew a girl at her place of work who would drive me to my match. We got the bus to the corner of Pendleton Church, outside Salford. She was supposed to pick us up at seven o'clock. It got to half past. 'Where is she?' I said.

'She said she would do it if she could,' my wife said.

'If she could?'

So that was one year gone.

After winning the Boys' Championship and the Youth, I grew frustrated at my inability to progress. My play on the club tables was good but I didn't seem to be able to translate that when it really mattered. I remember after one tournament failure someone said to me, 'You'd be an even better player if you lost that chip on your shoulder.'

I bristled when I heard that but he was right. At the time I didn't have any confidence. I was the archetypal Northerner but I thought that was the way to fire myself into these situations, by being a little bit arrogant. After all, it had worked for me in my previous finals but underneath I was actually quite shy. I thought I had to show that aggression to prove I belonged in that world.

I grew disillusioned. It felt as if there weren't a future in snooker, for the game or me. Snooker was still very much an underground sport in the mid-1960s. The amateur scene was strong and in many ways kept the game alive in the wake of the floundering professional scene. The English Amateur Championship was split into a north–South divide, with the winner from each region playing in the final. Oddly, Stoke-on-Trent was considered in the South region. Ray Reardon had emerged from the southern section in 1964 and beat another rising star, John Spencer, in the final. Subsequently, Reardon had quit his job as a policeman and turned professional in 1967.

Spencer was a player I'd first been aware of back when Stan Holden told me once that he was playing a challenge match with a guy from Radcliffe, Greater Manchester, called John Spencer. Apparently, Spencer had been a good player when he was fifteen but had stopped playing while completing his national service. He'd got a job working in a bookmaker's and had started playing again. Within two years he had reached the final of the English Amateur Championship, losing to Reardon.

The following year he reached the final again, this time against Patsy Houlihan, at Blackpool Tower Circus. I went along to watch. The only things I knew about Houlihan I'd read from reports in the snooker magazine. He was being tipped as a great potter and was from Deptford, east London, so it was certainly a North–South final that year. He had a number of backers with him from London who clearly fancied his chances. Spencer had improved dramatically over the year that had passed since his defeat by Reardon, but still lost to Houlihan, so I backed our local challenger; but, after hearing the hype around his opponent, I began to feel less confident.

Houlihan won the final easily, 11–3, in a match so one-sided it was over early in the second session. Because of the early finish the players provided an exhibition match for the audience. This time Spencer wiped the floor with Houlihan. The real match was over; there was no pressure on either player, so Spencer was able to perform. Just as I did, John found it difficult to produce when it mattered. But he had been playing at this level for only a couple of years. He had the ability; he just needed to believe in himself. Some of the snooker Spencer played in that exhibition was unbelievable. No disrespect to Patsy, but Spencer was producing shots that he simply couldn't play.

In 1966, Spencer had made the final for the third year in a row. His opponent in the final, at Huddersfield Town Hall, was Marcus Owen, whom I had played in Leytonstone billiard hall years earlier. Many people said he was the best amateur ever to have played the game. Spencer, however, paid no heed to that, nor did he show any signs of nerves as he beat Owen easily, making the first century break in the final in the process. I was present to watch every single frame of that match. Spencer was a joy to watch. In many ways he was the forerunner of the modern game. I was witnessing the future of snooker. He turned professional that year – no mean feat due to the closed shop operated by Joe Davis and the others.

But in 1969 the game underwent the first stage of a revolution. A new organisation, the World Professional Billiards and Snooker Association (WPBSA), took over the running of the game and, from being an invitation-only event, the World Championship was revived as a knockout tournament featuring four of the best players from the old era and four new professionals.

At his first attempt, John Spencer won the World Championship. In the final he beat Marcus Owen's brother Gary 37–24. In one frame he needed the pink and black to win. The pink was near the baulk line. He potted the pink and screwed back the length of the table for position on the black – a shot that was unheard of back then. Joe Davis's brother Fred, himself a multiple world champion, admitted that neither he nor his brother would have been capable of playing that shot.

Spencer was trying to make the game watchable – and the only way to do that was to make shots that the ordinary amateur couldn't play. The impact his victory had on the local game in the Northwest of England cannot be overstated. I'm not exaggerating when I say that he improved players in our area by twenty-one points.

For years I had read in the snooker magazine about all these players from the South. Now we had a player in our midst who was the best in the world. Spencer and Reardon turning professional would change the professional game for ever.

★ ★ ★

In 1969 another significant development happened. The BBC launched a new snooker series called *Pot Black*, an invitational featuring eight players. It was actually Ted Lowe, the man who would become the 'voice of snooker' thanks to his hushed tones, who persuaded the then controller of BBC Two, David Attenborough, that there was an opportunity to exploit the advances made in colour television. Snooker was back on the small screen and its popularity was growing.

There was another factor in my own enthusiasm for the

game's return. A player was emerging from Northern Ireland who would light up the sport like no other: Alex Higgins. Again, it was Stan who first drew my attention to the 'Hurricane', as he would come to be known.

Stan had been at a tournament in Bolton in which Alex played for the Belfast YMCA team. Stan told me everyone watching had been stunned by the speed that Higgins played at. When he had gone into the match, which was two frames on aggregate, his team had been 154 points behind. By the time he came off the table they were in front. There was an even greater signpost to come. After the match, John Pulman, now world champion, presented the prizes and played Alex in a one-frame exhibition game. Alex potted Pulman off the table and basically took the mickey out of him. This was no mean feat, not least because Alex himself admitted he was 'in awe' of Pulman. This was the first time anyone had begun to time how quickly a player made a break – after Alex made a century break in three and a half minutes.

His success was no flash in the pan. In 1970 Alex played six money matches and won every one of them, including one against the new world champion, John Spencer.

From the very start, Alex polarised opinion. In 1970, some said he would be world champion in two years' time; others said he would simply flash briefly across the sky like a meteor and then blow up. In a way, both opinions would eventually be proved right. Whatever the case, he was certainly an enigma, but the public quickly warmed to him. He sped around the table and made the most outrageous shot selections; his game was a joy to watch. Not only did he make the game itself more exciting, but he also brought added publicity to the sport. This was something it badly needed.

Snooker was being transformed before my eyes. It was impossible not to get caught up in it. As the seventies began, it was an exciting time – not just for the game but for me too. Away from the table I had more important considerations than how to get to snooker matches. Susan was expecting our first child.

* * *

In 1971, shortly before our baby was due, Granada Television in Manchester, perhaps inspired by the success *Pot Black* was enjoying and the popularity of the World Championship, organised their own snooker tournament. They invited the top eight amateurs in Britain to play in it. I was delighted to be one of the eight. It was particularly special for me because my father was able to come and watch. He hadn't seen me play but, as the tournament was held at Granada's studios, it was easy for him to get to.

Granada televised the tournament and it was my first time playing on TV. I didn't feel any added pressure, in fact I seemed to be able to channel it better. During breaks in the tournament my father and I would go into the canteen and he couldn't believe his eyes. 'Oh, look there's Hilda Ogden over there,' he said, as all the *Coronation Street* stars were in there at the same time. I couldn't help thinking back to the day of the England World Cup game in 1966 and his reluctance to switch from the soap.

It became even more special to have my dad there because I played some of my best snooker in a while and won the tournament. As I was an amateur I couldn't receive any prize money, so instead Granada awarded me £350 in vouchers. With our baby due I asked if the vouchers could be made out for

Mothercare. That tournament helped us a lot: we got a pram, a cot and all sorts of baby equipment from my 'winnings'.

I'd won a televised tournament and soon I was about to become a dad. Life was on the up. Could it stay that way?

CHAPTER 7

THE ART OF THE HUSTLE

Two days after I won the Granada tournament, my manager picked me to up take me to work. As I stepped into the car I felt a sharp stabbing pain in my chest.

'Are you all right?' he said.

'No,' I said, clutching my chest. I was in agony.

I was rushed into hospital. I had a collapsed lung, or, to give it the technical name, a spontaneous pneumothorax.

The timing couldn't have been worse. I'd just won the tournament and was starting to think I might get some accolade. There were tournaments coming up that I fancied my chances in. Instead, I was in a hospital bed for two weeks. There would be no snooker for me for a while. I was gutted. The specialist who operated on me was a Mr Bernstein. He explained it was the type of thing that could happen to any fit healthy young man.

Funnily enough, my path crossed with Mr Bernstein's thirty years later. I was a guest at a golf day at the Whitefield

Club in Manchester. A friend introduced us and asked me if I remembered the specialist. Of course I did. I also remembered his comment about being fit and healthy. At the interval I was desperate for a smoke, but didn't want Mr Bernstein to see me. He's saved my life, I thought. What will he think if he sees me smoking? Finally, I found a quiet terrace and slipped outside. Who should I bump into out there having a sly fag? Mr Bernstein!

While I was laid up in hospital recovering, Dad came in to see me. 'I told you all those late nights would do you no good,' he said.

At least on a personal front, I had cause to celebrate. Our baby son Gary was born shortly afterwards. My mother said he was the spitting image of me as a baby. Both Susan and Gary were healthy. I couldn't be happier.

And, while I had missed out on the amateur championship for another year, a silver lining came a year later. Granada TV approached me again. They had launched a number of *How to Play* series on sport. Would I like to present a seven-part series on how to play snooker? I certainly would. I was delighted. I assumed, because I'd won their event, they knew I would be recognisable to viewers and I was a local lad.

I would be presenting the series with Gerald Sinstadt, the football commentator. It was a fantastic opportunity to increase my exposure – but I had one dilemma. I knew how to play the game but explaining it to someone else was another matter entirely. Plus, there was the pressure of having to do it over seven twenty-five-minute programmes. I got Joe Davis's book *Snooker for the Complete Amateur*. All of my explanations were based on Davis's idea on how to play snooker. The series aired on Sunday mornings at eleven o'clock. When I first met

Left: In the arms of my Auntie Joan –
I've alwys looked good in a hat.

Below centre: My mum and dad at their
fiftieth wedding anniversary party at
the Talk of the North club, Eccles.

Bottom: Youngest child: wide-eyed
and innocent.

Above: Wearing the goalie turtleneck in my school football team. I played alongside Peter Done (front row, right), brother of Fred Done, co-founder of the Betfred bookmaking business.

Right: Growing up in post-WWII Salford. I seem to have already adopted a quirky smile.

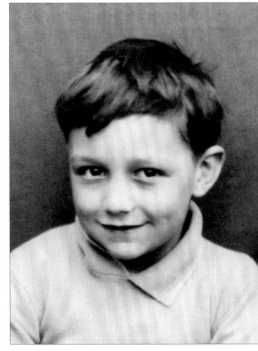

Above: It all began in Salford. A photo of myself (second from left) with my father (back row, second from right) at a local snooker tournament.

Left: Patsy Fagan and I are still in competition, but now only on the golf course.

Above left: The great Joe Davis in action – the snooker advice in his book helped me in presenting the *How to Play the Game* TV series in 1972.

Above right: The best and worst day of my life – arriving late for the 1979 UK Championship.

Below: The UK Championship after-party. I hold the cup with Freddie Frost (left) and my opponent Terry Griffiths (right). Fair play to Terry for joining the party.

Left and middle:
In action at the
table – my peak
years.

Bottom left: At the table
with Alex Higgins. He
always had the audience
on the edge of their
seats.

Bottom right: Relief;
tears; elation: I pose with
the cup after winning the
UK Championship, 1979.

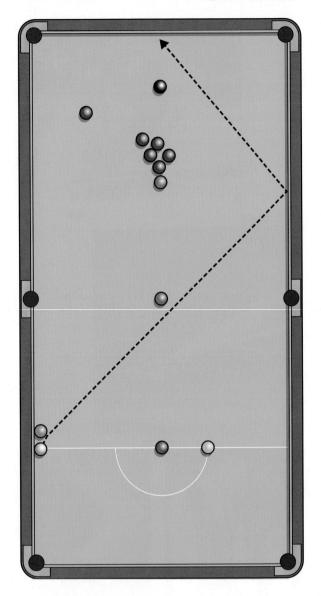

An illustration of Fred Davis's cheat shot against me, which would have been disallowed had the Miss Rule then been in force:

I had him snookered behind the green.

The right middle pocket blocked a one-cushion escape.

A two-cushion attempt would have nestled him into the cluster of reds, allowing me to pot the loose red into the left corner pocket.

He intentionally played thin of the green, leaving the cue ball tight on the cushion behind the black.

Left: (left to right) Tony Meo, Kirk Stevens, Graham Donkin, John Pullman, myself. Graham's father, Bruce was the first master of ceremonies to introduce the players at the Crucible Theatre.

Right: (left to right) Ex-Manchester United player Gerry Daly, Patsy Fagan, Alex Higgins, Con Dunne, myself – where did I get that jacket?

Below: Snooker professionals' teatime, backstage at Goff's, the Irish bloodstock auctioneers. From left: Doug Mountjoy, Steve Davis, John Spencer, manager Henry West, Kirk Stevens, myself and – no, not Roy Orbison – Dennis Taylor.

Top left: Geoff Lomas wanted to make Manchester's Potters the best snooker club in England. Geoff (right) and his father, Harry, with me at the opening in 1976.

Top right: Jimmy White vs Alex Higgins at the Embassy World Championships semi-final in 1982. A study in concentration in one of the most memorable matches ever at the Crucible.

Centre left: Presenting a well-deserved 'services to snooker' award to player and chairman of the WPBSA Rex Williams.

Bottom: Comedian Jim Davidson presents me with the trophy for Jokist's victory, years before we would work together on *Big Break*. 'You're really funny on that snooker,' he said.

Joe Davis, a couple of years later, he congratulated me on the series. I told him I'd taken everything from his book.

'Well done,' he said. 'Good idea.'

The exposure seemed to help my cause on the amateur scene. Up to 1972, I was under the radar. Soon, however, I was Lancashire amateur champion and I was playing for England in amateur team internationals. That was an eye opener in many ways. Some of the places we played were very basic. When we played Scotland the match was held in a school; I can't recall where. The dressing room was basically just a brick changing area. I asked a man who worked there if there was somewhere I could hang my jacket. 'Hold on a minute,' he said. He came back with a nail and a hammer and he banged it in the wall. 'Is that all right for you?' he said, and walked off.

That match was also notable because we had the first female referee in Vera Selby, a very good snooker player who would become the world's first ladies' champion. She wore hot pants and sleeve-length gloves.

England had a good team then. Six of us would be in the team and we'd travel with a couple of officials. It was another chance to evaluate yourself. The England team rarely got beat as we had Jonathan Barron from Cornwall and Ray Edmonds from Grimsby, both of whom had been world amateur champions. I was playing with all these top amateurs but I began to realise I was as good as they were and we were better than the other British teams.

Scotland struggled to produce that many exceptional players then, apart from Bert Demarco, who was a bit of a legend north of the border, and Eddie Sinclair, who was another good player who would turn professional later in the seventies. Someone asked Ray Reardon once why he thought no top snooker players had come from Scotland and he said, 'They drink too much.' This is the same Reardon who, when once interviewed on television on his political persuasion, answered quite matter-of-factly, 'Well, when I was a miner I was a very strong socialist, but now I've got a few bob I vote Conservative.' Only Ray could say that.

Right enough, there were some big drinkers in the Scottish team but there was a great camaraderie among all the nations. The England team travelled to Wales and Ireland. The first time I ever flew on a plane was for a tournament in Dublin. The amateur scene was thriving, while the professional game was being set ablaze by Alex Higgins.

The Hurricane's triumph in the 1972 final, defeating John Spencer 37–32 in a thrilling spectacle, took snooker to a whole new audience. I couldn't help but be amazed by the speed at which he flew around the table. In the year after his spectacular victory, I was to get a unique chance to view his talent at close quarters.

I couldn't believe my eyes one day in Chorlton when Higgins walked into the club. He'd heard this was where I practised and wanted to play me. I can still picture him waltzing up to me and saying, 'Do you fancy a game?'

This was the world champion! How many times do you get to play the reigning champ in your own club, on your own table? I racked them up immediately.

He gave me a seven start but I seemed inspired by his presence. Whenever we got to the stage where he needed snookers he'd rack them up again. Watching him play was an education. I marvelled at his flare and flamboyancy, how he built breaks, his cueing action, his ability to take on all pots. We played £2 a frame and kept going until 9 p.m. We played sixty-four frames and I finished fourteen frames in front – against the reigning world champion. I couldn't believe it.

After we finished he said he didn't have the money on him so he'd have to owe me. As he walked out he said he was going into town and could he borrow my jumper? Of course, I said, so out he strode with my pullover. He never did give me the money he owed, and I never saw the jumper again. That was my introduction to the one and only Alex Higgins.

It was an experience. It was good for me to play someone like him. To get the better of him was great and it gave me another insight into what I was capable of. Our impromptu session made me believe in myself a bit more but probably knocked me off the rails for a while afterwards. I began running around the table like a lunatic. I was playing so quickly but I was enjoying it.

Higgins was a breath of fresh air, but snooker was still frowned upon in some quarters – the sign of a misspent youth. It probably didn't help that both Marcus Owen and Patsy Houlihan served time in prison. I can't recall Houlihan's exact offence but he once described to me how he was found in a supermarket when it was closed.

As I had seen, Alex Higgins was prepared to practise for long hours when he was in the mood, but, by the time he had to defend his world title in 1973, his weakness for the temptations that would ultimately destroy him – drink, gambling and women – were beginning to be apparent. He didn't even make the final.

Higgins's next opportunity to show the world he wasn't just a flash in the pan came with the launch of a new tournament in Canada. As the country was trying to promote the game on a world stage, a number of players were invited from the UK

– and I was one of them. Given that the furthest I'd travelled was Dublin, getting the chance to fly to Toronto and Ottawa for three weeks of snooker was very exciting.

Canada's brightest talent was a young player called Cliff Thorburn, who had recently been crowned the country's national champion. Bill Werbeniuk, a player who would make a big impact, in more ways than one, on the UK scene, was also appearing as part of a strong Canadian contingent. Flying the flag for the home nations, alongside me, were Higgins, his fellow countryman Dennis Taylor, a young amateur from Leicester called Willie Thorne and Graham Miles, the unofficial second-best player in the world who had won *Pot Black* and was the defeated finalist in that year's World Championship.

It was fascinating to visit North America for the first time, and equally interesting to see how the public were taking to snooker. If anything, the crowds were even more enthusiastic than I'd witnessed back home.

In my first match I defeated Tino Malo from Montreal. In a close match I edged it 5–4. In the quarterfinal I came face to face with Higgins for the first time in a tournament. I wasn't able to repeat the form I'd shown in Chorlton and went down 8–3 in the best-of-fifteen match. Higgins would lose in the semifinal to Dennis Taylor, who then lost to Thorburn in a close final.

After Toronto it was over to Ottawa for an exhibition. Hard as it might be to understand now, the big draw for the public at the time was Graham Miles. Higgins found this hard to take and wasn't happy that he was going out at night to widespread indifference. Since he'd burst onto the scene in 1972 he had become used to the adoration and recognition.

Feeling a bit unloved may have been the reason he got on

the phone to Ciara, a girl he'd dated when he visited Australia after winning the world title. He asked her to come to Canada, on the promise that he'd marry her when they got back to Manchester. Knowing she was coming over seemed to relax him and we had fun, playing locals at snooker and our own card games.

One night Willie won $80 from Alex in a card game and, knowing that he was unlikely to see the money, asked instead for a 6 foot teddy bear that Higgins had won at a funfair. These bears were quite coveted on the trip because they were quite hard to come by. I had one but it wasn't through winning it: I'd bought it from someone who had. Alex duly obliged and handed Willie the teddy. It wasn't the last we were going to hear about the damn bears, however.

The Canada trip was life-changing for me in many respects. Not only was it the first time I got to see what life was like for professional players, but I felt I held my own with them. It also opened my eyes to the entertainment side of the game.

One night, we were playing an exhibition when the proceedings took on a bawdy edge. The announcer was reading out the scoreline as we went along in English and in French. When I reached sixty-nine points, the announcer said, '*Soixante-neuf*.' I gave him a knowing look and everyone started laughing. Then, halfway through a game, I noticed that my cue was getting a bit sticky. I didn't have a cloth handy to wipe it with, so I decided to wipe it with my tie, which was tucked into my shirt. The audience went wild with laughter. Even when Alex was trying to play his shot, they couldn't stop laughing. It was then that I realised that you didn't always have to play well to entertain an audience, but when I went back to my place you would have thought I had just made consecutive centuries, such was the ovation I received. The promoter, Maurice Hayes, approached me after the match and pointed out that, with my deadpan expression, anything I did that was silly became all the more funny. He said, 'You should try to do that whenever you can.' His words stayed with me.

The tables in Canada had even bigger pockets than those at Chorlton. I found these easier to play on because by concentrating less on potting the balls you were able to make bigger breaks and build up your concentration level. I also started working out different ways to break the balls and for going into the reds.

It was an eye opener in many ways. One night we were invited to a party, but, instead of offering a drink, someone produced a cigarette and said, 'Have a blast of that.' That was the culture in Canada.

Just as we were about to fly home, it all kicked off when Alex's girlfriend Ciara noticed the huge teddy bears and asked him why he didn't have one. He told her he had, but had given it to Willie.

'What did you give it away for?' Ciara said. 'I would have loved one of them!'

Ciara was boarding a different flight but left in a huff. Once we were on our flight, Alex started demanding his teddy back. Willie refused to part with it. He had already promised it to his own girlfriend.

I was stuck between the two of them as they traded insults and argued for the entire twelve-hour flight home. Alex accused Willie of being a cheat and at one stage threatened to tell customs the toy was stuffed full of drugs. 'They'll rip it apart and then nobody'll have it,' he seethed.

He didn't go through with it, thankfully, and, after what seemed an eternity, we disembarked with the bears intact. The incident didn't detract from what had been a wonderful trip. For the first time I started to think there might be a chance of turning professional – but how could I justify it with a young family to support?

★ ★ ★

Back in Chorlton, the club was becoming a hotbed for snooker. There were characters in there who liked a bet, and opportunities to play money matches with some of the best amateurs around. The better I became, the more backers I had, but the trick was finding people to play – and sometimes I had to become quite inventive to entice the competition. Apart from the normal points start, I would sometimes take on players with whom, after potting a red, I could go only for the yellow.

Patsy Houlihan once told me that to play a reluctant punter he had to agree to use the long cue. He had to open a window so he could cue properly. I didn't quite go to those extremes but my favourite was when one opponent complained that no start was enough because every chance I got I could make a sixty or seventy break. 'OK,' I said, 'any break over fifty doesn't count.' He agreed. He stood for it for six frames but never played me again.

Bets between different snooker clubs were popular, particularly when I had backers willing to put a stake on my winning. Paul Medati was in a similar position. He and I found success in an amateur doubles championship and we often got together for money matches. He was once challenged to go to Leicester and play Willie Thorne. One of Paul's backers told me they arrived at Willie's club, Osborne's, for a best-of-seven match. As they broke off for the first frame, Paul's backer went to the bar. The clubs were still unlicensed in those days, so he ordered a cup of tea and a sandwich. There was a bit of a wait and, when he got his order, he went to see how the match was going, just in time to see Willie get to the snookers-required stage in the fourth frame and win the match. The summary would have read, 'Went to Leicester, had a cup of tea and a sandwich, cost me £300.'

Occasionally, an opportunity arose to have a money match during the day. This happened when I had the chance to play a young, up-and-coming Irish lad called Patsy Fagan. I got a call at work one day asking if I could come to the snooker club the following day. If I did, it could be rewarding. I'd have to call in sick at work, but it seemed worth it.

Fagan's backer was a guy called Peter Careswell, who had a plumbing business in Putney, south London. What a character he was! His attitude to Northerners was a little underwhelming and his idea was to take Patsy around the country and play the best for what they liked. Patsy and his backer had been in Manchester for a couple of days. My friend Paul Medati had played him a couple of times but had no success.

Peter Careswell was no mug. He had heard that I was a better player than Paul. He didn't think we were an even match and said I should give Patsy a start. A little reluctantly, I gave Fagan a seven-point start. I came out on top but it was tough. I think it was about then that I realised that, to improve my game, I had to play more.

I also went to other snooker clubs, not necessarily to play the best player there, but perhaps to find someone we'd heard was good to play for money.

I learned one night that Cliff Thorburn had come over from Canada and was playing at the Bolton snooker club with John Spencer. Dennis Hughes and I went over to see if we could get a game. I ended up playing Spencer – he the professional, I the amateur – while Dennis played Thorburn. Cliff's sponsor was a chap called Terry Haddock. After my match he said to me, 'You're unbelievable. You don't look like a snooker player but, boy, can you pot a ball!'

I was thinking, What does a snooker player look like?

I was watching Cliff and he was a shadow of the player I'd seen in Canada. He could hardly string two balls together. A week later, however, I went back to Bolton and played him for the first time. This time he was on top form. His break building was of a standard I hadn't seen very often. He ended up taking money off me. However, over a meal afterwards, he confided that he was thinking about going back to Canada. He didn't think he had a future in Britain.

'Why are you saying that?' I said. 'You'd have a chance against almost anybody.'

'You think so?'

'I know so,' I said.

I think my little pep talk must have worked, because, as we know, Cliff went on to become a popular and successful figure on the circuit.

During my pursuit of money matches, one of my backers was a character called Sid the Monkey Man, so named because he worked the promenade in Blackpool. The monkey he owned would jump on punters' shoulders, Sid would quickly take the picture and charge two quid for the photo. Who could refuse an offer like that? Being a grafter and seeing me play in practice, he thought taking me out to play in another club would probably be more profitable. To be fair, he didn't pay me peanuts. He gave me fifty per cent of any winnings – a lot more than most would.

Word had it that, in Walsall snooker club, a guy called Market Mick would play for a 'nice few quid'. We went over there, met Mick and, after a bit of haggling, I agreed to give him a fair start. I guess you could call this hustling but it was the way of the world then in the snooker clubs. Market Mick was the perfect foil for a hustle. He couldn't resist a bet and he had a killer weakness: he thought he was a better player than he was.

We agreed to play a six-reds game. Not only does it make for a quicker game, but points-wise it's exactly half a full frame. I had offered him a forty-points start per frame. He didn't think it was enough, so I offered twenty points on a six-red frame. He accepted immediately.

We came away from Walsall with money in our pockets and smiles on our faces. Half of £600 might not seem like much these days but back then it was a windfall. We could have won more that night but Sid couldn't help himself. Mick looked as if he was going to win one frame. He just needed the pink and the black, which was over the corner pocket. Just as he was about to play his shot, Sid, who was sitting behind the line of the pocket, started counting out the money to pay him. Mick missed the pink and blamed Sid for putting him off. It didn't get violent but it certainly got tense. Mick refused to play another frame.

At the Northern Snooker Centre in Leeds a character dubbed Mervyn the Jeweller was the big attraction. Sid and I travelled through to meet him. Mervyn was on the ball and demanded a sixty-five-start per frame, so I had to be at my best. The bet was always per frame; in this instance it was £80. After two and a half hours we were £640 in front. Sid came over and told me this was 'case money', which meant if I won the next frame we had cleaned him out. I potted the brown to go twenty-two points in front with only eighteen left. Mervyn needed a snooker, which, surprisingly to me, he got. I then missed and he went on to pot the blue, pink and black to beat me.

Another two and a half hours later we were level. He won the next seven games. I would have played on but Sid knew I was tiring. Our chance to wrap it up came and went with the case money game. When you give someone a huge start you have to be on top form for every frame and, as I tired, the more mistakes I made. It was a long drive back from Leeds with just the fiver in my pocket I had started with.

Nights like that illustrated how fickle the business was. Although I was still working in Trafford Park, I was struggling financially and was desperate to earn extra money either through snooker or on the horses. It was difficult providing for a wife and child on my meagre salary.

I got the offer of an exhibition in Oldham from someone who remembered me from the Granada series. I earned £15 a night, the same I was getting for working. That got me thinking: just two exhibitions a week and I'd be on more than earned by my full-time job.

I would go to a local club, play the best players in the club. Sometimes, if it was best of seven frames, I'd give them on aggregate a two hundred start and, during the course of the evening, if they beat me on the aggregate, it was a case of no win, no fee. It was John Spencer who'd come up with the idea.

For a short time it proved quite popular. I think I lost one evening when I didn't get paid, but, even if that happened, we used to raffle a cue off to make money and the proceeds I'd split with the promoter.

I thought about a job change that could tie in paid employment with my snooker. An occupation I thought fitted the bill was that of postman. It should have been great. I could work in the morning delivering mail, finish at 1 p.m. and have the rest of the afternoon to practise. I got a job in Rochdale post office but very quickly I realised it was not the dream role I'd hoped for.

I was getting up at 4 a.m. delivering letters all morning. We had first and second post in those days. By the time I finished I was knackered. If I had a money match in Bolton I was catching the bus and falling asleep. It was actually costing me money, as I wasn't at my best when it came to matches and I didn't have the time I wanted to practise.

This was no good to man or beast. I didn't live far from the post office but it came to a head one Saturday morning after I'd had a late night. The alarm went off but I thought, No, I'm not going in.

The next thing I knew there was a banging on the door. The guy from the post office had come to knock me up.

'Are you coming in?'

'Yeah, all right,' I said and reluctantly got up.

It was nearing Christmas and when I got into the office there were all these presents to be delivered. The van drivers normally delivered awkward-shaped items such as footballs, as they wouldn't fit in the mail sack, but to make a point they'd left them for me to deliver. It was the straw that broke the camel's back, as they say. I grabbed a wrapped football and kicked it the full length of the post office sorting room.

'Sorry, lads, that's it for me,' I said. I walked out and never went back.

★ ★ ★

For the first time in my life I was out of a job. I thought I could make ends meet with the exhibitions but, coincidentally, they dried up. I felt extremely self-conscious, as though people were judging me. Here I was, a guy who had been on the telly – in those days that made you a minor celebrity on a local level – but I wasn't able to make ends meet. I almost wanted to walk around wearing a balaclava because I didn't want people to see I wasn't working.

I tried to make more money betting and by gambling on the snooker, but when you're in a rut nothing seems to go your way. I was in a state of flux. What should I do? Should I give up the game I love and get a steady nine-to-five and just settle into family life like everybody else? My head said yes, but my heart told me that wasn't for me. As long as I still had a bit of talent I hoped I might be able to continue playing. But how could I juggle playing snooker with earning a living?

One day, in February 1975, the door to Chorlton snooker club swung open. I was about to find out.

CHAPTER 8

MR PERFECTION

T hose moments when your life can change dramatically? This was one of them.

The man standing before me in Chorlton snooker club was Geoff Lomas, whom I had met only briefly, years before. He had a proposition for me.

'I'm opening a snooker club in Salford,' he said. 'And I want you to join me.'

Geoff's great name for the club was Potters. He was taking over the old Riverboat Club in Great Cheetham Street, where Gerry Dorsey used to compere, before he found fame as Engelbert Humperdinck.

Geoff wanted me to be his partner and help run the club. He thought that my name, as a well-known amateur, would attract other people to come down and play, which it did. He showed me the plans and said that, if I agreed, he would pay me £40 a week, nearly double what I had been earning in my last job. I couldn't believe it. It sounded like my dream job.

The club was to open the following year.

I went home that night and talked it over with my wife. Understandably, she wasn't sure. It sounded unpredictable, a bit of a gamble, which it was. However, I think she could see how excited I was about it. Although she wasn't too happy, I rang Geoff and said yes.

From that moment, my life changed – not always for the better.

Geoff, like a lot of other people, could see that snooker's popularity was soaring – and in the Northwest particularly. When Higgins won the World Championship in 1972 it was at Birmingham's Selly Park British Legion, but the following year it came to Manchester and the City Exhibition Hall, where Ray Reardon triumphed. Reardon won his third title in 1974, when it returned to Manchester, this time at Belle Vue. The following year had seen the competition travel to Australia and another title for Reardon, but in 1976 it was going to be returning to the UK, with some of the matches at Wythenshawe Forum, Greater Manchester. *Pot Black* was a success on television, and in 1975 the Masters tournament was launched and, for the first time ever, television lights were used throughout the competition. Increased coverage meant greater audiences. It really felt as if we were on the cusp of something.

Unfortunately for my wife, that was exactly what she was afraid of. Although the club was a long way from opening, I'd given her a taste of what life as a professional might be like, with my trip to Canada. In addition to that, after the world championship every year a pro–am tournament was held at the Pontin's holiday camp at Prestatyn, North Wales. Anyone who *was* anyone entered. They used to get more than nine hundred entrants. The amateurs fought it out and then eight top *Pot Black* professionals would come in to make up the last thirty-two players. The professionals had to give us amateurs a twenty-five-point start if we played them.

In 1975 I reached the final stages but, when I rang home to tell my wife of my progress, she got really upset. Our son was still a toddler and, obviously, it wasn't great that I was away from home. She simply didn't want me away and would have preferred me to have a normal job. That was what she had been brought up with. Now I could see another way I could go and she didn't want me to be away. The only way I could succeed was to go away for these tournaments and I began to feel guilty for doing so. I got the impression she was saying, Why don't you stop playing snooker and start being realistic here? Try to get a job. We have a child. We need to live as our parents did.

I got to the final that year and faced the formidable Ray Reardon. He gave me the twenty-five-point start. I thought I was as good as he was, but I became overawed by the situation. He beat me convincingly. Still, I got £500 for runner-up, which was a lot of money to me then. While I was there I could feel the groundswell of interest. The holiday camp was packed. It was a phenomenal atmosphere. We stayed in the chalets and we'd arrange money matches away from the main tournament. The game was really beginning to catch on. *Pot Black* had clearly been a big influence.

After the tournament was over, Geoff took me to the club before it opened to show me his vision. As soon as I saw the distance between the tables I said, 'There's not enough room.'

'No one will notice,' he said.

His belief was that by squeezing in another table he could

maximise revenue. It was his club. He did have a match table, however.

While he was still doing up the club, he said to me one night, 'We're going into town. We'll order a taxi. Here's the number. Ring up the taxi company and tell them to pick us up at Potters.'

At the time there wasn't even a sign above the door.

'They won't know where it is,' I said.

'They soon will,' he said, 'and so will everyone else.'

That was his attitude right from the start – to make Potters one of the best snooker clubs, not only in the Manchester area but also the country.

Geoff took me to a nightclub called Blinkers, which was owned by a bookmaker called Selwyn Demmy. It was a popular hangout for many of the United and City players. Until that night I'd never been to a place like that. It made me realise what a sheltered life I'd been leading. For years, if I wasn't out playing snooker I'd been at home with my wife and child.

Geoff would open my eyes to a whole new world. He not only got me involved in the snooker club but he effectively became my confidant and best friend. He gave me direction and focus.

I'll give you an example of his influence. When he heard I was without a car he set about changing that, to make me more mobile. I had first taken lessons with Stan Holden, back at Small Street. Stan used to take me out in his car and taught me the basics. I had tried to pass my test but had failed three times. On the first occasion, I was nervous enough but when I arrived for the test my examiner told me an inspector would be sitting in. What chance did I have? I thought, I'm going to have to be Stirling Moss to pass this!

I knew how to drive and borrowed a car, although I didn't have a full licence.

Incredibly, a pal who worked for an insurance company insured me, even though I didn't have a full licence. I didn't think that was possible. Nor did the police when they pulled me over one night driving home. I hadn't been drinking and I don't think they even had breathalysers in those days. I think they were just making random checks.

'Have you got your papers?' one of them said.

It was about 2 a.m. I didn't have any documents. They took me down to the police station and they charged me with driving without a licence or insurance.

When the case called at the magistrates' court, I pleaded not guilty and defended myself. I had a suit and waistcoat from Burton's that I paid for weekly. I thought I was Perry Mason. When the police officers gave evidence I interrupted them and when I finished I said, 'I rest my case,' just as they said on television.

When it was my turn in the witness box I pleaded my case. I said I've got insurance and presented my documents.

They didn't believe me because I had only a provisional licence. They rang up the insurance company and asked for a representative to come to the court. They delayed the proceedings until they could hear from him.

The guy turned up, confirmed I was insured and said if I had been in an accident they would have covered me.

I ended up getting fined £60. They couldn't take my licence off me because I didn't have one!

After that, the mate who lent me the car said, 'Next time you get pulled give them my name and when you have to produce you can take my licence.'

So I did! There were a few times during that period when I had to remember what name I'd given. I know it was illegal but it didn't feel as if you were doing anything wrong. Passing a test in those days was very hard. You had to drive in the car they gave you, with a clutch that was sharp as anything. I'd stall it every time.

Not long after my court drama, one of the guys at Chorlton said to me, 'Give me the money, you'll have your driving test tomorrow and, I promise you, you will pass.'

I went along in the morning and I passed. I've no idea, to this day, whether he knew the fella, or any deal was done, or whether I just didn't make any mistakes this time because I had been driving for a while.

I came out with that pink slip thinking, Woah!

My only problem now was how to get a car.

Once again the guys in Chorlton snooker club came to the rescue – sort of. I bought a three-wheeled Robin Reliant for £50 from some of my backers in my match against Patsy Fagan.

My first trip was to Bolton with one of the lads. On the way into Bolton there's a set of lights. When the light changed to green the car wouldn't move. I gave it some gas and it shot into the car behind. There was hardly a dent on that car but the back was nearly torn off mine.

The next day I went into the club and said to the boys I'd bought it from, 'This is a liberty. It won't go up a hill.'

'Yeah.' They shrugged. 'It's not very good.'

They gave me back £40, so it cost me a tenner to go to Bolton!

I still needed to get a car, so I went to the bank and borrowed £600 to buy a Triumph Herald. It was such a relief to have my own transport. There was nothing worse than having to go somewhere with my cue. There were no two-piece cues in those days, so I protected it in a big metal case. I used to sit there on the bus with it standing upright beside me and people would think it was a handrail and grab hold of it. I'd pull it out of the way because I wanted to protect my cue. Many a time I had people falling down the bus because of what they thought my cue was!

★ ★ ★

Potters Snooker Club opened its doors on 4 June 1976. To mark the occasion Geoff came up with the idea to put 'WANTED' posters in the snooker magazine. He devised a series of posters, featuring a host of top amateurs such as Ray Edmonds and Willie Thorne. The text read, 'Wanted: £1,000 reward is waiting for you if you can beat John "Mr Perfection" Virgo at Potters Club.'

I had earned the nickname in Potters because, if I wasn't on perfect position on the ball I played for, I put my hands on my hips, shake my head and tut. I was a bit embarrassed by the advert in a way because I was playing with these people in the English amateur teams and I remember walking into the bar one day and I felt like a gunslinger stepping through the door of a saloon bar. They were all holding up these magazine ads. But none of them took up the challenge. No matter what they thought.

The only one to give me a game was Cliff Thorburn. Geoff said to me one day, 'We've had Willie Thorne on the phone. He wants to know if you want to play Thorburn.'

Since our previous match and my little chat with him, Cliff had been down in Leicester practising with Willie and had been producing the type of snooker he'd shown when he'd first come over, when I'd first seen him. They came to Potters and set up a game. Many of the lads from Chorlton came with me to Potters, keen for a piece of the action.

The money was set at £1,000 – a lot of money in those days. All the members of the club had a bet – £50 here and there. Cliff and Willie had arrived with a number from the Leicester crowd. One character was called Relentless Reg, so called because, whenever he was down on his luck, which was often, he would shake his head and sigh, 'It's relentless.' They were all backing the Canadian.

We agreed to play the best of nine frames. I was expecting a tough match but in just over an hour I'd beaten him 5–0.

We were all elated and I was desperate to get to the bar to celebrate the victory. However, in front of everybody, Thorburn said, 'Right, I'll play you double or straights, but this time it's for your own money.'

That was a bit of an insult, I thought. He was implying that I didn't have as much to lose as it wasn't my money at stake. That wasn't the case. I had my own money on the previous match, like the rest of them. It seemed that to save face he now wanted to play me for my own money. I gave him the only reply I thought was appropriate: 'Fuck off.'

A little while later I had another opportunity to play Patsy Fagan. He had a new backer called George Jackson. My challenge was to play Patsy in his home club, the Ron Gross Snooker Centre in Neasden, northwest London. How much money was bet on the game I never knew, but, by the time the match was tied at eight frames all, the pot was over £1,000. In the deciding frame I needed to clear the table to clinch the match 9–8.

After potting the last red I came a bit high on the black. I didn't get into the cue ball enough and somehow went in off in the middle pocket. I lost, but Ronnie Gross, a former World Championship player himself, said afterwards it was one of the best matches he had ever seen. It was small comfort for Geoff and me. However, as we travelled back to Salford, we felt the money was only lent.

Two weeks later I was playing Patsy in a tournament sponsored by J. W. Lees, who were the brewers for Potters. When Geoff asked George Jackson what he wanted to bet his reply was, 'I haven't brought much money with me. After John lost in Neasden I didn't think you'd want to play us for money.'

What a liberty! We had gone to London and played him on his own patch. Eventually, we managed to get a couple of hundred quid on and I won the match 5–1. It was not Patsy's fault.

Sometimes I had to travel far and wide for a money match. The snooker grapevine was very informative. Word had got round that there was money to be earned in a snooker club in Jersey. A guy from the Midlands had played over there and won £1,500 from a player who was backed by the owners of a Chinese restaurant.

One of the members of Potters Club, Derick, worked on the oil rigs. He overheard the conversation about the club in Jersey. Without much encouragement he offered to pay the travelling expenses for a group of us to go over there.

Two problems faced us as soon as we arrived. First, where was the snooker club? We didn't have the luxuries of a satnav or Google Maps. Eventually we found the only place it could be. It was called the Mechanics Club. It had only six tables but was the only place on the island that resembled a snooker club.

We signed in on the premise that we were on holiday for a few days. We had a few games on our own, while Derick discreetly asked around who the best player was. A young lad told him the club's star player wasn't in that day, but would play anyone for money. The lad even rang him up, informed him that we were looking for a money game. He assured us he would be in the next afternoon.

Our next problem was then finding a place to stay. It was just our luck that the day we arrived was slap bang in the middle of Battle of the Flowers week, an annual celebration and a must-see festival that attracted visitors from all over Europe. There wasn't a hotel room to be found anywhere. The only available hotel was in neighbouring Guernsey.

Oil workers must have earned good money, because, undeterred by this setback, Derick hired a private plane. The cost of the trip was escalating, but we were confident that the next day we would be in the money.

When we arrived at the Mechanics Club we once again signed in. I used the name John Duncan, just in case my own name was recognised. After a short while our man arrived. We chatted for a while before we set the balls up. To our consternation, he wanted to play for only £2 a game. I told Derick we would have a few frames before we asked to raise the stakes. He was only an average player. I won the first four frames but was reigning it in so as not to show my hand too much.

Derick asked him if he wanted to raise the stakes.

'No,' the man said. 'I recognise him from the snooker magazines.'

He'd seen the 'WANTED' posters Geoff had used to advertise Potters.

Desperate to recoup his air fares, Derick told him we had heard he had some backers. Where were they, and what start did he want?

Yes, the man said, he did have some Chinese guys who used to back him, but, after losing a lot of money to a player from Birmingham, they said they would never back him again. Reading between the lines, it sounded as if they were close to giving him a good hiding.

We walked out of the Mechanics Club with £8 – our entire winnings. A rough estimate of the cost of our trip, with hotels and air fares, was about £500. To be fair to Derick, he didn't complain. That's gambling. Thank goodness he paid all the expenses! I didn't have the heart to ask him for half the winnings.

When I got back to Potters the next day Geoff thought it was the funniest thing he had heard.

★ ★ ★

The better I got to know Geoff Lomas, the more I realised how much we had in common. Like me, Geoff loved a bet. His grandfather had been a bookmaker and what he didn't know about betting wasn't worth knowing. He completely changed my approach to gambling. Having worked for his grandfather, he had built up quite a few connections in the racing game but the cornerstone of his opinion was times. He had a good friend in Bob Nathan, who called the handicap book his bible. Other angles that Geoff brought to my notice were trainers at certain courses and jockeys who were riding at their minimum weight.

Until I'd met Geoff my philosophy, like my father's before me, had been the formbook. The problem with this system is that you have no idea what condition the horse is in at the time it's running. Although I'd grown confidence in my own opinion, I had learned not to go too crazy. I would always bet twice as much on a strong tip than I did on my own opinion.

Apart from playing snooker for money, my main betting was still horseracing and occasionally going to the casino. Casinos were not really my bag, however, because in those days it was either blackjack or roulette. The problem with these games was that you had to make a decision every minute. Do you stick or twist? Or what number appeals to you? It was very hit-or-miss.

To give you an example of how much our love for betting influenced us in those early days, when Geoff had been trying to secure the deal from J. W. Lees to supply drinks to the club, our meeting with the rep clashed with a big meeting at Epsom. Nathan was going nap on a horse called Quiet Fling in the Coronation Cup.

As we sat down to talk, the horses were going behind the stalls. Geoff was telling him how many barrels we would want a week. Me? I had half an eye on the television. When they came around Tattenham Corner I couldn't sit still any longer. With two furlongs to go, Quiet Fling went to the front. One moment I was having an important meeting, the next I was on my knees cheering the horse home. I learned in later years that shouting your horse home wasn't the done thing. But, as any punter will agree, the rush I got from backing a winner was up there with anything I could do on the snooker table.

It wouldn't be the last time my two passions clashed – at times it would prove extremely costly – but I enjoyed that night.

★ ★ ★

We weren't just winning at the races. Potters was thriving. At the tournaments Geoff held in there we'd attract crowds of a hundred and fifty people. It may not sound much but the atmosphere generated was something else. Every taxi driver quickly knew where Potters was and that was a way of getting name awareness. It was on its way to becoming known as one of the top clubs in Britain.

Snooker clubs in the mid-seventies were buzzing. There were no fruit machines, no card tables. It was all snooker. If you wanted a bet you either played or backed someone else.

Snooker was now my life full time. I thought it would be great, because, being in the club all day, I thought, I could practise when I wanted, but the reality was not as straightforward as that. Someone had to change the barrels behind the bar, make sandwiches and ensure the place was ticking over. By the time I'd done all of that and the staff came in, the idea of practising went out the window. The only time I'd really get to practise was if Alex Higgins came in and I'd practise with him and a couple of other players. Playing with Alex continued to be a revelation – but his presence in the club could occasionally be volatile.

Geoff had suggested I bring in some of my trophies to display behind the bar. They were not the most prestigious trophies or awards, but they brightened the place up and I was proud to have them there. The next time Alex came in he took a look and said, 'What are all these babe?' When I told him they were trophies I'd won he offered to bring some of his own in. The next thing we knew he arrived with a whole series of trophies. A bit of one-upmanship perhaps. They didn't last long, though. He got in a bad mood after having a bad run in a kalooki card game. He was convinced someone was cheating him. 'You're all cheats,' he declared, 'and I want my fucking trophies back.' He gathered them all up and took off down the stairs. 'Fuck you all!' he shouted over his shoulder as he went. The next thing we heard was a great clanking din as he fell down the stairs, his trophies noisily falling alongside him.

Alex was a loose cannon, but his impact on the game cannot be overstated. After he won the World Championship, suddenly everybody was running round tables at 100 m.p.h., bumping into one another, balls flying everywhere. It was the Higgins's movement.

* * *

At a time when my fortunes seemed to be changing, I had to come to terms with the shock of losing my father. He had continued working at the docks well past retirement age. The union had got him an extra £3,000 pension, so he stayed on until he was sixty-eight. He was able to enjoy the benefit of only six years' retirement. He was struck down with cancer of the stomach. I couldn't believe it when he was gone. So much of how I thought and who I was had been shaped by him. It was my dad who first ignited the desire in me to play snooker and it was always a sense of sadness to me that he passed away before I hit my prime. It was a pity, but that was one of the problems of turning professional so late. It just wasn't to be.

I channelled my energies into trying to make a name for myself. I was hoping for more exhibition work but my snooker club duties were getting in the way of playing.

It wasn't conducive to a happy home life either. I was throwing myself into my new role at the club and playing.

In 1976, the year Potters opened, it was Geoff who encouraged me to turn professional. After my Canada trip I'd been giving it serious consideration, but it wasn't was easy as it sounds. Spencer and Reardon turning professional had opened the game up – but only so far. At the time there was a rule that you had to have won the English Amateur Championship before you could apply to go pro. That was a title that had so far eluded me.

There was another chance, however. After the World Championship that year at Wythenshawe, which Ray Reardon won, a tournament for the top amateurs in Britain was held. I was among those invited to compete. In the semifinal I faced Doug Mountjoy, the newcomer from Wales who had recently won the World Amateur Championship. It was a close game, but I managed to beat him. Doug was turning professional at thirty-five, the age many considered a snooker player reached his peak. Terry Griffiths told me after the match that Doug had gone up to him and said, 'I'm nearly as good as him, aren't I?'

I went on to win the tournament. I was starting to believe in myself that I could compete with the better players – but how would I earn a living? I was thirty years old. If I turned professional now I might only have five years before I was past my prime.

Doug turned professional in his first tournament and won the Masters. Seeing the impact Doug was having made me think I could at least emulate his success. With Geoff urging me on, I applied to the professional association, the WPBSA, and later that year I was accepted.

Twenty-one years after I first picked up a snooker cue and potted a ball I was becoming a professional. I was finally going to find out, having spent all that time wondering, if there was money to be made in the game.

It was an exciting period, but I was conscious I was on

borrowed time. The clock was ticking. In five years I could be washed up. I had to hit the ground running, make a quick impact.

I think my wife despaired at the direction my life was taking, but was powerless to stop me. Reluctantly she accepted that I needed to prove to myself I could compete with the top names.

I was stepping into the unknown – and almost immediately it would have devastating consequences for all of us.

CHAPTER 9

VIRGO'S REBELS

There were snooker tables nearly as far as the eye could see – thirty of them – packed with people. On my other side table-tennis balls were flying around from thirty-six tables. Amid all this were people crammed in to see my latest exhibition of snooker trickery. There was I in the middle. I explained my next trick shot to the compere beside me, resplendent in his red jacket.

'John is now going to try to pot the pink in off the black.' His voice bellowed out of the loud hailer he was carrying. That was the only way he could be heard. A few people in the audience to his left nodded. He then turned to face the audience on his right: 'John is now going to try and pot the pink . . .' He turned again. 'John is now going to try . . .' Round the hall he went. When he was finally done I played my shot.

Turning professional might conjure images of a snooker

player travelling the world, going from tournament to tournament, staying in the top hotels. It can be true of today's players, some of whom complain there are too many tournaments. However, back in 1976, the reality of a professional's life was much different. There was only one tournament – the World Championship – plus the Masters, *Pot Black* and the Pontin's, all of which were invitational. So snooker players had to supplement their income by playing the holiday camps.

I was delighted when I landed a contract for a whole summer at Butlin's camps. It was for only £150 a week but it was guaranteed income. I couldn't believe the size of these places. Skegness was the biggest. When it was at capacity it had twelve thousand holidaymakers staying there. The snooker room, if you could call it such, had, as we've seen, thirty tables plus those thirty-six tennis tables; but there were also a dozen air-hockey tables and twenty dart lanes. The place was absolutely huge. Its size made it difficult to do an exhibition. My Red Coat assistant needed the loud hailer to explain what was going on, but constantly having to repeat himself didn't do much for the flow of the show. On the other tables, matches were going on. Invariably, when I bent down to take my shot, a ping-pong ball would hit me on the head. It was mayhem.

It was a steep learning curve. My slot lasted two hours and the only way I could have the crowd leave with smiles on their faces was by learning how to entertain. The tables were dreadful – there was no guarantee the ball would go where I wanted it. I had to hone the trick shots to suit the table. It taught me how to play the audience. If you could take some people with you, it got the whole room going.

I was also getting an education in how *not* to do it. The Red Coat who regularly helped me was a funny guy, but one day he took his humour too far. After my stint, he was taking charge of the donkey derby. I went down with him to take a look. There were all these little kids holding on – they had bars on the tops of the saddles. He said, 'Right, children, hold on to the reins tightly. If for some reason when you're going round the bend you lose grip of the reins, grab hold of the handle on top of the saddle. If for some reason you miss this and you're going underneath the donkey you'll see another handle. Do not grab hold of that.'

I was in bits. All these kids were looking underneath their donkey to see what handle he was on about. When I went back the following week the Red Coat wasn't there. Some of the parents had complained and he'd got the sack. I felt for him but it was a reminder that you needed to know and play to your audience.

Skegness was my first port of call on Mondays. I would drive straight there from Manchester, do my stint there on Monday and Tuesday. On Wednesday morning I would drive from Skegness to Clacton-on-Sea, do two shows there on Thursday and Friday and then drive back to Manchester on Friday night. It was exhausting. Then I was hanging out in Potters. Geoff was one of the first people in the country to apply for a late-night licence. When croupiers at the casino finished at one or two in the morning they could come to Potters for a late-night drink.

If we didn't hang out in Potters, we were going to nightclubs such as Blinkers. From the kind of bloke who liked going to his local pub I was now someone who liked to be out all night.

If I'm being honest, I must say that my head was turned

once Potters was opened. I seemed to be living the life many young people lead before they settle down and get married. My problem was that I had a wife and young son at home. My excuse was that I was focusing on my career and that I had to put myself out there, get known. I had come to the professional scene relatively late in life. I had to make the most of it before it all ended.

My life completely changed. Up until that point I hadn't had a lot of excitement. I'd always struggled for money. Yes, I'd had the tournament wins and the odd money-match success. And I was lucky that I had a loving wife and son and a nice home – but I didn't see it like that at the time.

All my life, snooker had been simply a parlour game, something done away from the limelight in local clubs. Now it was opening up, it was exciting. It was on television. I was playing against the top names in the game. We were getting recognition. Believe it or not, snooker attracted some groupies back in those days. There was even a bit of a pecking order. Willie Thorne was considered the best-looking snooker player at the time – this was back when he had hair. It was said that was the reason he was invited onto *Pot Black* – because he looked good in front of the cameras. It's not as if I were suddenly raking it in or getting a lot of attention. I was way down the pecking order and I was still working in Potters. But my life was changing.

Willie turned professional, purely on the back of his *Pot Black* invitation, in the same year as Doug Mountjoy and I did. Patsy Fagan also made the step up in 1976. The game was opening up yet further.

At the Northern Snooker Centre in Leeds, run by Yorkshireman Jim Williamson, a British Junior Billiards and Snooker Championship was played. I was in the club to watch and saw a young ginger-headed lad called Steve Davis for the first time. I could tell by the way he got down and hit the ball that he looked useful.

Steve was beaten in the snooker tournament but won the billiards competition. Not long after that I played him in a pro–am event in Enfield. Although I beat him and he was just a raw fifteen-year-old, I could tell he was a good player. Little did I know that the young boy would go on to become the bane of my and many other players' lives!

On the next table was another very promising youngster, from Tooting, south London, Jimmy White – just fourteen but brimming with natural ability.

Changes were happening apace on the organisational side. Maurice Hayes, the promoter who took us to Canada, had secured the sponsorship of the tobacco brand Embassy, a move that would do wonders for the game in general. Sadly, the World Championship was dogged by financial problems in 1976 and, while Maurice did a lot of good work, it was necessary to find someone new for the game's showpiece. Mike Watterson was the new promoter. One of his first moves would be one that helped cement the game in the minds of the British public. His wife Carole had been to the Crucible Theatre in Sheffield to watch a show and returned raving to her husband what a good venue it could be for snooker. With Embassy agreeing to continue their sponsorship, the 1977 World Championship was the first time snooker had a proper home of its own and the Crucible would become synonymous with the game. The prize pot was £17,000, the highest it had ever been.

Such was the expansion of the game that a qualifying round had to be played. In their wisdom, the WPBSA decided that, of the sixteen that would play at the Crucible, fourteen should be seeded. That meant that Mountjoy, Thorne, Fagan, Roy Andrewartha, the English amateur finalist, and me had to play down to two.

Geoff Lomas thought seeding fourteen with only two qualifiers was wrong. I shrugged and asked what we could do about it.

'Call an EGM,' he said.

Given that I had struggled to understand what a GCE was as a kid, what Geoff was saying sounded like Morse code. When he explained it was an 'extraordinary general meeting' and that we, as professionals, could call it, we set about trying to make it happen. We rang around the players who were having to qualify and with their support requested a meeting to state our case.

Rex Williams was the chairman of the WPBSA at the time but before we even got into the meeting threats were being made. Willie Thorne was in tears. He said John Spencer had warned him that if we won the vote he'd never play in *Pot Black* again. That wasn't something that concerned me as I hadn't been invited to play in *Pot Black*, but I could see for Willie it was a big deal. That would cut off one of the few tournaments to play in. The message was clear: go against the establishment and there would be no more invites.

It seemed rich, given the difficulties John Spencer had in turning professional, that he would seek to block the chances of new players on the scene. I spoke to Spencer about his remark. He said, 'All you and your rebels are going to do is ruin the game.'

The five of us were dubbed 'Virgo's Rebels'. Actually, we should have been called 'Lomas's Rebels' but at the time it didn't seem like a big deal. Events later would cause me to reconsider that opinion.

Amid all this antagonism, the meeting started. I spoke for the so-called rebels. The meeting got very heated and, to be fair, the chairman, Rex Williams, kept a very firm grip. Remarkably, we won by the odd vote. We came so close to losing: if John Pulman had turned up to the meeting as he had promised the vote would have swung in their favour.

Still, the anger from the established players did not abate. Dennis Taylor challenged some of the players for money; not me, however. The insinuation was that he was better than we were. Dennis seemed to feel that, as he had been a professional for three years, he was entitled to be seeded to the final stages. Dennis may not have got his way in 1977 but, the next time he intervened on the issue of seeding, it nearly ripped the game apart.

Emerging from such rancour wasn't the ideal preparation for my first crack at the world title, but, come the championship, I tried to focus. I beat Andrewartha 11–0 to set up a meeting against Yorkshireman John Dunning, a match I came through 11–6.

As fate would have it, my opponent in the last sixteen was John Spencer, the rebel versus Mr Establishment. We shook hands and the match started without any mention of the previous arguments over seedings. Had it all been forgotten? I was about to find out.

Early in the match, I led 4–1. In the next frame I potted a red, intending to run through for the black, but I got a bad contact, so, instead of being straight on the black, I was left with a thin cut. I asked the referee to clean the cue ball. In those days, referees just used a coin to mark the place where the cue ball had been. This referee just picked it up, rubbed it in his hands and put it back on the table, now in a position from where I could no longer pot the black. I complained but he denied the ball was in the wrong place and told me to carry on. I asked Spencer for a second opinion, but he just ignored me. Instead of carrying on with my break, I had to play safe. I lost that frame and, being unable to shake off my sense of injustice, lost the next two after that.

I'm not making excuses, but that incident upset me. In the mid-session interval I spoke to the promoter, Mike Watterson, to complain. He said he had already spoken to the referee about what happened. The reply he'd got was, 'You know that Virgo – he's a trouble causer.'

Clearly I had built up a bit of a reputation for myself, rightly or wrongly. I did make trouble for the referee, however, which might have explained why I never saw him back at Sheffield again.

I lost the match to Spencer 13–9, disappointed that I'd let a small incident get to me. However, I was pleased with my overall performance and it was great to experience playing in a World Championship. Spencer went on to win it, beating Cliff Thorburn in the final.

After the tournament ended and the season officially over I went back to Butlin's – the same routine and travelling as the previous summer. This time, however, the long drives only left me more time with my thoughts, which, believe me, were not pleasant.

★ ★ ★

My marriage, which had been struggling for a long time, was over.

Susan and I had been growing apart for some time and it was all my doing. It was a good time for me in the sense that I had ambition then. I was beginning to see I had a future but I could also see that the life I had started had crumbled, and that was tough.

It's easy to say now that the grass isn't always greener, but back then, when I was being introduced to a completely different lifestyle from the one I was used to – from the one I grew up with – it was so hard to stay focused.

I was a guy whose manager once said wouldn't amount to anything. I would be selling shoelaces in the park. Now, here I was, playing the World Championship, partying in the Playboy Club with bunny girls all around, which was one club Geoff took me to. I almost defy any young man in that situation not to have his head turned.

In hindsight, I should have stuck it out, but you don't know what's around the corner. I'd thought my life was being mapped out for me, and now here I was living for the day. I wanted to see where this new life would take me.

Susan and I had different goals. I wasn't even sure what my goals were, but I didn't want to live out a mundane existence like my parents – I knew that. I didn't want to be just scraping by – although there have been times in my life when scraping by would have been a blessing in disguise. It certainly hasn't all been champagne and caviar. But I wanted to push on.

I take full blame for everything that happened with my first marriage. I find it hard thinking back to those days, because I'd always considered myself a better person. I hurt people I loved dearly and it still saddens me to think about it. I thought I was better than that. I fell short of the standards I'd set myself, and that's a hard thing to accept.

Maybe if I'd gone to university and had a degree, I would have had something to fall back on, but I was convinced my life, outside snooker, was going nowhere. Snooker was my only route out of my existence. The lure was there and I didn't have time for anything else. I had to be available to play snooker. If it was going to London or Leeds, I wanted to have that availability, and that is very difficult when you're married. It's as if I had these growing pains that I needed to spread my wings to heal.

I have nothing but good to say about my first wife. None of it was her fault. She only wanted the best for her family. The only time we ever had a disagreement was when she just wanted me to find a steady job that could provide for us all.

Maybe I married at the wrong time. I was too inexperienced. I hadn't lived a life, but there was a feeling of pressure to conform to how my contemporaries were living in Salford. At the time, I had no idea how things would change. The simple truth is that, by the mid-seventies, I wasn't the same person she had married.

I've done things in my life of which I'm not proud, of which I didn't think I was even capable. I know you have to live your life and face up to it, but I can't help having regrets at the way things turned out. I could have acted a whole lot better. I ended up making a mess of it all.

You do things on the spur of the moment and from there there's no going back.

My actions and the impact they had weighed heavy on me as I used to take those long drives across the country. There was a big roundabout at the edge of a motorway I passed every week and a few times I thought about driving straight over. It wasn't the answer, of course, but I hated the hurt I caused so much there were times I just wanted to wipe myself out – just disappear.

I found great difficulty in coping with it and I still do when thinking back. I wouldn't wish it on anyone else.

The cause of all the hurt was myself. I met a girl who came into Potters. Her name was Avril. She'd only popped in looking for a guy she knew. I met her again a week later in Blinkers when I was out with Alex Higgins. She was older than I and seemed more streetwise, more in tune with the life I was leading now.

On the night we got chatting and hit it off, Alex was also trying to chat her up. She chose me.

Given the way things turned out between us, that was the one occasion when I look back that I think, Why couldn't Alex have won that night?

CHAPTER 10

IN OVER MY HEAD

In 1977 the UK Championship was held for the first time. Although a non-ranking tournament, it was nevertheless another chance for me to prove myself.

I hoped playing might take my mind off my personal turmoil. Held in the Tower Circus in Blackpool, the tournament didn't quite match the prestige of the Crucible, but I didn't care. I equipped myself well, beating Dennis Taylor 5–2 in the last sixteen, then in the quarterfinal came from 2–1 down to defeat Graham Miles 5–2. In the best-of-seventeen-frame semifinal against Patsy Fagan, I raced into an 8–5 lead, needing only one more frame to reach my first major final. I couldn't close out the match, however, losing 9–8. Fagan would go on to lift the title, beating Doug Mountjoy 12–9 in the final. There was no disgrace in losing to the eventual champion, but I had a feeling it was a chance missed.

The tournament was notable for a number of reasons. Three

of the four semifinalists were all newcomers, something that wouldn't have gone unnoticed among the game's hierarchy. The championship was also remembered for Willie Thorne's bitter last-sixteen clash with Rex Williams. During the game, Williams accused Thorne of playing deliberate misses, tantamount to calling him a cheat. The match went to a deciding frame and, during the tense finale, Rex complained to the referee about one shot Willie played trying to get out of a snooker. The referee decided that, in his opinion, Thorne made a fair attempt. Willie clinched the match 5–4 but the furore did not end there.

Later that night, back in the hotel, someone asked Willie about the incident. Willie said he hadn't really cared whether he had got out of the snooker or not. The conversation was overheard and the promoter, Mike Watterson, was so alarmed he called an EGM consisting of the WPBSA secretary, Mike Green, senior referee John Williams and himself. In their infinite wisdom they decided to disqualify Thorne and give the match to Williams.

Watterson rang Rex with the decision. Although Williams disagreed with the reinstatement he was told in no uncertain terms that, if he didn't come back, he would be fined for nonappearance. During his drive from Birmingham, the decision was changed again. After some second thoughts and the possible threat of legal action, Thorne was reinstated.

The story made headlines along the lines of 'WILLIAMS CALLS THORNE A CHEAT'. The fact that he never said that was immaterial – something that I would discover to my cost in later years.

For the first time snooker and the integrity of the players was being questioned. It would not be the last time. The incident also served to show that the press were not solely interested in what happened on the snooker table.

★ ★ ★

By this time I was now living with Avril, having moved out of the flat in Rochdale. In the short period from before I got married to this point, attitudes had changed so much there wasn't the same stigma attached to couples 'living over the brush'. I was building up a name for myself. I had people ringing up to book me for exhibition work.

Ged Ford usually promoted country-and-western shows but he had a snooker table in his house in Peterborough and he often booked players for matches. One night I was there to play the great Fred Davis. I must have let all the talk about Mr Perfection go to my head. I turned up in a white suit, white shirt and white bowtie, and I painted a pair of black shoes white. If it had started snowing I'd have gone missing. I don't know what Fred Davis must have thought of me. The next morning before breakfast I went out for a run in a bright-red tracksuit. I came back sweating, my face the colour of my tracksuit. Fred looked at me. He must have wondered what had happened to his game.

Another person to whom I was grateful for bookings was Del Simmons, who would be instrumental in getting me more involved with the political side of the game in the years to come. I first met Del while he was working for Bristol Coin Equipment (BCE). He lived in Weybridge and started putting on exhibition matches with John Spencer, Alex Higgins and Ray Reardon. Like Geoff Lomas, Del had spied an opportunity with snooker as the game became more popular.

He rang me one day and said he had a booking for John

Spencer for an exhibition that the former world champion couldn't make. 'How much do you charge a night?' he asked.

'Fifty quid,' I said. Given I'd only just turned professional, I could hardly command large fees.

'Fifty quid?' he said. 'I'll get you more than that.' Immediately, I was on £75 a night. I was so keen to get any work I might have said I'd do it for £25, but now I was on £75 a night.

Doing exhibitions allowed me to develop my trick shots. Every professional has a repertoire of entertaining shots he can perform. It's part and parcel of the game. Gradually, however, I began to develop another way to entertain.

I remember one evening going to watch the Northern Irish professional Jackie Rea. Jackie was the leading player out of the country before Higgins came along. He wasn't the best professional but he was a good player and his antics earned him the label 'the Clown Prince of Snooker'. He did all the exhibition circuits. The night I saw him he did an impression of Joe Davis. It wasn't the most accurate but the audience loved it. As I watched the reaction I thought, What a good idea! I started thinking of the impersonations I could do of other players.

One night in Potters I was called from the bar to do some trick shots. The tricks weren't working very well, so I said, 'I'm going to do something different.' I started impersonating John Spencer, sticking my bottom out and sniffing, as he was prone to do. It got a few laughs. Then I did Higgins, as he had lots of mannerisms people recognised. That went down a storm.

For a while I just did the impersonations for laughs in the club. When we hosted amateur tournaments, I tried them out. I did one of John Hargreaves, who was a well-known amateur from Stoke-on-Trent, then Ray Reardon. I had one of Cliff Thorburn, which I thought was quite funny, but it didn't get the laughs I expected.

I used to study the top players for ways to improve my game so that was how I could notice their little idiosyncrasies. In the age before television completely took over, players developed their own individual way of doing it.

When it came to my own game, I felt the 1978 World Championship was a chance for me to make a real impact. In my qualifying match for the chance to play at the Crucible with the last sixteen, I drew Fred Davis, then sixty-four, which was some age to be still competing, let alone at the highest level. The match was to be played at the Forum, in Romiley, Stockport. I have to be honest: I thought at his age he didn't stand a chance of beating me. I started well and moved into a 4–1 lead. Although he came back, I had other good leads at 6–3 and then 7–4.

In the following frame I had him in trouble and was looking forward to going 8–4 ahead and just one frame away from victory. I had him snookered by the green, which was lying near the cushion on the baulk line. The one-cushion escape was not an option: the right-hand middle pocket was stopping that route. To come off two cushions, he would have nested into the cluster of reds. If he had done that he would have left me a pot on the loose red into the left corner pocket. His choice was to play purposely thin of the green and leave the cue ball tight on the cushion behind the black. I had walked back to my seat thinking it was impossible for him to leave the cue ball safe. How wrong I was!

Davis proceeded to play the most blatant deliberate miss I have ever witnessed (see plates, page 6). I couldn't believe it. This was the great Fred Davis, brother of Joe. I looked at the referee, Jim Thorpe, but didn't say anything. I was too stunned. The referee allowed play to continue. I was rattled. I lost that frame and the next two. The match was level at 7–7. I managed to compose myself enough to win the next frame to take me one frame from qualifying. But Fred rallied again and won the next two to clinch victory.

As we shook hands at the end of the match I realised that behind that famous smile was a man who wanted to win at all costs. In some strange way I admired him for being so ruthless, but it didn't stop me feeling absolutely gutted.

Losing out in the qualifiers was a big blow, particularly as, for the first time, the championship was televised from Round 1. For once, viewers weren't just being shown highlights but could watch a frame from beginning to end, allowing them to see there was more to snooker than just potting balls.

Fred went on to reach the semifinals that year, narrowly losing to the South African Perrie Mans, which was a remarkable achievement. To mark the event 'When I'm Sixty-Four' was played, heralding the beginning of the musical item, which would become a big hit with armchair fans over the years.

In that semifinal Fred needed only a straight pink to take his match with Perrie Mans to a deciding frame – and he missed it. Given their intense rivalry over the years, people often wondered what the relationship was like between Fred and his more illustrious brother Joe. Once, when someone asked Fred if Joe had ever helped him, he said the only advice his brother ever gave was him was, 'Take that smile off your face.' I had some insight, however. After Fred's semifinal defeat, I walked through the exit door and came face to face with Joe

Davis. He was sitting in a chair, ashen-faced and clearly upset, muttering, 'How did he miss that pink?'

Whether Fred ever found out how genuinely concerned Joe had been I'll never know, but if he had seen the look on his brother's face he'd have realised how much he cared.

I may have seen another side to Fred Davis that year but I have to say that the reason he continued to be so good right into his sixties was that of his attitude. He was a great competitor but didn't take the game too seriously, something many players, myself included, couldn't say.

Fred had been awarded an OBE in 1977, the year before he reached the semifinals. He received letters from all over the world congratulating him. Then a local radio station rang him and the female interviewer asked him whether he still played the game. Fred told me, 'That brought me back down to earth.'

He also told me that, when he went to Buckingham Palace to receive his honour, the Queen Mother asked him what he did for a living. If he was winding me up he never cracked a smile.

Ray Reardon won the final in 1978 once more. We didn't know it then but it would be the last of his six world titles. To almost everybody, Ray was undoubtedly the best on the planet. The one person who disagreed was the Australian Eddie Charlton. Despite having never won the World Championship or beating Ray Reardon in a major tournament, Charlton laid claim to the title of world champion because he'd beaten the Welshman in a WPBSA-sanctioned tournament in Australia called the World Matchplay Championship. At the time there was concern that using the term 'world' could be dangerous. That concern was justified. Both the BBC and ITV sports programmes reported that snooker had a new world champion. It led to a bitter war of words between Charlton and Ron

Atkins – the Australian amateur champion who'd challenged his fellow countryman's assertions – and consternation within the WPBSA over how to resolve the dispute. Eventually, they took the decision to cancel the following year's World Matchplay Championship in Australia at the eleventh hour, after pressure from the BBC and Embassy.

The episode would give further insight into the workings of the game's ruling body, something of which I would soon have first-hand experience.

* * *

On 10 July 1978 the snooker world was in mourning over the passing of Joe Davis, aged seventy-seven. Some said he never recovered from an illness, which came at the time he was watching Fred play in the championship that year.

'My life has been immeasurably enriched by knowing Joe Davis,' said Phil Bull, the owner and founder of the racing book *Timeform*. At the memorial service for the great man at St Margaret's, Westminster, which I attended along with the other professionals, it was a view everybody seemed to share. I felt a loss, not because I really knew him, but because I wished I had.

In October that year, shortly before the UK Championship took place, the young ginger-haired lad I'd seen two years earlier in a junior event in Leeds turned professional. Not only would Steve Davis dominate the sport in years to come, but his manager, Barry Hearn, would also make his presence felt in a big way. A new era was beginning. Obviously, we had no idea then how much of an impact Davis would have on the game but early controversy around the young player should have served warning of what was to come.

Almost as soon as he turned professional, the BBC announced that he would be appearing in the 1979 series of *Pot Black*. 'He has the magic name,' *Pot Black* commentator and consultant Ted Lowe said, referring to Davis's legendary namesakes.

It was certainly surprising that Davis, having turned professional only two months earlier, was in the popular television series. Patsy Fagan, the 1977 UK champion, was overlooked, as I had been ever since I'd turned pro two years before. Davis's inclusion was all the more startling as there was no place for Alex Higgins. The biggest box-office attraction the game possessed, rejected for someone who had been there for five minutes.

Ted defended the decision by claiming Higgins had not performed well on *Pot Black* and that they were trying to introduce the audience to new names. I have always been a great admirer of Ted and in later years was privileged to sit alongside him in the commentary box, but he made no secret of the fact he disliked Higgins. He thought Higgins would drag the game down from its professional level. He didn't appreciate my view that Higgins was the man responsible for bringing a new aspect to snooker, that he had spectators on the edges of their seats and inspired young players to take up the game.

★ ★ ★

Away from the game, 1978 was a tough year for me financially. I was feeling the brunt of leaving home and trying to provide for my new girlfriend. I was gambling more than ever, thanks in part to George Best!

Manchester United's mercurial talent had long since fallen out of favour at Old Trafford. Despite his goals and brilliance, his star status diminished when it emerged he wasn't training properly and his wild off-field partying was affecting his performances. It's still incredible to think he was still just twenty-seven when he left Manchester United in 1974.

The following year George joined the Los Angeles Aztecs of the North American Soccer League. While over there, he recommended to his new manager his good friend Bobby McAlinden, a Salford lad. Not only was Bobby a big pal of George's and a footballer, but also they shared a deep love of gambling.

McAlinden flew out to join George at the Aztecs in 1976 and the two of them shared a house. They would even go on to own a bar together in Los Angeles. In 1978 George asked Bobby to be his best man when he married Angie Janes.

I knew Bobby's brother Kevin from the snooker club. While Bobby played in America, his brother went over there to visit him. During his stay he met Cliff Lines, the head work rider for Michael Stoute, a trainer who had come to prominence in 1972 when a horse called Sandal gave him his first win at Newmarket. Cliff had also worked for Sir Noel Murless, trainer of nineteen classic winners. With that sort of background, it was clear Cliff was a good judge of a horse. He told Kevin to give him a call if he ever saw a Stoute horse running, and he would give him the lowdown on whether it was worth a bet. This chance meeting would turn out to provide the best information we'd had up to then. So, inadvertently, it was George Best who got me gambling like never before. I suppose I have to blame someone.

As the 1978–9 season commenced I vowed to myself it would the year I would make an impact. I tried to recapture some focus ahead of the UK Championship in November.

In the qualifier I beat my former amateur teammate Ray Edmonds 9–4, setting up a last-sixteen tie against seven-times former world champion John Pulman. Perhaps daunted by his record, I didn't start the match well, slipping to 2–0 behind. As the game wore on, however, I grew in confidence and, from tying the match at 3–3, I won the next six frames to take it 9–3.

My quarterfinal opponent was David Taylor, the player I'd read about in the snooker magazine capable of amassing century breaks. Taylor had entered the record books earlier in 1978 for compiling three consecutive breaks, totalling 409, during an exhibition at Butlin's holiday camp at Minehead, in Somerset. At the time it seemed no one had been counting but Eddie Charlton, while defending his right to be recognised as world champion, also claimed he held the record for consecutive break building, with a highest combined score of 272. Unfortunately for the Australian, that was another claim to fame taken from him. I'm not taking anything away from David, but it now seemed that, whether you were playing Joe Bloggs in a holiday camp or Ray Reardon at the Crucible, you could go into the record books.

Taylor, in practice, was one of the best players I'd ever seen, second perhaps only to Higgins. However, after winning the English and World Amateur titles in 1968 he hadn't really set the professional game alight. He'd beaten Patsy Fagan on his way to meeting me at the UK. Was this to be his year?

Perhaps, because I didn't get close to him, losing 9–2. Taylor didn't demonstrate his break-building skills but still ran out the winner. Although David showed what a good player he was by beating Higgins in the semifinal 9–5 before coming up short against Doug Mountjoy in the final, losing 15–9, I was bitterly disappointed with my form. Once again, I believed it was a match I could have won.

I came home disillusioned.

When your partner is effectively your manager as well, it doesn't make for a happy home life. I was out of the tournament and the exhibitions had dried up. Having it pointed out that the reason the phone isn't ringing is that you played terrible on television isn't the most wonderful motivation.

To be frank, it was a volatile situation. We would have screaming rows and then not talk for two days. It wasn't a healthy situation to be in.

I was despairing where to go from here. I'd given up everything for the game, yet couldn't seem to produce my best form when it mattered. It was not a happy time.

Plus, I had the money worries. Gambling on horses was unpredictable at best. The odd good win was almost the worst thing to happen as you over-speculated, hoping to emulate it. And, although I had the odd exhibition, it wasn't enough to sustain any kind of lifestyle. With only two or three tournaments a year in which to prove myself, the financial pressure was always at the forefront of my mind and I was not able to play my best snooker. It was difficult to concentrate when I was trying to get through the next round just to pay the electricity bill.

I wondered what I was doing with my life. Had I made the right decisions, both personally and professionally?

To some people sport is black and white. If you are one of the best players around and you've beaten your rivals before, why aren't you beating them every time? Why aren't you winning every tournament? It's hard to explain.

I had a consultation with a sports psychologist. It was

unheard of then – to go and speak to someone about your issues and try to find a solution. The man we'd found was, remarkably to me, the son of my father's doctor in the general practice in Salford. He was keen to discuss everything about my situation and he asked me outright how things were at home. He needed to know everything so he could work out how best to tackle my issues.

I opened up about the guilt I felt over my marriage, the hurt I had caused and the fact that my new relationship had been a volatile one.

He came up with coping strategies for me to use in high-pressure situations and taught me self-hypnosis. Whether it would be helpful I would have to wait and see.

Interestingly, after our sessions were over, he said to me, 'Best of luck, John, but I really think things won't get better unless you leave this woman.'

I was quite surprised he was so forthright. It's an indication of the type of thoughts I'd been sharing.

I should have listened to his advice. I should have walked away – but I didn't. I think I persisted because I just felt all this aggravation and hurt I'd caused everyone. Was it all going to be for nothing? Maybe I didn't want to be on my own, to be without a girlfriend. I'd never lived on my own. Perhaps I was afraid of what that would be like.

Whatever the reasons, I walked away thinking, What does he know?

What we did agree on was that I could do with a proper manager, one able to secure me more lucrative bookings. If I could sort out my financial affairs I could concentrate more on honing my game.

I spoke with Henry West, a manager based in Surrey. His

other player, Patsy Fagan, was doing the Warner holiday circuit but didn't want to continue with it. Henry was happy to sign me up and almost immediately got me to take over the entertainment slots from Patsy.

I was delighted. Hopefully, this would mean an end to my short-term money worries.

My first gig was at Hayling Island, off the Hampshire coast, at an event to raise money for charity, with five other professionals, including Doug Mountjoy, Dennis Taylor and Willie Thorne. We would play a mini-tournament and all perform some trick shots.

What could possibly go wrong?

CHAPTER 11

MAKING AN IMPRESSION

It was nearing the end of the night on Hayling Island and I'd drawn the short straw. Of the six players who were to go to the table one at a time to perform trick shots, I was up last. At first I didn't think it was that big a deal. But, as I watched the others do their turns, it was with growing consternation. The trick shots they performed were all the ones I knew. By the time Willie Thorne expertly executed his last shot and the audience clapped their appreciation I was feeling decidedly uneasy. I was up next. This was my first stint at the prestigious Warner holiday camps. Perform well and it could lead to more work.

I didn't know a trick shot that hadn't been done. I had to think fast. I went to the table still trying to work out what I would do. Fortunately, a piece of wood fell off one of the table legs, so I made a quip about it and got the audience laughing and on my side. They seemed like a good crowd. Maybe this was the moment to try out the impressions I'd done up until then only in Potters.

I said, 'We have different types of players and different mannerisms and I'd like to give you an example of how, in my opinion, these people would pot the black.'

I started with Spencer. That went down well. Next I did Reardon, who, despite his Prince of Darkness appearance, was always laughing with the crowd. It was another hit. Then there was my impersonation of Alex, which was the simplest of the lot. He was always rushing round the table, pulling faces and twitching.

People seemed to like it but I was just happy to get through my slot without looking like an absolute idiot. I didn't think much more about it. I had no intention of doing it again, particularly in public.

From cursing my luck a moment earlier at not being able to perform a trick shot, I was now thanking my stars that I'd been forced into a situation to come up with something different. It was a bit of fun but, although I wouldn't see the benefits for years, that night set me on a different path from my contemporaries.

Being with Henry West was immediately paying dividends and I looked forward to 1979, hoping I could at last do myself justice when it mattered in the big tournaments.

Armed with the sports psychologist's self-hypnosis techniques, I felt confident I was better equipped to deal with the pressure.

My first qualifier for the World Championship was against Maurice Parkin, a player who hadn't won a match in six years before he eventually tasted victory while trying to qualify in 1978. I started well moving into a 6–0 lead in the best-of-seventeen match. In the seventh frame I cleared up with a break of 137 and closed out the match emphatically, winning 9–0.

My victory set up a final qualifier with Willie Thorne to see who would make it to the Crucible. I thought history was about to repeat itself when, in a game where momentum swung from player to player, Willie went 8–5 ahead, needing just one more frame. My mind drifted back to the previous year when I led Fred Davis and he managed to come back. Using the techniques I had been taught, I tried to remain calm. I just needed to win one more frame and hope some doubt crept into Willie's head. I did that. Then in the next I made a break of 120. The momentum was back with me. I won the next two frames to complete my comeback and take the match 9–8. What a difference a year makes! After each tie, players are required to fill in a match report, making any comments they feel are relevant. Willie's read, 'Why does it always happen to me?' Funny, that could have been me writing the same thing the year before.

Henry West had recently taken on the young player from Tooting who'd caught my eye a couple of years earlier, Jimmy White. He had just won the Southern area section of the English Amateur Championship at just sixteen and was the best exponent to emerge so far of the style first displayed by Alex Higgins. Jimmy had combined a natural cueing action with a tremendous temperament. Nothing seemed to faze him, even then. I knew he was destined for great things.

In April 1979, before the draw for the Crucible took place, Jimmy was vying for the title of English Amateur Champion and was due to play the Northern area champion Dave Martin, from Middlesbrough, in Helston, Cornwall. Henry organised a coach to take Jimmy's supporters to the match. Jimmy, Henry and I went by car. If this was the biggest match of Jimmy's life, you wouldn't have known it. He was so laid back he arrived in Cornwall without an evening shirt, cufflinks or a suitable pair of shoes. Instead of finding a practice table we went on a shopping expedition.

Despite the less-than-ideal preparation, Jimmy started the best-of-twenty-five-frame match like a whirlwind. He won the first frame and in the second made a break of 130. It would have been a championship record but the governing body, the English Association of Snooker and Billiards, had deemed the pockets too big, so it could not be ratified. When Jimmy took the first frame of the third session to lead 10–3, it looked to be all over.

In that final, however, I saw for the first time a weakness in Jimmy's game that would haunt him in years to come. He became too casual, too adventurous, and let his opponent back in. By the end of the session his lead was just 10–8. I don't think he panicked but Henry and I did. I was reminded of Higgins and the fact that he never won easily – mostly because, when he was well in front, he became more interested in entertaining the crowd than winning the match. Jimmy scraped home 13–10. Martin was an excellent player who played well but, if he had gone on to win, it would have been a case of Jimmy's losing it.

While we were in Cornwall the draw for the World Championship was made on television. I was drawn against Cliff Thorburn, a player I was confident of beating, given our history together. I arrived in Sheffield, therefore, in the best shape of my life. My confidence was high. I had good support from both Salford and London, through Henry and I knew that, if I could produce my best form, I had a chance of winning the title.

Despite my confidence, I started slowly, falling 3–1 and then 5–3 behind in the first session of the best-of-twenty-five encounter. By the end of the first day, however, we had tied at eight all.

We had one session left to play, which would be held in the morning – the first time that had happened.

We arrived at the Crucible the following day to find the arena packed. This wasn't the norm back then. During my first visit to the theatre the players sat in the arena and watched the other matches; it could be that quiet. The crowd this time, however, weren't for Cliff and me. Alex Higgins was starting his quarterfinal against the newcomer Terry Griffiths on the adjacent table.

As anyone who has watched snooker on television will know, the two tables are separated by a thick plywood screen. This is so players are not distracted by what's happening on the other table. What the screen doesn't stop, though, is the noise – as if Cliff and I didn't have tension enough! It seemed every time we bent down to play a shot the audience would go wild at some shot or incident on the next table.

I started that morning session as I'd finished the previous day's and worked myself into a 12–9 lead. I was down on frame ball – the moment when a player goes further ahead than there are points left on the table. If I potted this it was the frame and the match. I bent down and was just about to strike the cue ball when a tremendous cheer went up. I swear my heart stopped beating. One of the most important shots of my life and, just as I was about to play, there was bedlam. Later, I found out this was the moment Alex made his second consecutive century break. But that's the Crucible. It's the same for both players, and it's and what makes it special. Fortunately, I managed to stop myself before I struck the ball, regained my composure and potted the ball that won me the frame and the match.

I was through to the quarterfinal, where I would play another Canadian, Bill Werbeniuk, who had knocked out John Spencer 13–11.

I was delighted to be through, but the big talking point of the day – and of the round – was the Higgins–Griffiths match. I didn't see the majority of it because I was playing, but some say it was the best match ever at the Crucible. Both players were operating at an unbelievable standard. When Higgins won the first session 6–2 you thought that was it. However, as was Higgins's wont, being well in front, playing well, in his mind it was time to entertain. Griffiths was having none of it. He may not have been a household name at that moment but he was a two-times amateur champion and had been brought up in a tough snooker environment.

The match went to a deciding frame, which Griffiths won with a magnificent break of 107. For the third year in succession Higgins was beaten by the odd frame.

Personally speaking, I believe that, when Higgins was knocked out, the tournament lost some of its magic. I am sure Terry didn't feel that. What a confidence boost he'd just had – beating Higgins, playing at his best, on the biggest stage in snooker!

Another early casualty that year was Terry's fellow Crucible debutant Steve Davis, who lost to Dennis Taylor. What I always remember about that match was the moment when, while Dennis was at the table, Steve started eating a sandwich. Apparently, being inexperienced and not used to long matches, he got terrible hunger pangs and decided he needed to eat something. A lot of the players watching it on television in the players' room thought it showed a total lack of respect for Dennis. I had never seen it before or since. But I suppose, if you're hungry, you've got to eat.

In my next match against Werbeniuk I made the perfect start and after the first session led 8–1. At the start of the final session I led 11–5, just two more frames from a semifinal place. As I got down to break off in the seventeenth frame, I noticed that the end red was loose from the triangle. Instead of asking the referee to re-rack them I decided to improvise. The result was that I left an easy red destined for the middle pocket. Bill cleared the table with a magnificent break of 142, equalling the world record for the championship at the time. This gave him such a boost in confidence that in the end I was glad to struggle over the line 13–9.

My opponent in the semifinal would be either six-times world champion Ray Reardon or Dennis Taylor. Most people assumed that I wanted to face Taylor. Far from it. To play Reardon at the Crucible in the semifinal of the World Championship would be a dream come true.

It didn't happen. To everyone's surprise, Dennis won 13–8. So the semifinal line-up was Griffiths versus Eddie Charlton and Taylor versus Virgo. No Reardon, no Higgins, no John Spencer. I can't imagine any of the other players gave this any consideration but I started to think about the last four and wondered from where the entertainment would come.

This year was the first that television cameras had been there for the entire seventeen days of the championship at the Crucible. That was going to be over one hundred hours of snooker. In one of the early rounds Griffiths's match was still going on at 2.30 a.m. and the BBC stayed with it. The commitment was there from the corporation but I still felt there was an onus on us all to sell the game to the wider public. The game was still in its infancy. We couldn't afford for that interest to dissipate.

With the biggest entertainers in the game out, who was going to stand in for them?

I prepared for the beginning of my semifinal by having an early night, leaving a few people still drinking in the hotel bar. At half past three in the morning there was a loud banging on my door. After I'd gone to bed, a merry party had kicked off downstairs. Some people had even ended up on the hotel putting green. I couldn't get back to sleep. It was hardly the ideal preparation for the biggest match of my life.

That this could happen today, with the spotlight there is on the game at the Crucible, is unimaginable. Back then, however, it was a different culture. It was only the third year we'd been at the Crucible and only my second time there, because I'd been beaten in a qualifier the year before.

I'm not using what happened as an excuse. We've all done it, saying we'll have one more, getting caught up in the moment, chatting to everyone, things getting out of hand. I'm explaining this only to give an indication of where my head was.

When the match started I got carried away and tried to attack like Alex Higgins, while using the mannerisms of Reardon. I had it in my head that he was the reason people were watching the game. It is a terrible admission to one's ego. It is all about results but I had it in my head that I was trying to show the public it was watchable.

There I was in the semifinal of the World Championship and I was doing impersonations!

I got off to a terrible start in the best-of-thirty-seven match, falling 4–0 behind. I did rally to bring it back to 6–4 at one stage but slipped behind again and, before I knew it, I was 10–5 down. At 17–10 behind, I was staring defeat in the face and, although I did manage to claw it back to 17–12, Dennis closed out the match 19–12.

I take nothing away from Dennis. He played well but I came away thinking I could have done so much better.

I wasn't ruthless enough. I won't name names but there are certain people who play the game in such a manner that if we all played like that you would be struggling for an audience. Sport has to strike that balance between the entertainment side and the winning. You can say that about all sports. In football there are the teams that park the bus. In golf, there are players who keep churning out the steady rounds without anything spectacular.

When pitched together, the contrasts in styles can be great. Reardon's matches with Higgins were like chalk and cheese; Higgins with Steve Davis; Davis and Jimmy White; White against Stephen Hendry. Stephen was not by any means a boring player but his ruthless efficiency and calmness under pressure against Jimmy's swashbuckling style made for a great match-up.

In the other semifinal Terry Griffiths defeated Eddie Charlton 19–17 and went on to win the title at the first time of asking, beating Dennis 24–16. It wasn't the most memorable of finals but at the end of the day it's the record books that count. The headlines were the same as when Higgins won it for the first time.

To compound my disappointment, I lost the third-place playoff with Eddie Charlton 7–3 but by then I just wanted to leave Sheffield. In a year that had promised so much, I ended the snooker season wondering how I had ended up with nothing.

I vowed not to make the same mistakes again – and next season I'd come back stronger.

CHAPTER 12

PLAYING POLITICS

In the days following the end of the World Championship, the WPBSA held its AGM in a hotel in Sheffield. Since the tournament had moved to the city it had become a tradition. In 1979 a decision was taken that threatened the game's very future.

Nothing in the early stages of the meeting gave an indication of the controversy to come. It was only when the issue of seedings came up that things went awry.

The meeting was well attended, particularly by overseas players. For some it was their first time at the Crucible, but they were entitled to an opinion and, rightly or wrongly, were given a vote.

For any motion to be passed it only took one person to propose and another to second it. This is what happened when, after a lot of discussion about how many should be seeded at Sheffield, a South African player called Derek Mienie – who in his first appearance in the World Championship that year had been knocked out in the initial qualifier – made a suggestion. He proposed that only the winner and runner-up in the previous World Championship should be seeded for the following year. Dennis Taylor, the runner-up that year, seconded the motion and, unbelievably, it was voted through.

I left the meeting feeling very frustrated to say the least. It meant that the likes of Reardon, Spencer and Higgins – former World Champions and players who had done so much to open up the game – might not play in the final stages at Sheffield, our shop window.

Three days later I got a call from Del Simmons, the promoter who had helped me with some exhibitions after I turned professional. For the last few years he had been promoting snooker matches at the Tony Club in Weybridge, Surrey, and had also been working closely with Reardon and Spencer. Del relayed the fears for the game expressed by Ray and John. I sympathised with them. This was different from the time that I, with others, changed the seeding system. This time someone who, in my opinion, had no chance of making it in professional snooker had changed the complete fabric of the game.

'We can't have these people telling us how to run the game,' Del said.

He explained they had formed a new company called the Professional Snooker Association Ltd (PSA). By this time Dennis Taylor had realised what a big mistake he had made and had joined the new body. The next step was for the PSA to call an EGM to try to get the WPBSA to change the decision. Fred Davis became chairman of the PSA. Our proposal to the game's governing body was that only players who received World Championship points would be allowed to vote. This would hopefully stop the fiasco that happened in Sheffield.

The future of the game would be settled at an EGM slated for a date in August.

★ ★ ★

In the meantime, I had my own immediate future to sort out. My relationship with my new partner was complicated. Over several years we split up and got back together many times. During one break and with no place to live, I moved in with my manager, Henry, and his family in Sunbury-on-Thames, in Surrey. After such a period of upheaval and stress, it was refreshing to practise in different snooker clubs. Ronnie Gross had his snooker club in Neasden, where I'd played with Patsy Fagan, and eventually Henry opened a place of his own in Kingston upon Thames. Over the summer I was booked for exhibitions at the holiday camps and it was great to be working flat out as I tried to put my money worries behind me.

My main gig was at the Hayling Island resort. Playing the camps gave me the opportunity to meet other entertainers. One of the other acts at the camp at the same time was the popular television ventriloquist Roger De Courcey with his puppet Nookie Bear. I remember getting drunk one night and pinching Nookie out of Roger's bag. I took it back to my room and tried to have a conversation with it.

Guitar legend Bert Weedon – the man whose *Play in a Day* tutorial guides inspired the likes of Paul McCartney, John Lennon, Keith Richards and Eric Clapton to take up the guitar – once got me and a dart player to strip to the waist and do a muscle jig to the famous tune 'Wheels'.

From Warner's I had another arrangement to get the ferry over to the Isle of Wight to play an exhibition there at the request of club owner Nobby Clark. What a character he was! In return for playing at his club he gave me priority boarding for the ferry. On the way back to the mainland I arrived at Ryde and was told to wait in a particular lane. The ferry arrived and all the cars and caravans started boarding. All of a sudden the tail started to rise but I was still stuck in my lane. I was wondering why I wasn't getting on when I heard someone shout, 'Stop that ferry!'

There was Nobby running down the slip. 'John, hold on,' he said. I swear to God they reversed the ferry, dropped the back, reversed two cars off and I got on. That was Nobby Clark – wonderful.

Another character I had a lot of fun spending time with was John Taylor, nicknamed John the Arab, mainly because it was Arab businessmen he drove around London, but also because he looked like one. He came with me on a few of my trips to camps on Hayling Island and the Isle of Wight.

I had first met John at the Ronnie Gross Snooker Centre. Living life on the road can be a lonely affair, and it was nice to have a companion with me. Like me, he liked a flutter.

I was playing at Bembridge, a Warner holiday camp on the Isle of Wight. We arrived early, with time to have a coffee and look at the paper to check if there was a horse worth betting on. The snack bar was on a raised platform, looking down on the dance floor. It seemed the average age at Bembridge was over sixty. As we sat down I noticed some of the guests were having an aerobics class. There were probably twenty people in the class, split evenly between men and women. Some of the guests took turns in dictating the moves for the others to perform to the music.

I had my head in the paper and it was only when I spoke to

John about some horse that was running that I looked up to see he wasn't there. To my astonishment he was on the dance floor in the aerobics class. The pace of the class was pretty sedate given the age of the participants. That was until John got up to conduct the next set of moves.

At first he did a few arm exercises, the gentle hoop rotations everybody followed. Just as I was beginning to relax he dived to floor and started doing press-ups. A few of the ladies looked as if they were thinking about it but declined. Most of the men, however, whether they had just got carried away or thought they could still do it, were down on the ground. Now John was quite fit and in no time at all he had done ten press-ups. Then he leaped to his feet into star jumps, clapping his hands above his head. A few of the ladies followed, at least with the clapping part.

Not so the men. After their exertions they were still trying to get up off the floor.

'What the hell?' came a shout and one of the staff came in running. I quickly caught John's eye and we made a sharp exit. It was funny watching all these old guys still trying to get back to their feet.

John Taylor was one of those people who one minute would have bundles of money, the next nothing.

Doing the holiday camps was hard work but it was just a relief to be playing snooker as a professional. It was still new to me and it was good fun.

The camps reinforced that it wasn't enough just to play snooker: you also had to entertain people. It wasn't just a case of their being entertained by potted balls. Some of the tables weren't so good that you could rely on them. Without really thinking about it, I was honing my act.

I wasn't the only one. Established entertainers such as Bradley Walsh and Des O'Connor learned their trade on the holiday-camp circuit. And, long before I knew him or had even met him, Jim Davidson first came to my attention doing a stand-up routine at a Pontin's holiday camp. You were appearing in front of quite a big audience. It was a good learning curve. Not only were they good places to cut your teeth at, they were also a good source of income for acts.

When I finished my own circuit I had the chance to fill in for Ray Reardon down in Devon. Ray liked to take a couple of weeks off because he enjoyed his golf. Funnily enough, it was while filling in for Ray that *I* took up golf. Ray used to do his shows in the morning so he'd have the afternoons free. At all the other holiday camps the schedule was morning and afternoon, but Ray had worked out all his holiday camps down in the south Devon area to fit around his golf. It was the same for me. After lunch I had the whole day free, so gave the game a go.

Ray is the president at Churston Golf Club near Torquay. He was playing one day when a stranger who had hit his ball onto Ray's fairway said to him, 'You're Ray Reardon, six times champion of the world. Can you answer a question that I've always wanted to ask? What do you think is the difference between golf and snooker?'

Reardon replied, 'Well, I've been playing snooker for fifty years, never lost a ball.'

I've not regretted taking up golf as I've had some lovely times, but I do find that golf is a bit too time-consuming, particularly if you're a professional snooker player. It's not as if you could go out and play golf for an hour. It's an all-day job.

It was the summer, there weren't many tournaments, so what the heck!

Ray was so popular at the time that he even released a record. It came out during one of the times I filled in for him at Pontin's. Before I did my slot, I was trying to remember the tune to some of the other guys. The manager was a big fan of Reardon, so I asked him, 'Ray's record – how does it go?'

'Very well,' he said smiling.

I wanted to know how the tune went, not how it was selling!

Back then if an act had merchandise to sell, they had to sell it through the official shop and the camp took a third of the percentage. I know this because Roger De Courcey used to sell a host of memorabilia – little toy Nookie Bears, mugs, slippers, pencil cases, the lot. When they informed him that any merchandise had to be sold through the shop he wasn't too happy, so he worked out that, if he went out of the main gate and dropped the back of his car, he was outside the camp and could sell his merchandise. At the end of his show, he used to explain to people, 'Give me ten minutes, I'll be outside. You'll see a Cherokee Jeep where I'll be selling all this lovely merchandise. I can't sell it on the camp because they want a third of what I'll sell it to you.' And out he went. And then he wondered why he never got another run at the camps. That was Roger – a law unto himself.

As the summer drew to a close, I tried to take stock and refocus for the new season. There would be two tournaments before the end of the calendar year in 1979, with a new event in India scheduled to follow directly after the UK Championship.

However, before a cue ball was struck in earnest, my life was to take another turn – and I'm not convinced it was for the better.

★ ★ ★

In August, the EGM for the WPBSA was held to discuss the breakaway faction that had led to the establishment of the PSA. In the battle for the game's future, the actions of the new company proved crucial. The WPBSA won the right to continue but agreed to the PSA's stance on seeding. Two factors stopped the split. First, vice-chairman Rex Williams found some common ground between the warring factions, and the BBC played their part by making it clear they didn't like working with breakaways, but preferred to work with official associations.

The WPBSA agreed to change the seeding and held another vote. This time there was a proposal that eight players would be seeded, with the top eight qualifiers joining them to make up the last sixteen playing at the Crucible.

A consequence of the upheaval was that both the chair, John Pulman, and vice-chair, Williams, stood down. Williams had been instrumental in keeping the WPBSA as it was. If it hadn't been for him, the governing body would have changed its name to the PSA.

A new board was to be elected. Ray Reardon and Graham Miles were elected as chair and vice-chair respectively.

Del Simmons, who was becoming increasingly involved with the promotion of the sport, had rung me up ahead of the meeting. 'They could do with someone like you on the board,' he said. Because I was opinionated and not frightened to speak up, he thought I could make an impact.

At the meeting they were looking round for people to be on the new board. From my own point of view I thought going on the board might be a chance to protect myself. I was only three years into life as a professional. In two years I would have reached my peak. The game was changing. It was an opportunity to be at the forefront of that.

'OK,' I said and I put my name forward. Before I knew it I was elected onto the committee of the WPSBA. So began ten years of politics.

If I'd known then what I know now I would have resigned immediately.

CHAPTER 13

UK CHAMP AND BOMBAY DUCK

Going into the UK Championship in 1979, I was feeling confident. I wasn't the only one. John the Arab, companion and prankster, put a bet on me at 20–1 to win the title. John's problem was that he liked to bet everything he owned, which meant I often had to lend him money. For me to get back the money I was lending him I would have to play the tournament of my life. Nothing like a bit of pressure. In some ways it was a hark-back to those early days in Small Street and playing to win because I couldn't afford to pay the lights.

Held at the Guild Hall in Preston, the tournament meant I was heading back North again for the first time since the summer, but, as I had no place to stay, I booked a room at the Charnock Richard services on the M6. Henry West travelled up with John Taylor and me.

My first opponent was Tony Meo, a former classmate of Jimmy White, who had recently signed to Henry's stable.

Although Tony had not turned professional till earlier that year, he was hotly tipped and had been the youngest player to make a maximum break at the tender age of seventeen.

In the first frames he showed just why he was considered such a prospect, racing into a 5–0 lead. By the end of the first session I was 5–2 down and struggling to get a foothold in the match. If this continued I could forget thinking about even the quarterfinal, let alone winning the tournament.

During the opening frame of the next session I made a break of 102, which gave me the spark I needed to push on. Although Tony put up a good fight, I won four frames in a row to take the match 9–6.

My next match was a quarterfinal encounter with the player everyone was tipping to be a future world champion: Steve Davis. Although Steve had yet to win a major title, such was his reputation – earned after a series of impressive performances in challenge matches and a convincing win over defending champion Doug Mountjoy in the previous round – that he was favourite to win.

I knew I was going to have to be at my best to win and in the early exchanges there was nothing between us. Only when I edged into a 4–3 lead did I feel I had the game to beat him.

I got myself into an 8–7 lead and was among the balls in a frame that would give me the match. I was in the process of clearing up when I bent down to play my next shot. All of a sudden there was a crash. Luckily, it didn't put me off my shot. I turned and saw what the noise was. Steve had laid his cue on the seat and, as I prepared to play, it had rolled off the chair and crashed to the ground. You can imagine the look I gave him. Steve says it was the only time that he hoped his opponent wouldn't miss. I didn't but, after the sandwich incident in Sheffield, this showed Steve still had a lot to learn.

The semifinal line-up was Griffiths versus Werbeniuk, Taylor versus Virgo – almost a repeat of the World Championship back in May. Griffiths had been at the top of his game throughout the tournament. After beating Higgins in the quarterfinal, I overheard Dennis Taylor say that 'nobody can beat Terry'. When the Welshman beat Werbeniuk 9–3 in his semifinal there weren't many people in Preston disagreeing with that statement.

I exacted partial revenge on Dennis for my World Championship defeat. The result was never in doubt once I moved into a 4–1 lead early on, and I kept the pressure on to run out a 9–4 winner. It helped that this time I had no middle-of-the-night dramas. I just focused on the job in hand and went into the first session of the best-of-twenty-seven-frame final feeling good. In my head it was a chance to put the record straight. I took my growing confidence onto the table and raced into a 5–0 lead. As Friday's play went on I enjoyed a lead of 7–2 and ended the day 11–7 up.

The events of the following day – when I was docked the frames for being late, as recounted in the opening chapter – should perhaps have left me speechless. However, after somehow managing to come from behind to win the UK title, in my victory speech, holding back the tears, I thanked nearly everybody I'd ever known. The audience, after booing me hours earlier, put that behind me to give me a wonderful ovation.

When I came out of the arena Bill Werbeniuk said, 'You must a have balls of steel.'

That night to celebrate we went back to Potters Snooker Club. It was disappointing that my father wasn't alive to see me win a major title. I wonder what he would have made of it, all those years after getting me that table.

I couldn't celebrate for long, however, as I had to get on a plane to India to compete in the Bombay International in what is now called Mumbai. To be honest it wasn't what I wanted to be doing. It was three weeks to Christmas, and I'd just won the biggest tournament of my life. I wanted to celebrate properly.

The following day, one of the write-ups in the paper suggested that, because Terry was world champion at the time, he probably would have gone on to win but felt guilty over the two-frame deduction.

What a liberty! But, then, I did think that maybe the injustice I felt fired me up; but, if that hadn't happened, I had a four-frame advantage and was playing some of my best ever snooker. Maybe they did have a point. It took away that bite that I needed sometimes to get over the nerves I used to feel when I was playing.

The win was the highlight of my career, but a sad legacy of that triumph is that because of the BBC strike no highlights reel exists. I haven't been able to look back and relive my moment of glory.

While I was at the airport to catch my flight to India, one guy shouted, 'Well done, John!' The final frames may not have been televised but some people were aware of what happened. It was nice to get some small recognition at least.

And John Taylor was happy. He won his bet so headed back to London with his pockets bulging.

Having never travelled outside of the Western world, I was completely unprepared for the shock of landing in Mumbai. The heat was oppressive, the air dense. I felt I could hardly breathe.

We were there for two weeks but the tournament was scheduled for only the second seven days. For the first week we relaxed, tried to acclimatise and had the tough job of being wined and dined by the sponsors.

The tournament was being held at Bombay Gymkhana. Every player had a suit made by the sponsor. That was another revelation: that you could have a suit made in two days.

During the day we'd lie by the pool. John Spencer and Del Simmons – now employed by the WPBSA as a contracts negotiator – would be playing backgammon. Dennis Taylor was looking for volunteers to put sunscreen on him because he'd had a bad experience the year before. Being fair-skinned, he'd been badly burned. Thinking he was buying something soothing he could put in the bath, he'd accidentally bought a muscle heat treatment instead. It was so hot he had to lie in a bath of cold water for four hours before he had cooled down enough.

Steve Davis came woefully ill prepared. I had to give him a pair of my shorts.

In that first week I could relax. I felt on top of the world. Steve and I were practising one day. He said, 'Do you mind if I go and practise on my own, John? I'm not getting a shot.' I was so full of confidence that, if he missed a shot, I'd be clearing up.

We were warned not to drink the water but forgot that this applied to ice cubes too.

The hotel we were staying in was the first in which there was a phone in the bathroom. After a couple of days with a funny tummy I began to see why.

One night a few of us went out for a walk. A man approached me holding a baby, asking for money. I gave him five rupees.

He sat in the gutter holding the child. Initially I assumed that was their abode for the night but I came to suspect it was simply a ruse to extract cash from foreigners.

Seeing such poverty, however, did have an effect on me. I even penned a couple of poems, I was so moved. The contrast between the conditions in our hotel and that on the streets unsettled me. I had never seen anything like it before.

When it came to the snooker there were also cultural differences to get used to. The referee sat in an umpire's chair calling the scores out and there were two guys dressed in white taking the balls out of the pockets.

The eight players were split into two groups and we played a round-robin format, after which the top two players from each group would battle out semifinals.

I was in a group with Dennis Taylor, Cliff Thorburn and Indian snooker and billiards champion Arvind Savur. The other group comprised Steve Davis, Doug Mountjoy, John Spencer and a Canadian player I'd first met when I'd travelled to Canada with Higgins, Kirk Stevens.

In my first match I defeated Dennis comfortably 6–2 and was on even better form when I beat Savur 6–1. Cliff Thorburn got the better of me 6–1 and we both progressed from our group.

In the other section, Spencer was on impressive form, winning all his matches. Steve Davis joined him in the semis.

I met Spencer in the last four and my fine form continued as I came out on top 8–6. My opponent in the final would be Cliff Thorburn, who took care of Steve Davis 8–5.

After losing to Cliff earlier in the tournament, I was wary but going into my second consecutive final I felt in great shape and ran out a comfortable 13–7 winner.

★ ★ ★

Returning home from India five days before Christmas, I never felt better. I had money in the bank and with two titles under my belt I felt the world was my oyster.

I was looking forward to getting back North to see my friends. Henry West met me off the plane at Heathrow. He told me the following night he'd arranged for me to present some prizes at his snooker club in Kingston. As I'd already made arrangements to go back to Manchester I told him I couldn't make it. He wasn't happy and ordinarily I would have backed down, but the lure of going back to Potters and seeing my friends was too much. Plus, he hadn't mentioned the prize night when I'd rang him from India.

On the morning of the 21st I headed North. I was back with my partner and she lured me to a hotel under the ruse that she needed to drop off something. As I opened the door to the bar all hell broke loose. All my family and friends were there – my mother, sisters, brother, Alex Higgins and his wife Lynn, Geoff Lomas and many more. My mother was over the moon. My father may not have been alive to see it but she couldn't have been more proud.

The surprise had worked beautifully. I was just baffled that my manager could double-book me when he knew I had a big party coming.

As I had gone to India straight after the UK Championship I hadn't had a chance to read all the newspaper reports – apart from the one that said Griffiths would have won. I was handed a book of press cuttings with the inscription: 'UK CHAMP AND BOMBAY DUCK.'

It was a fantastic night and worth waiting for. At one stage Alex Higgins and I were chatting at the bar when Lynn joined us. 'Why don't you do things like this for me?' he asked her.

'I will do, when you win something,' she replied.

Well, then, Alex predictably took the hump and an argument kicked off, which meant they both left early. Typical Alex.

Lynn had a point, however. For all his great ability, he hadn't won anything major for years. This was the start of the 1980s and the game had taken enormous strides.

We all faced new challenges. As I looked ahead to the next decade, I did wonder if I could keep this momentum going.

New players were emerging – Davis, Jimmy White, Tony Meo. Could I sustain this hot streak I was enjoying?

CHAPTER 14

BLOWING HOT
AND COLD

In the aftermath of my UK triumph I'd moved again, this time to Northampton. A central location made it easier for me to get around the country. However, it meant cutting all ties with the life I'd left behind.

On the playing side, new sponsors were appearing from everywhere. One new event, the Wilson Classic, was held in Manchester in January 1980. I lost in the semifinal to John Spencer, who went on to defeat Higgins in the final. Alex caused controversy when he was reported for verbal abuse to referee Jim Thorpe.

Another new tournament swiftly followed. The Tolly Cobbold Classic, at the Corn Exchange, Ipswich, was a group format with the top two contesting the final. I beat Terry Griffiths but lost to Higgins and Dennis Taylor. Higgins went on to beat Taylor in the final but was at it again, abusing referee Nobby Clarke this time and accusing Dennis of being a cheat.

The Masters was up next and, despite being UK champion, I had to play a qualifier, which I lost to Cliff Thorburn. Higgins lost in the final to Griffiths but caused further controversy when he accused Terry of standing in his line of shot.

The World Championship was extended to twenty-four players at the Crucible. I got off to a strong start, beating Jim Meadowcroft 10–2 and was up against Eddie Charlton in the last sixteen. In the best-of-twenty-five encounter, neither of us could build momentum with the lead swinging each way. At 11–10 up I thought I had a chance of winning, but Charlton showed his experience to edge it 13–12. Given the fine form I'd been in, I was hoping to have made a bigger impact in Sheffield, but it wasn't to be.

Cliff Thorburn upset the odds that year, defeating Higgins in a tense final that would be memorable for two reasons. With the scores tied at 13–13 I was in the WPBSA room when Cliff's wife Barbara came rushing in, saying Alex had just called her husband a 'cunt'. After Higgins's run-ins already that year a disciplinary hearing was nearly called there and then. Thankfully, that was averted. After the match, which Cliff won 18–16, I approached Thorburn in my capacity as a Snooker Association board member.

'Is it true Alex called you a cunt?' I asked him.

He shook his head and said, 'No.'

Given that Alex was not always coherent, it's hard to know exactly what went on. It was this sort of scenario that Alex created in the arena and backstage.

The match was also significant because it took place at the same time as the Iranian Embassy siege in London. When the BBC left the snooker coverage for an update on the siege, the switchboards were jammed with complaints. People were more interested in the final of the Embassy World Snooker Championship and after ten minutes the corporation bowed to their pressure and returned to the snooker. If we needed any reminder of how popular snooker was becoming, that was it.

Directly after the World Championship was the Pontin's Professional in Prestatyn. My form returned and I beat Fred Davis and Steve Davis before coming from 3–0 down in the final against Ray Reardon to win 9–6.

The 1979–80 season had easily been my best yet. I hoped to carry my form into the next snooker year but after another busy summer at the holiday camps, and as I prepared for the new season, I was surprised to find myself not invited to the new series of *Pot Black*. I wasn't invited to the Benson & Hedges Masters, either. I thought that, as reigning UK champion, I would be in with a shout. Was I still considered a troublemaker, still suffering a reaction to the 'Virgo's Rebels', my involvement in the breakaway PSA and my late arrival to the final session?

I also received some very sad and disturbing news. John 'the Arab' Taylor, my companion throughout some of my highlights of the previous year, had suffered a terrible time of it. As we've seen, he was the type of person who rolled from having hundreds of pounds in his pocket one minute to having nothing the next. We all thought he was capable of bouncing back from any setback, but life got too much for him. In a fit of despair he shut himself off and committed suicide by taking a drug overdose. Tragically, his body was not discovered for twelve weeks. It was awful to think of somebody being so alone.

As the season began there was yet another new tournament. The Champion of Champions was an invitational group format but the organiser of the event had struggled to find a sponsor. At one stage the WPSBA looked to block it but the organiser managed to find enough money to pay the winner, but no one else.

I was playing so well that in the early stages of the tournament – a group format held at the New London Theatre, in the capital – I beat Dennis Taylor, Steve Davis and Kirk Stevens. I was playing out of my skin.

In the final I faced Doug Mountjoy. I should have won comfortably, given the form I was in, but for some reason I was up and down like a yoyo. It was as if I weren't bothered. I had to gee myself up to play but if I got too up I became all jittery and if I was too calm my concentration levels weren't there. The fact that I was winning tournaments and still not getting into the Masters or *Pot Black* probably had an effect. You start to think, Why bother?

I wish I had been more focused. I was on borrowed time. My life at the top as a professional was short.

My game returned for the World Challenge Cup, a World Cup-style team event devised by Mike Watterson that had been played for the first time in 1979. I was in an England team with David Taylor and Fred Davis. We reached the semifinal, where we played Canada, comprising Cliff Thorburn, Bill Werbeniuk and Kirk Stevens. During the match big Bill bent over the table and his trousers split. Play was halted while his trousers were sewn back together. I remember David Taylor had bought a new suit for the tournament and he was concerned that all they'd show on television was Werbeniuk's wardrobe malfunction.

Although I lost only three of the fifteen frames I played, we lost to Canada, who went on to beat Wales in the final.

My lacklustre start to the season was brought home to me all too painfully when it came to defending my UK title in Preston in November. It was an altogether pathetic performance. Despite being seeded through to the last sixteen, I lost my first match to Tony Meo 9–1. As in 1979 I slipped 5–1 behind, but this time there would be no comeback. I couldn't explain why I played so badly, which was even more frustrating.

The tournament was to be Steve Davis's big breakthrough. He blew away the Hurricane 16–6 in the final.

I made the decision that year to take a more active role in the running of the game and one thing I was determined to see happen was Steve Davis in the Masters. After my own snub, I felt strongly that Davis shouldn't likewise miss out. For the UK champion not to be there competing for the Masters made a mockery of the game.

The man who brought snooker to the Crucible, Mike Watterson, was fast becoming the biggest promoter in the game. Apart from the World Championship, he was also responsible for the UK and the World Team championships. At the start of 1981 he brought in another one, the Yamaha Organs Trophy, in the Assembly Rooms, Derby. The tournament was significant because for the first time ITV were going to televise an event nationwide. It was a round-robin format but I couldn't get going, losing all of my matches, to Jimmy White, Cliff Thorburn and Steve Davis.

Aside from my poor performances, snooker was booming. Widespread coverage was helping it become one of the most popular sports on television. One of the main reasons for this was, in my opinion, the resurgence of Higgins as a major force. He won the Masters at Wembley, beating Terry Griffiths. His doing well, however, caused headaches for the establishment.

One such battleground was Alex's insistence on not wearing his bowtie. Other players were beginning to copy him. It may seem a trivial matter, but there was a belief, one that I agreed with, that part of snooker's appeal was the dress code and the conduct of the players. It added to that sense of theatre. Some players were choosing to wear white suits. There wasn't an issue with that, but Kirk Stevens was ditching the tie and having his shirt open nearly to his waist. That was the main reason bowties were compulsory in evening sessions.

Higgins may have felt he was being unfairly singled out for attention but at the table he had bigger worries, as 1981 would be the year when Steve Davis truly arrived, winning his first World Championship. Davis beat Higgins in the last sixteen on his way to securing the title.

Davis combined technique with incredibly hard work. Up until then, players had relied on a natural ability to see them through. Davis was utterly dedicated. In Barry Hearn he had a manager who was equally as committed to ensuring his player reached the very top. Hearn also saw the potential of the game overseas and was about to make Davis, if not the most popular player, the biggest earner.

I had another disaster at the hands of Tony Meo, losing 10–6. After the previous year, which had delivered so much, I was bitterly disappointed with my form and was glad to see the back of the 1980–1 season.

By this time I was living in Shepperton in Surrey. I enjoyed London. It was a different way of life from what I had grown up in. It was very upbeat. In Salford if you were short of money it could be depressing, but in London there seemed endless opportunities. People seemed to have a different outlook on life and probably more aspirations than I ever had.

Shepperton was a great location for racing. Just off Walton Bridge was Kempton Park. Go the other way and you were in Esher, the home of Sandown Park. As my form dipped my love for racing was in danger of overtaking snooker as my number-one passion.

I also started going to Windsor races on a Monday night. One night took a more bizarre twist than usual. My good friend Rodney Hutton, former professional golfer, rang me. We should go to Windsor that night, he said. His bookie pal Neville Berry had called him with some interesting information about a race there that night. A punter from Yorkshire had asked Neville for a £20,000 bet on a horse in the first race.

Neville didn't know the name of the horse. The conversation hadn't got that far because the bookie hadn't wanted to take the bet as he would have had to cover his liability by backing the horse with the other bookmakers. That would not have gone down well.

But Neville told Rodney he had arranged to meet the guy half an hour before the race. It would be a good move for Rodney if he saw the chap and followed him to see what he was backing. I don't know if you remember the *Two Ronnies* characters Charlie Farley and Piggy Malone, the two private investigators. Well that was what Rodney and I must have looked like.

Every time the punter looked in our general direction we would hide. He had two binocular cases, which, according to Neville, had £10,000 in each. By the time we were certain which horse it was it was now down in price to 6–4. We put our bets on and hoped for the best.

The horse took up the running two furlongs out and won by two and a half lengths. It was worth the trip, as Rodney and

I had a good bet. It was only after the race that I noticed that my pal Geoff Baxter had been riding the horse. I asked Geoff what the trainer had said to him. He told him to kick on when he could and keep him going to the line. I assumed the guy got his £20,000 on. There was 8–1 on offer early but only for small money. But somebody knew that was the day, even if the jockey didn't.

Moments like that stirred the blood and took me right back to those first experiences at Manchester Racecourse with my dad and The Black Horse.

Not every night produced the same feelings, however. One evening at Kempton I wasn't having the best of nights and was chasing my losses. It was the last race of the night and the favourite was the Arthur Pitt-trained Tom Forrester at 6–4. The odds were too short for me to get my losses back. I was more interested in the Michael Stoute-trained Stepple Bell, ridden by Walter Swinburn. My American pal Terry Rogan was all over the favourite. I went down to the rails and was surprised to see 8–1 about Stepple Bell. I had the bet with a bookie I knew, Tony Coullie, from Fairmile Racing. My wager was £200 to win. As I was heading for the stands to watch the race I bumped into David Smalley, who wrote a column in the handicap book.

'John, the owner of Kingsfield Flyer, has had his biggest bet ever on his horse,' he told me. I had never done it before but I nipped back to the bookie and asked him if I could have my £200 on Kingsfield Flyer at 11–2 and cancel my bet on Stepple Bell. Tony said that he didn't have any big liabilities on the race and agreed to my new transaction.

The race began and as they turned into the straight I knew I had done my money. Kingsfield Flyer was last and going nowhere. Tom Forrester and Stepple Bell were fighting out the finish. To say I was cheering on the favourite along with Terry is an understatement.

Tom Forrester won by a head, but a photo finish was called. I turned to Terry, who wasn't sure. I offered to halve his bet. The result was announced before he had a chance to reply. He had a good bet on the favourite, while I was just relieved that Stepple Bell hadn't won.

'Two bottles of your best champagne,' shouted Terry as we got to the bar. We were talking more about my relief that changing my mind had not cost me. Over in the corner I noticed Arthur Pitt as we were just starting into the second bottle of champagne.

I raised a glass to him, but he didn't respond and didn't look happy.

'I would leave him alone if I were you, John,' said a guy at the bar.

'Why?' I said. 'He just had the last winner.'

'The stewards have disqualified it and given the race to Stepple Bell.'

You could not make it up. We were all losers. Terry had done his money and if I hadn't changed my bet I would have recouped my losses on the night.

The main reason I changed my bet was the price. Invariably, when a Stoute horse was fancied 8–1 it was too big a price. Tom Forrester was disqualified because he gave the winner a bump at the two-furlong marker. I never did tell Dave Smalley the story. He only passed on his information to do me a favour.

If only I hadn't bumped into him. But, as I have found out all too often, 'if only' was a running theme in my life.

And, as I was about to discover, when my two passions of

snooker and horse racing clashed it could only mean one thing for me – disaster.

CHAPTER 15

WHEN TWO WORLDS COLLIDE

It was the year everything was thrown out of kilter.

In 1982 the snooker world was stunned when Steve Davis, the hot favourite to retain the World Championship, was knocked out in the opening round by a young man from Bolton hardly anyone had heard of: Tony Knowles.

Davis's 10–1 defeat – to this day still one of the biggest shocks in Crucible history – meant Terry Griffiths was then the new favourite. Like the passing of a curse, he too soon fell, losing 10–6 to Willie Thorne.

Alex Higgins was still in contention but, after being caught urinating in a plant pot, and getting into a spat with a security guard, in which he ripped off the man's lapel badge, people wondered whether his head was in the right place.

I had come into the tournament playing some of my best snooker since 1979. In my opening match I'd beaten the relative newcomer from Grimsby, Mike Hallett, 10–4 and felt in good shape. Although I hadn't featured at the business end of tournaments that season I had posted wins over Dennis Taylor, John Spencer and Ray Reardon, and had beaten Tony Knowles in the International Open. Aside from Davis, it had been a patchy season for a number of players. And, with the other favourites falling by the wayside, the bookies installed me as the best bet to take the title.

The seventeen days of the Crucible can be a test of endurance and my next match wasn't for four days. Talking to the jockey Geoff Baxter, he suggested meeting at Chester racecourse. It sounded like a good idea – a day at the races to relax. We had a good day and I didn't lose any money. A winner in the last race of the day got me out.

Thanks indirectly to George Best and Kevin McAlinden, I'd got to know Cliff Lines, Michael Stoute's work rider, very well. As I did on most racing days, I rang Cliff the following morning.

He thought that Dawn Johnny, ridden by Walter Swinburn, would run well in the Chester Cup but said the horse would want firm ground. I assured him that it was firm as I had been there the day before.

'It should win, then,' he said.

He also told me about another horse, trained by Major Dick Hearn in a later race.

I placed my bets on the two races and went for my scheduled practice session. I was pleased to find my game was still there. I was potting well and looking forward to my next match.

After finishing my practice session I went to find a television to watch my bets. As Cliff predicted, Dawn Johnny won the Chester Cup at 16–1. It was already a good day but as I watched the later race I was amazed to see the Major Dick Hearn horse also romp home at 7–2. What a result!

With my single on Dawn Johnny and the double on the two, I had won a bumper payout – in fact it was nearly as much money as I'd get if I won the World Championship after seventeen days' hard battle at the Crucible.

In two days' time my match with Ray began. It should have been quite the occasion – playing the six-times world champion at the home of snooker. However, from being in a frame of mind where I couldn't miss a ball, now I couldn't hit one to save my life. It was as if the pockets had shrunk to the old billiard-table size. What was happening?

I lost the first session 6–2 and, unless I pulled something out of the bag, I was staring defeat in the face. I rallied slightly but Ray was too good and he won the match 13–8. Another favourite for the title had fallen.

Trying to analyse what had happened, I didn't think it was the actual money I'd won that was the problem. It was the elation from having two good days with the racing. My karma had been disturbed. Calm, cool and collected was how I had arrived in Sheffield. All that went in the blink of an eye.

Going to Chester had thrown me off course. It spoiled my second-best chance of winning the World Championship and gambling had got in the way. Would I ever learn?

Even though I'd lost I stayed on at the Crucible because of my role on the committee of the WPBSA. My own disappointment aside, I felt the 1982 championship was the best ever.

With Davis out, the tournament was wide open. Alex Higgins fancied his chances and, with a passionate crowd behind him, who would bet against his winning a second title ten years after his memorable triumph?

In the semifinal, Alex faced Jimmy White, which meant a

conflict of interest for me. I'd loved Alex since I first saw him. He was the one who inspired me to become a professional but I'd watched Jimmy from such a young age that I was desperate to see him fulfil his potential.

Jimmy began the match oozing confidence, taking the first four frames. Even Alex's wife Lynn was worried for her husband and took the drastic step of reaching out to Geoff Lomas for some advice on how to get Alex focused. Geoff suggested she phone Peter Madden, Alex's old jockey pal. Geoff thought that, if Alex could see Peter's calming presence in the arena, it might help him focus. Sure enough, Peter took his place in the front row.

Normally I watched the snooker on television backstage. But for that match I sat in the players' boxes for the last five frames. Jimmy was still playing the match of his life and when he moved 15–13 ahead, just one away from victory, I felt sure he had the match won.

In the next frame, however, Alex made a break of seventy-eight, which included a shot on the blue that was simply mesmeric. Even watching it back now, I find it hard to believe he managed it. That shot could almost be his epitaph.

In the decider Jimmy missed a straightforward red, which let Alex in. It was another glimpse into that vulnerability of Jimmy's game.

Alex, from looking down and out just moments earlier, seemed like a man possessed and produced some of his best snooker to clinch the match.

'I've got the ten-year itch,' he told the BBC. 'There's nothing wrong with my marriage but I've got a ten-year itch for the world title.'

In the final he faced Reardon, who, despite not being at

his best, looked to have the edge over Higgins because of his history in world finals.

After the first day, which ended with Alex ripping off his tie, Higgins was 10–7 up. From then on he was unstoppable.

The scenes when he won the title are part of British sporting history. All etiquette went out of the window as he beckoned Lynn and their baby daughter Lauren to share in his glory. 'Bring my baby, bring me my baby,' he said through tears.

Once the elation of Alex's stunning victory had died down we, as the committee, had the small disciplinary matter of his earlier behaviour to attend to – when he'd peed in the plant pot and assaulted the security guard.

The AGM was held the morning after the final, as many of the top players were still in Sheffield. Before we got to the issues with Alex we were working through some other matters when there was a knock on the door. A waiter came in with a trolley with six bottles of champagne, jugs of orange juice and glasses. They were presented to us 'with the compliments of Mr Higgins'. John Pulman, the acting chair and a legendary drinker, was delighted. 'Oh, good old Alex,' he said. It was only 10 a.m., but he got stuck into the champagne as we went through the agenda. Not everyone joined him, because of the early start, but by the time the minutes had been read three bottles had gone.

Then there was a second knock on the door.

'Morning, babes,' said the newly crowned world champion as he came into the room.

We gave him a round of applause for his victory and Pulman in particular thanked him heartily for providing the champagne.

Alex said, 'Listen, there's a lot of press outside and I'm keen to leave and get home with my wife and baby. So, what's the decision here?'

We told him we'd get to his business in due course and that he could go home and we wouldn't put out a statement on our decision until he'd been informed.

He made an impassioned plea about wanting to turn over a new leaf.

'It's taken me ten years to win the title again,' he said. 'I'm going to be a great ambassador for the game. This is just what I needed and I'm so happy. Just forget what happened to the security guard. He wound me up, but it's all in the past now.'

And out he went. His words and the fact that he'd won his second title in such style worked in his favour. The general feeling was that we shouldn't punish him too harshly for what he'd done.

Eddie Charlton raised an objection to Alex's playing in a forthcoming tournament in Australia. Some sponsors had banned him from playing there ever again. When I asked what the issue was, Eddie said Alex had pulled a gun on someone. Whether it was fake we didn't know, but he had threatened to 'blow their brains out'.

'I suppose that is a slight problem,' I said.

We were still having a discussion when Alex appeared again, holding his baby. He was going all out for the sympathy vote. We ushered him out again and got back to business. Eddie was adamant he couldn't go to Australia but despite that it was looking as if Alex would get off with a small fine and a ticking-off.

Just then, however, the door flew open. Unbeknown to us, Alex had been on the other side, listening in.

'Listen,' he snapped. 'I don't give a shit whether you fucking

184

want me to play or not.' Turning to Charlton, he added, 'And as for you – I wouldn't go to fucking Australia if you paid me. You can stick snooker up your arse!'

We all sat there stunned. There was no choice now but to up his punishment.

'He's not changed, has he?' Terry Griffiths said. It was hard to argue with that.

Alex was deducted ranking points and fined. He was his own worst enemy.

That meeting was my first experience of the committee's disciplinary procedures – but it was something I'd soon get used to.

That summer I joined Alex Higgins and Jimmy White for a tour of Ireland. Higgins had already been involved in a bizarre bit of drama when, while being driven about with the World Championship trophy, their driver, fearing he wasn't getting paid, took the trophy and held it hostage until Alex paid up.

During the tour I witnessed some of Alex's antics for myself.

On one evening I closed the exhibition with a few trick shots, not realising that Alex had disappeared back to the hotel. There were four hundred fans queuing for autographs from the newly crowned world champion and all they got was me. Luckily most were sympathetic but it could have turned ugly.

On another night, Alex did stay on to sign autographs but, as I got my pen out, he produced an inkpad and a stamp, on which was carved 'A. Higgins'.

'It's a time saver,' he said.

As I was busy signing away with my pen all I could hear from next to me was the sound of Alex's stamp. The fans were a bit confused but in the main they went along with it. Such was the level of fame and the aura he had that people were mostly too scared to complain. One fan did ask Alex if he would consider a conventional autograph. 'No, sorry, babe,' he said. 'I'm only stamping tonight.'

We had finished the signing when a guy walked over. 'Alex,' he said, 'I didn't want to ask you in front of everyone else. But my son Christopher thinks you are the greatest snooker player in the world. He loves you. I've got his book here and I've got a pen. Would you please sign it with "To Christopher, best wishes"?'

Alex looked around to check nobody else was looking. I could see his mind ticking over. Then he said, 'OK, come here.' He took the book and the pen from the man and wrote, 'To Christopher, best wishes' and then stamped his name underneath it. The guy was stunned, shook his head and stormed out. I couldn't believe it.

'I just like to keep people on their toes, babe,' Alex said with a shrug.

★★★

The 1982–3 season saw Steve Davis regain his world crown, and his manager Barry Hearn's influence was growing. He had added Terry Griffiths and Tony Meo to the stable of his promotions company, Matchroom, but the feeling was that Davis was the main attraction.

Davis won the World Championship with a session to spare, 18–6 against Cliff Thorburn, but the Canadian was clearly tired after his two previous rounds had gone to a deciding frame. And, of course, making the first maximum at the Crucible.

As Davis's stature grew, so his supporters became even

more vociferous and intimidating. It wasn't just his opponents who were noticing. I met Sebastian Coe, who originated from Sheffield and had been to the Crucible a few times. When I asked why I hadn't seen him there for a while he said he couldn't stand Steve's supporters and the barracking that went on.

Steve was, in my mind, one of the best snooker players ever but he was beginning to distance himself from the others. He would be content to stay in his room when he wasn't playing or practising, playing Space Invaders.

Throughout that season my form had continued to yoyo but was more down than up. In the UK Championship I had a good win over Doug Mountjoy, making a 127 break in the process, but fell once more to Tony Meo in the quarterfinal.

In the International Open I reached the semifinal but lost to David Taylor, while in the Professional Players' Tournament I beat John Spencer and former Yorkshire champion Joe Johnson on my way to the semifinal, but lost out to Jimmy White. And in the World Championship I once again failed to get into the last sixteen, losing 10–3 to Willie Thorne.

Since that great year in 1979 I had lost some of my hunger for the game. I hadn't fallen out of love with snooker but it was frustrating to be playing well in practice but not able to translate that to the table when it mattered. I was still practising regularly for six or seven hours a day. In my experience, six hours of hard practice used to equal six frames in a tournament. One night at Henry's Kingston Snooker Centre, I played 'points' snooker with Cliff Thorburn and Kirk Stevens and the session lasted seven and a half hours. At the end I was playing as well as I've ever done.

What I didn't appreciate at the time was that getting more

involved with the running of the game was harming my potential in tournaments. I was in my peak years but being on the committee was a distraction.

★ ★ ★

That Christmas my mother came down to stay for the festive period. She had never been to London before. To bring in the New Year we went for dinner to the Ferryboat Inn at Hampton Court. It was the first time my mother had seen caviar.

'This is nice,' she said. 'What is it?'

'It's fish eggs,' I said.

'Oh, I'm not eating that,' she said and didn't have another bite.

That night I met for the first time a man who would become one of my greatest friends: Rocky Taylor. Rocky was a stuntman who had appeared in dozens of big movies. His claim to fame at the time was that he had just stood in for two James Bonds in the same year, as Roger Moore in *Octopussy* and then as Sean Connery during filming for *Never Say Never Again*. He started working in show business at the age of fifteen, teaching Cliff Richard judo on the set of *Summer Holiday*, and was the original voice of the Honey Monster in the Sugar Puffs adverts. He was actually born Laurie and his dad Larry was an actor who appeared in *Zulu* alongside Michael Caine. When father and son were appearing in the same celebrity football charity match, the entertainer Bernie Winters said, 'We can't have two.' So he changed his name to Rocky – long before the Sylvester Stallone movies.

Rocky had recognised me from the snooker coverage on television and came over to introduce himself. We got on straightaway but it was the fuss he made of my mother that showed me what a decent guy he was. By that time Mother wasn't as mobile as she once had been, but he got her dancing in her seat. 'Come on, Mrs V,' he said. She loved the attention.

It was a special time and all the more poignant because it was the last Christmas and New Year we spent together. Tragically, she died before the year was out.

By the mid-eighties snooker was booming. Tournaments were being added to the schedule every year and sponsors were queuing up. There was more money in the game than ever before. Everyone's a winner? Not quite.

CHAPTER 16

MY BIGGEST BREAK

One of the new tournaments was a Professional Snooker League, featuring twelve of the top players, with the exception of Steve Davis and others from Barry Hearn's Matchroom. The matches were held in various venues across the country from November 1983 to April 1984. The winner was supposed to get a gold cue and £50,000. However, the sponsor ran out of money halfway through so by the end the prize pot was completely empty.

Trust me to produce some of my best form for years. Of my eleven matches, I won eight, drew two and lost only one. Along the way I beat Alex Higgins, Ray Reardon, Dennis Taylor, Jimmy White, Kirk Stevens and Tony Knowles. I ended up without a penny and there was no sign of a golden cue!

Davis continued to dominate the game, winning seven tournaments that season, although, notably, Alex Higgins took the UK Championship, meaning he'd won a career 'triple crown' of the World Championship, Masters and UK, emulating a feat achieved by Davis and Terry Griffiths.

At the Benson & Hedges Masters at Wembley, the interest the game was generating in the showbiz world was illustrated when the famous actor Donald Sutherland arrived. He took his place in the front row, just in time to see Kirk Stevens make his maximum break against Jimmy White. He stayed for only the one match and yet witnessed only the third 147 to be televised. That must be how it is for Hollywood stars, I thought. No wonder they always seem to get a parking space outside a bank in all the movies.

In that season's World Championship I was 9–8 up against Willie Thorne, needing only one more frame to win, but lost 10–9.

On his march to the final, Steve Davis beat Dennis Taylor 16–9, while Jimmy White came from behind to pip Kirk Stevens 16–14. An early finish to the semifinals meant the spectators were going to end up short-changed. I was still at the Crucible and the promoter Mike Watterson came up to me. 'I hear you do impressions,' he said. 'Would you mind doing some now?'

Why not? I thought. It was the Crucible, it was the first time I'd performed them on television, but I treated it as I would any other exhibition.

'What I'm going to do,' I said, 'is have a little bit of fun and I'm going to do a few impersonations of some of the professionals you've been watching this week.'

I started with 'my old favourite' John Spencer. He was a commentator for the BBC's coverage by then, so I added that John was, 'taking elocution lessons and had a walk-on part on *Coronation Street*.'

For a long time Spencer had been one of my star pieces,

but I'd noticed at exhibitions that, because he had been out of the picture for a while, I wasn't getting the same reaction. Audiences in the clubs only recognised players who had been on television and, when John hadn't had much exposure during a lean period, a lot of the audience didn't know who he was.

However, I began with the old head shake, stuck my bottom out and started sniffing and showed the audience how I thought he might pot the black. The Crucible crowd seemed to appreciate it.

After I potted the black there was a slight pause as I had to get back over to my seat to use the microphone.

'And now,' I said, 'your friend and mine, Mr Ray Reardon. Probably a lot of you have come along and wanted his autograph. Well, he's just gone back to Transylvania on a refresher course.' That got a big laugh. I went on: 'Ray, from the sitting position, would probably eventually play the black something like this . . .'

I sat down and gave some knowing smiles to the audience, as Ray was prone to do. When I stood up and shook myself down, the place erupted, which allowed me to do the mock 'give over' gesture that was another Reardon favourite. Ray was such a well-known character in the game that his mannerisms were instantly recognisable.

Once, when I had been doing a show with Ray, out of deference I omitted to do his impersonation. 'What about me?' he asked, 'I thought you did me.' So I did – and Ray laughed along with everyone else.

He did get his own back on me one year when, while I was in the middle of my routine, he appeared with a bushy beard on, mimicking me. The audience loved it.

Back at the Crucible, I actually missed the black doing the Reardon impression but that only got a bigger cheer and enabled me to do Ray's little giggle.

'A man I've not done very often, but I think his performance in this year's championship deserves it, is Dennis Taylor,' I said, before reaching for the prop I needed to do the Northern Irishman – a novelty pair of oversized glasses. I then pretended to struggle to see the table, which went down well.

My next one, I said, was going to take a lot longer than the others because it was Terry Griffiths. The former world champion was well known as being one of the slowest players but did have some mannerisms it was easy to mimic: his bemused expression and funny way of sizing up every possible angle for what seemed like an eternity.

When it came to doing the then current world champion, Steve Davis, I started by taking a sip of water. People recognised the rise of his little finger and then how he liked to flick his nose while weighing up a shot. There wasn't a great deal in Davis's cuing action to mimic but once the black went in I rose with a few fist pumps, which were very much his trademark.

'I'm not going to do Jimmy White,' I said. 'He's left-handed and he pots too quick for me.' Referring to Kirk Stevens's open-neck style, I added, 'I'd like to do Kirk but I haven't got that many hairs on my chest.'

At that moment, a woman called out, 'Why don't you do John Virgo?'

'Well I did that the other night and got beat 10–9 by Willie Thorne,' I said.

I closed by saying that I thought the audience was in for a great final that night, praising Jimmy for the way he had come back in his match. I closed my little ten-minute stint by doing

194

the 'one and only Alex Higgins'. I left him until last because not only was it the one that always got the biggest reaction but I had to take off my tie and undo my shirt to give it the full effect. Doing Alex's swagger-cum-stagger and lightning-fast walk around the table always got a laugh, and I potted the black to loud cheers.

When I came off, the presenter, David Vine, said to me, 'You just got £25,000 of free publicity out of that.'

Not everyone was a fan. After my impersonations were televised, a teacher at a special-needs school wrote to me asking if I realised that when I was doing my impression of Alex Higgins I was also taking the mickey out of every disabled child in the country?

I showed it to the producer but he took one look at it, said, 'Have you ever read anything like that,' and ripped it up.

It was unbelievable. Surely people could see I was just having a bit of fun. At the exhibitions, after Ray Reardon had experienced a dip in form, some spectators had felt my impersonation was a little cruel, but my take-offs were never meant to be like that. I always had great respect for Ray – it's just he had so many mannerisms he was a godsend to me.

Over the years I'd added to my repertoire by using props. As well as Dennis's trademark glasses, I got a bald cap for Willie Thorne and had an earring to look like an eyeball to do my Graham Miles impersonation because he used to sight as if he was looking out of his ear.

From then on, if a session finished early the producers would ask me to fill in. The public reaction was great but what people didn't know is that I used to sit there at the Crucible praying I wasn't needed. I may have looked all jovial and comfortable in front of the cameras and making the audience laugh but the early fears I'd felt back when I first did exhibitions never left me. I was always terrified of making an idiot of myself.

One year, instead of doing my impersonation of Steve Davis, who continued to dominate the sport, I said, 'I'd like to do Steve Davis – but wouldn't we all?'

As more people saw the impersonations, to keep my act fresh and hone my jokes I recruited a professional scriptwriter.

David Vine was right, though. Getting that kind of national exposure did do wonders for my profile – but, given what it would lead to in later, life it was more like £2.5 million!

CHAPTER 17

I GOTTA HORSE

After those first impersonations on national television I became instantly more recognisable. And with the increased recognition came a perception that because you were on television you must be worth a few quid.

Now when I went to Windsor races on a Monday night I had trainers coming up to me. They were like car dealers but, instead of trying to sell me a motor, they were trying to flog me a horse. Owning a racehorse wasn't something I'd ever considered. It just wasn't something a boy from Salford did. However, in the wake of that 1984 World Championship appearance, the exhibition work had picked up.

After getting back together once again, Avril and I tried to cement our commitment to making it work by getting married. We had relocated to Normandy, near Guildford, and, although we were reasonably settled for a while at home, there was one complication.

Kirk Stevens was being managed by Geoff Lomas but living in London was proving too much for a young player who had been battling a cocaine addiction. Kirk had been partying at the famous nightclub Tramp with the likes of Status Quo musician Rick Parfitt. Geoff and another former snooker player turned businessman called Noel Miller-Cheevers, who was also looking after him, suggested to me that Kirk needed to get away from the bright lights of the big city. As we were out in the countryside we might have been able to help Kirk battle his addictions. So he came to live with us for a while to get away from those temptations.

It was under these circumstances that I met Colin Williams, then a trainer but in his day a very talented and strong jockey. He rode Peter O'Sullevan's Be Friendly when the famous BBC commentator's horse won the Vernons Sprint at Haydock. As I had a decent knowledge of the formbook, talking to Colin about his achievements was a delight. He had been a trainer for a couple of years and asked me, did I fancy owning a horse?

My good friend Geoff Baxter, who was stable jockey for Bruce Hobbs, told me that Colin was a decent trainer and could get one ready, but I still wasn't sure about buying a horse. It wasn't so much the price tag but the training fees that were the problem.

As I chatted to Colin at Windsor one night, he told me he would have a winner on the following Wednesday. The horse was called Making Tracks. I rang Geoff and asked him what he thought.

'What kind of race is it?'

'A seller,' I replied, meaning it was a race in which the winner would be put up for sale afterwards. That was Geoff's sphere.

'Back it,' he said.

I told Kirk about the tip. He'd been making progress since living in my house and had been beginning to stabilise, although he wasn't at the stage of wanting to practise snooker. Kirk, like most snooker players, was brought up gambling but he didn't have a clue about betting on a horse race. The horse's starting price was going to be around 10–1. I told him I was going to invest £400 – £300 to win and £100 to place. The place money, I explained, was so that if he got beat I would have recouped my stake money. The horse was beaten in a photo finish, but he got the race in the stewards' room. What a result!

When I got back home, Kirk was in his bedroom, with all this money strewn all over the bed. His bet had been £390 win and £10 place. Beginner's luck or what? His place bet would never have covered his stake. Not that it mattered in the end. He was very excited and, when I told him that the trainer wanted me to put a horse with him, he said, 'Count me in.'

With Kirk on board, I asked my punting buddy 'TV Steve' if he was interested. He was, and so we agreed to go three ways on the £6,000 it was going to cost to buy the horse. Colin Williams had sourced it in Ireland. Its sire was called Orchestra, which was a mile-and-a-half horse, but the dam was called What a Picture, which Colin had ridden. His view was that although it was a short runner – so barely stayed five furlongs, which was the minimum trip for a flat horse – it always had plenty of pace and he thought if you could combine that stamina and speed we could have a good horse. Steve came up with the name – 'Jo' for John, 'Ki' for Kirk and 'St' for Steve, hence Jokist.

The day after Making Tracks' famous victory, Kirk had

packed his bags and had headed back to Canada for a few days. He had to be back in Britain in a week's time as he had a tournament to play. He did get back in time, but looking a complete wreck and with no money left. He'd obviously blown his winnings back home. In hindsight, it might have been better for him if the horse had lost, or I hadn't told him about the tip. It was very sad.

By the time of Jokist's maiden race at Warwick, Kirk had forgotten all about his 'count me in', remark. Steve and I were co-owners but we decided to stick with the name, as losing the 'Ki' would have sounded silly.

For that maiden outing at Warwick, we went up to see how he would perform. My pal Geoff Baxter had agreed to ride him. The word was that Jokist was working well and Colin thought he would take all the beating. Those were the days when there were no early prices – particularly on two-year-old maidens.

Steve had stayed in London and had a few people who would be in the betting shops and take the opening show. With a not-so-fashionable trainer, the opening show of 11–4 was disappointing to say the least. I took up my position in the owners' viewing area. Standing there with my binoculars at the ready, I saw the ITV commentator Graham Goode.

'Got an interest?' he asked. I told him that Jokist was my horse and I was hopeful of a good run.

My first race as an owner and I've got Graham Goode, with his binoculars, giving me a commentary! When they turned into the straight, he said, 'I don't think you have any worries here.'

Jokist pulled away and won in fine style by ten lengths. It was such a thrill going into the paddock and being there when he came in as a winner.

I was obviously delighted that he'd won but, unfortunately,

Geoff Baxter's valet had overheard him talking to Colin and from what they had said realised that this horse was expected to run a big race. He told somebody who'd gone to a Warwick bookmaker and put a couple of hundred on and all of a sudden the alarm systems go. That's why the best price I could get was 11–4. I had a five-hundred win on it so I was happy enough but for a first-time-out two-year-old trained by a small trainer we should have got a bigger price.

Buying a racehorse was living beyond our means but it was easy to get carried away by this perceived celebrity status.

Unfortunately, that race was the only time he got his head in front as a two-year-old. The last race he ran that year was at Newbury and Steve Cauthen, the great American jockey, was booked to ride him. I didn't think Jokist would have much of a chance but at least I'd get a chance to meet Steve. It didn't turn out that way. He arrived into the paddock late, jumped on the horse, rode off to the start, trailed in about second last, jumped off before it got to the paddock and ran off to the weighing room before I got to meet him.

To add insult to injury, Colin Williams's first words to me were not what Cauthen had said about the horse, but the fact was he was going to sack the head lad. When I asked why, he replied, 'Look at the size of the horse. He's been overfeeding it.'

Steve and I weren't happy. Steve spoke to Cliff Lines, who suggested we move the horse to another trainer. He recommended Richard Shaw, who with James Fanshawe was one of Michael Stoute's assistant trainers. Cliff assured us Richard would be a good trainer given the opportunities. Colin Williams wasn't pleased when I told him. In fact, he even offered us another sprinter to replace Jokist. We were not for turning, however, and put the horse with Richard Shaw.

Speaking to Richard on the phone during the winter months, I learned he was pleased with the horse and assured me he would win races.

★ ★ ★

Kirk Stevens may have been right to back out of all the issues that came with owning a horse. But he had his own troubles. In the 1985 Dulux British Open he knocked Steve Davis out in the semifinal but was trailing the South African Silvino Francisco 9–5 going into the last session of the final. Kirk began mounting a fightback but during a toilet break Francisco confronted him, grabbed hold of his lapels and accused him of taking drugs. Once play resumed, Silvino's wife was then giving Kirk the evil eye every time he returned to his seat. This sort of behaviour wasn't on. Kirk pulled it back to 9–8 but eventually lost the final 12–9. After the match Kirk's management duly complained.

A hearing was arranged but, in the weeks running up to it, Francisco was quoted in a newspaper accusing Kirk of being 'high as a kite, out of his mind on dope'. Kirk then gave his own interview, where he admitted to being a drug addict.

When the meeting was held it was the unanimous decision of those there that to physically and verbally abuse an opponent during a match was intolerable. For his unacceptable conduct, the South African was fined £6,000 and deducted two world ranking points.

Coincidentally, 1985 was the year that drug testing was introduced at the World Championship. This had nothing to do with Stevens's case; the moves had already taken place. The Sports Council had been putting pressure on all sports to have drug testing. The governing bodies of tennis and golf refused. The council threatened us that if we didn't fall in line we would not be regarded as a sport. We felt we had to agree.

At the Crucible that year every test proved negative. But once Kirk had admitted to his drug problems everyone, it seemed, was taking up Francisco's cause. The newspapers and snooker magazines were pillorying the WPBSA. The verbal and physical abuse appeared to be forgotten. Silvino, it was said, was being punished for telling the truth.

I didn't think this was the case. Although I'd known for some time that Kirk had a problem, I had never seen him take drugs and I believed him when he told me he had never taken them while playing. After Kirk's public admission, my wife was quoted saying that she and I had tried to keep him clean while he was staying with us. This was interpreted as my keeping the issue from the board. Why should I have mentioned it? That wasn't what the hearing was going to be about and I was trying to help a friend who had a problem.

Now there was drug testing, if Kirk failed then he'd be letting himself down, as well as me. He never failed a drugs test.

It seemed from that moment on that snooker was under a microscope and the game's relationship with the press would never be the same again.

By the time the hearing was held, in June that year, Kirk had been attending rehab in Toronto. In terms of testing he was clean and was getting help, yet many people, along with Silvino, thought he should be punished.

The criticism continued unabated. Snooker's 'rulers', it was claimed, had turned on someone for rocking the boat when parts of the boat were 'rotten'. We were accused of trying to bury our problems rather than tackle them.

There was further controversy when it came to the Sports

Council's guidelines on banned substances. Their advice was to follow the International Olympic Committee's list. At the time beta blockers were not on the IOC list, but that changed when at an Olympics it was discovered that beta blockers helped slow the heart rate down, which could give users an advantage. Our chairman at the time, Rex Williams, had been taking beta blockers for several years. Suddenly, questions were being asked of Rex: could the chairman of the WPBSA pass an IOC drugs test? Rex's stance was that the board did not have to follow the IOC list. That is what we thought, naïvely as it turned out.

It was obvious that the WPBSA needed professional help.

Francisco had appealed his punishment and several months later, in front of Gavin Lightman QC, acting on behalf of the association, his fine was reduced to £2,000, with £1,500 costs. Lightman did say that he thought the South African had brought the game into disrepute. Francisco would later serve a prison sentence for smuggling cannabis.

Snooker was in the spotlight but, thankfully, looking back on that year, I remember that time well, but for all the right reasons.

For me, 1985 was the pinnacle of modern-day snooker. How could it get any better – the World Championship, a rank outsider and the seemingly invincible defending champion, a deciding frame that went down to the final black?

Against all the odds Steve Davis lost to Dennis Taylor, as 18.5 million viewers watched at home – the highest ever audience for a sporting event, the biggest recorded on BBC Two and the largest after midnight.

After the final there were all these rumours that Davis had let Taylor win. I'm not sure why that started circulating;

maybe it's a peculiar British trait of trying to take the gloss off it or something. There's no way Steve intended that finale. He still has nightmares about it today. 'I won six world titles but the only thing I'm remembered for is being beat by Dennis Taylor,' he says.

But that's what Dennis Taylor has done his whole career. He sneaks up on people. He did it to me plenty of times and he sneaked up on Steve Davies in 1985.

After that stunning last frame – and the post-match interviews that saw Steve give monosyllabic answers and Dennis wind up the Davis camp by announcing himself the best in the world – I knocked on Steve's dressing room. Barry Hearn opened it. 'You're the only person I'd let in here,' he said.

Steve was in floods of tears, absolutely crying his eyes out. 'Don't worry about it, son,' I said. 'You're still the best player in the world.'

We had a hug and I walked out. Anyone who had seen Steve in that state would never have questioned his integrity.

★ ★ ★

That championship was also special for me because it was the one where I first started commentating for the BBC. I'd been knocked out and the producer, Nick Hunter, said, 'Do you fancy having a go in the commentary box?'

When I said I did, he said, 'Just do a couple of days and we'll see how you get on.'

After the first day, Nick came up to me. 'How did you find it?'

'I enjoyed it,' I said.

'We like what you did,' he said, 'but just one thing to remember, John: we've already got one Ted Lowe!'

Without even realising it, I had been doing an impression of the legendary Ted Lowe, whose hushed tones had rightly made him the 'voice of snooker'. I think I have my impersonations to thank for their thinking of me. That and being on the board possibly helped, too.

I did a three-day trial alongside Jack Karnehm in the commentary box. 'The way to do it,' he said, 'is, once the frame ball's gone in, you leave it to me to close the frame.'

'Oh, OK,' I said.

I can't recall who was playing but, as the frame neared its conclusion, I told viewers that, when the leading player had potted one more red and a colour, it would leave his opponent needing snookers. The red and the colour were potted and Jack came in: 'Well, that should be good enough for it to be 1–0.'

As it was the opening frame, the other player came to the table and, even though the frame was gone, was potting some balls just to get a feel for it. Jack said nothing while this was going on. I felt some viewers may not know what was happening, so I chipped in: 'Well, the reason he's playing on—'

As I was speaking, Jack threw his microphone down on the desk. I finished my sentence, turned off the mic and said, 'Is there a problem?'

'I told you I finish the frames off.'

'Well,' I said, 'I'll tell you something. You don't tell me what to do. I was only saying it because it's something I think the viewers will like to be told.'

This was the same Jack Karnehm who was chair of the amateur snooker and billiards association when I was selected to play for England and went over to Dublin to play the Irish team. During that trip I was surprised not to see him there for the afternoon's play. 'No,' he said later, 'I went to the races with a bookmaker friend.'

He then added, 'To be perfectly honest, I hate snooker, can't bear watching it.'

As said, he was the chairman of the amateur snooker and billiards association. I thought, Now he's commentating on snooker and he hates the game and he's trying to tell me how to commentate.

The man I always tried to emulate was Ted Lowe. Viewers hung on his every word. Everyone remembers, though, his great line when they transferred over from black-and-white to colour TV and he said, 'For those of you watching in black and white, the yellow is behind the blue.'

After the 1985 World Championship final, the next tournament was the following season's Rothman's Grand Prix, which saw Steve Davis and Dennis Taylor in a rerun of their Crucible final. The tournament was held in October, just as the clocks went back. Ted's opening line, when Steve broke off for the deciding frame, was, 'Last night we put our clocks back one hour. These two stars turned theirs back to April.'

With Ted by my side, I felt I was learning from the master.

I must have done OK in my trial, because they asked me to come back the following year – and they've kept me ever since.

CHAPTER 18

A TASTE OF THE HIGH LIFE

O ne of the advantages of owning a racehorse was becoming a member of the Racehorse Owners Association. In November 1985 the ROA were organising a trip to America for the annual Breeders' Cup, that year held in New York at Aqueduct Park. We would be flying Concorde, staying at the Sheraton Hotel in Manhattan with club tickets for the two-day meeting. The trip would cost £2,100 but I figured it was the chance of a lifetime so I booked up.

Earlier that year I'd met a former New York Jets American footballer called Terry Rogan, who lived in Chiswick. We had shared loves of golf and racing. When I told him about the trip he said he would be back in America at the time so he'd meet me. I took that with a pinch of salt but he was a man of his word.

No sooner had I arrived at the hotel and opened my suitcase when the phone rang and it was Terry. 'Hey, big fella,' he said. 'I'm downstairs in reception.'

Across the road from the Sheraton was an Irish bar

called Rosie O'Grady's. As soon as we walked in everybody recognised me. The staff were mainly Irish people who went over there to work in the bars. That made for a good night.

The Breeders' Cup was in its infancy back then but the horses on show were top-class. The first day we arrived at Aqueduct Park you couldn't help but see the marked difference between British and American racing. I suppose you could describe their tracks as being like Chester Racecourse.

Looking at the race card, I noticed in the last race there was a horse called Infantry. The horse had raced in England, trained by Barry Hills, owned by Robert Sangster.

Robert Street, a jockey Geoff Baxter had recommended to me to ride Jokist, had told me that Infantry was one of the best horses that Barry Hills had ever trained. In the Breeders' Cup it wasn't listed as being trained by Barry Hills. Sangster had sold it to America and it was now owned by Sugar Maple Farms. Infantry had run in the King George at Ascot the year before and at the two-furlong marker had shot a couple of lengths clear but didn't stay for the mile and a half. This race was over ten furlongs, a shorter race at a mile and a quarter.

'We've got to back this,' I said to Terry. I passed the information on to the rest of the ROA group as well.

The race got under way and, as they turned into the straight, Infantry made his move. As he went clear, to a man we all shouted, 'Go on, England!' Out of the corner of my eye I could see a few people flicking through the race card, obviously thinking, England? Where's that come from?

The horse won and my winnings paid for the entire trip to New York. Not a bad result!

The next day was the Breeders' Cup itself. I backed Strawberry Road, ridden by Steve Cauthen. It came in second, behind Pebbles, ridden by Pat Eddery – the first time a horse from England had won the Breeders' Cup.

The night called for a celebration and we went back to Rosie O'Grady's, where an Irish band were playing. I was a great fan of the Fureys and Davey Arthur. After a few drinks and feeling full of myself, I went up to the lead singer and said, 'Do you know "The Green Fields of France"?' Not only did he know the song, but he recognised me. It was amazing. There I was in New York and it seemed everybody knew me.

'Would you like us to sing it?' he said.

'No,' I said. 'I'd like to sing it myself.'

It was one of my great claims to fame, singing 'The Green Fields of France' in Rosie O'Grady's in Manhattan.

If only I'd backed Pebbles it would have been the trip of a lifetime. And, sadly for Infantry, that was his last race. He broke down in training not long after and never raced again. I will certainly never forget him, however, or that weekend.

★ ★ ★

The following year was a new season and a chance for us to see if Jokist would fulfil his early potential.

'TV Steve' and I travelled to Musselburgh, near Edinburgh, for his first race as a three-year-old. We had high hopes, but Jokist was drawn badly, came all the way round the bend, ran wide and finished stone last.

The jockey, Richard Lines, Cliff's son, said to Steve he didn't think Jokist could win even a seller, the lowest grade of race you can run in. I had a word with the trainer and told him the jockey's view. Richard Shaw didn't agree. 'That's not what he's been showing me on the gallops,' he said. 'I just don't think he handled the bend.'

We had lots to think about. I was beginning to wonder whether we should get rid of the horse, since you don't want to throw good money after bad. To keep a horse in training was costing even in those days £10,000 a year. We trailed back down South thinking that the only good thing to come out of our trip to Scotland was the round of golf we played on Royal Burgess – the oldest golf society in the world and to this day one of the nicest courses I've played on.

Jokist's next outing was at Chepstow. Geoff Baxter had recommended Robert Street, the former work rider for Barry Hills. I asked him if he would ride Jokist and give us his opinion. With Robert at the reins he ran a terrific race. With a furlong to go he was still disputing the lead, but was worn down in the last fifty yards to finish second at 20–1. The horse that beat him, Young Jason, would go on to win the Stewards' Cup at Goodwood. 'You've got a good horse,' Robert said afterwards. 'He'll definitely win races.'

His third race was at Windsor on a Monday night, but I couldn't be there because I had to play a snooker exhibition in Manchester that evening. I rang Richard Shaw before I left home. He was very bullish about Jokist's chances. Reading the *Racing Post* that morning, I had noticed that Shaw also had a runner at Edinburgh that day called Sweet Alexander. When I asked him what chance she had, he said, 'If it doesn't win I may as well give up training.'

Sweet Alexander won on the bridle at 7–2. I had backed her in a single and had a £100 win double the two. It was a good start to the day.

Come the exhibition, I was due to start at 7.30 p.m. Jokist's race began at 7.25 p.m. I rang up my bookie at 7.24 p.m. to hook me up to the commentary. The race was late in starting.

The organiser was beside me tapping his watch. Just as they were coming inside the last furlong, Jokist came clear in the last fifty yards to win comfortably. My winnings were, for once, an awful lot more than he was paying me. But the show must go on. By the time I was introduced I was on such a high I wanted to share my joy with everyone. I apologised for starting the show late, but explained that I was listening to my horse win at Windsor at 12–1. 'You never told us,' they all cried.

For his next outing, my mate Rocky and I travelled north to see him run in the Nottingham Stewards' Cup. Jokist had a chance but he was up against the favourite, Ra Ra Girl. Before the race I told Rocky that, as we were in the owners' area, we had to act with a little decorum.

The race started and I could see Jokist coming up on the outside. 'Here he comes,' I said to Rocky.

All of a sudden this woman beside us shouted, 'Come on, Ra Ra Girl!'

That was the cue for us to start. 'Come on, Robert, give him his head.'

Jokist won by three lengths. We went ballistic. So much for decorum! He passed the winning line and we stormed down the stand from the owners' area to the winning enclosure on a wave of euphoria. We were there so early it must have been another five minutes before the horse arrived in the enclosure. It was a magic moment – an excitement I wasn't getting out of snooker at the time.

Like me, in my early days with snooker, he was improving, but I didn't know how far he could go. He was a three-year-old and he was improving out of all proportion.

Then he went to the Norfolk resort of Great Yarmouth and won there in an unbelievable time. After the race, the comedian Jim Davidson, who was doing a summer season there, presented me with the trophy. 'I think you're really funny on that snooker,' he said. There was no inkling then that years later we would work together.

Jokist had won three races on the trot.

I was on a high. Those were good times. Avril had given birth to our beautiful daughter Brook-Leah in 1986 and it really felt as though things were falling into place. I wasn't making much of an impact at snooker tournaments but the commentating and the horse racing were providing thrills and income, even if snooker wasn't.

Next up for Jokist was the Ayr Gold Cup in September. In the build-up we didn't have the best preparation. Steve wanted Richard Lines to ride him, but I said we couldn't really take Robert off because they'd been doing really well. Steve didn't take this well and said if that was the case he didn't want to be involved any more.

However, come the race meeting, we all went up to Scotland – even Jimmy White came with us.

The Scottish horse riders' association invited me to speak at the dinner prior to the race. Jonjo O'Neill, one of the best jump jockeys of all time and nicest people you could meet, who had won the Cheltenham Gold Cup, was there, recovering from his cancer treatment. Considering what to say in my speech, I thought it might be funny if I likened snooker players to horses, using the type of comments you saw in the racing papers.

So, I described them as: Terry Griffiths – very slowly away; Bill Werbeniuk – stuck in stalls; Dennis Taylor – blinkers helped; Kirk Stevens – strong challenge, got nose in front on line. That one raised a bit of a titter.

When it came to Alex Higgins, I compared him to a two-year-old – bit backwards, speed for three furlongs.

When it came to the race, Jokist was the antepost favourite. Robert rode him but finished twelfth – yet beaten by only four and a quarter lengths. There was a gap early on in the race and I don't know whether it was the horse or the jockey, but they didn't fancy going for it. It's easy for us to sit there and say the jockey could have done this or that but, when they're going along at 40 m.p.h. and there's a field of thirty runners and they're all concertinaing into the rail, would you be brave enough to push for that gap?

It was a blow. After the tremendous run he'd had he missed the big one.

I was in a snooker club in Ealing when Jokist lost in his last race as a three-year-old. The legendary Pat Eddery, who that year had ridden the winner in the St Ledger, rode him. I thought Jokist could have been placed but, once Pat saw he wasn't going to win, he just eased him down. As Jokist had won three races as a three-year-old he went so far up in the weights. From starting the season racing in the high forties, he was running nearly 80 pounds. He had to carry more weight. That meant that, although he'd improved from age two to three, that improvement stopped.

John Ferguson, an agent and adviser to Sheikh Mohammed bin Rashid Al Maktoum of the Godolphin outfit, told Steve we could get £40,000 for Jokist by selling him in Belgium. He was keen to sell, but I, like an idiot, had done what I swore I wouldn't do and had grown attached to the horse. To be fair to Steve, he did offer me £20,000 for my share but, at the time, I was miffed with him for wanting to sell, so I ended up giving Steve £20,000 for his share. I got the horse, but I lost a good friend. It drove a wedge between us and we never spoke again for nearly twenty years. Not only that, but I stopped ringing Cliff Lines as a result. Talk about cutting off your nose to spite your face!

What possessed me to buy his share I will never know. I just felt that to sell, after all the enjoyment he had given us, wasn't right. I should have known what would happen: Jokist didn't win another race for eighteen months.

It got worse.

Two weeks after the Ayr Gold Cup I had been at a snooker tournament when Alex Higgins came storming up. 'I'm going to sue you, JV,' he said.

'What have I done, Alex?'

'A friend of mine was at the Scottish horse riders' association . . .'

I thought, Oh, no!

My mind went back to the 'bit backwards' comment. 'What did he say, Alex?'

He said, 'What's all this about "speed for three furlongs"? I've got loads of stamina.'

I breathed a sigh of relief. Obviously the part about being a bit backward never bothered him in the least, so I got away with that one. I wouldn't be so lucky the next time.

Mike Dillon, of Ladbrokes, invited me to speak in Ireland at Leopardstown. I was still very inexperienced at giving after-dinner speeches. Instead of sticking to a routine that worked, if I saw four or five faces I recognised from an earlier event I'd spoken at, I changed my script, so it would look fresh.

I should have told the same joke about the snooker players and horses, which had gone down very well in Ayr but I knew a few people would have heard it so I decided to change.

Somebody had told me a joke the week before and I thought I'd tell that.

The joke was about a priest who, before going away on a sabbatical to Rome, says to his second-in-charge, a young priest, 'While I'm away, I'd like you to take over my duties in the church.' So the young priest says, 'What about confession, I know nothing about that.' The older priest tells him not to worry, he'll leave him a list of the penances.

At his first confession a guy comes in and says, 'Forgive me father, I have sinned. Last night my wife and I were shopping in the supermarket and I stole a packet of cornflakes.' The young priest looks down his list and sees what to say for stealing. He says, 'Go to the front of the church, say three Hail Marys, and don't let this happen again.

Next, a man comes in and admits to having a few drinks and hitting his wife. The young priest checks on the list for violence and says, 'Go to the front of the church, say four Hail Marys and don't let this happen again.'

Next up is a young girl. 'Forgive me, father, for I have sinned. Last night I gave my boyfriend a blow job.' Looking down the list, the young priest can't see anything that fits the bill. He opens the back of the curtain and one of the choirboys is running past. 'What does the father give for a blow job?' the young priest asks.

The kid shouts back, 'A bag of crisps and a glass of lemonade.'

Well, there was silence.

What I didn't realise was that on every table there was a priest. David Elsworth, best remembered for training the iconic Desert Orchid, said, 'We all wanted to laugh but what could we do because there was a priest on every table?'

It didn't end there.

The *Sporting Life* carried a big spread: 'VIRGO LEAVES RED FACES IN IRELAND.'

I thought, Oh no, what have a done?

I learned a painful lesson in Ireland. Be careful what you say and make sure you know who's in the audience. It still makes me shudder, just thinking about it.

CHAPTER 19

CHAIRMAN OF THE BOARD

S nooker might have been enjoying big television audiences and with it increased scrutiny, but, in the face of the controversy surrounding drug taking and players' conduct, on the green baize the game was coming to its own rescue.

For sheer drama, the climax to the 1985 final would be hard to beat, but in the months following that audiences were treated to some classic encounters. Sadly, I didn't contest any of them!

Steve Davis beat Willie Thorne in the 1986 UK Championship final but Willie missed a simple blue, which would have taken him 14–8 in front. Instead, momentum swung and Steve stormed back to take the match 16–14.

Great matches continued with Jimmy White beating Cliff Thorburn 13–12, after needing a snooker in the deciding frame. The game was doing a good job of papering over the cracks. The World Team Championship didn't have a sponsor after Guinness pulled out, even after Ireland had taken the title. There was criticism of the contracts negotiator, Del Simmons, as it was the first time since the game's boom that a tournament had gone ahead without the full complement of sponsors. Lots of reasons were being put forward as to why this was. The game was being dissected every month by *Snooker Scene* magazine, a publication that only a couple of years before had celebrated its ten-year anniversary and the success it had enjoyed off the back of the sport's popularity.

Everybody seemed to be fair game – the players and the association. It felt every big decision by the World Professional Billiards and Snooker Association was frowned upon. I still don't know why. Although I was on the board and had a vested interest, the criticism didn't seem constructive. It was, to me, purely and simply antagonistic.

Thankfully, there was enough interest in what was happening on the table to keep fans hooked. The 1986 final produced yet another shock. Joe Johnson defied all the odds to beat Steve Davis in the World Championship final 18–12. I had seen Joe play many times but never anywhere near the standard he produced that year. In his quarterfinal match against Terry Griffiths he trailed 12–9, only to produce four frames that were as good as I'd seen at the Crucible. He won 13–12 and was on his way.

For the second time at Sheffield, I made more of an impact with my impersonations than I did playing. In my first-round clash with Jimmy White we were tied at 7–7 but he pulled away to win 10–7.

When Joe Johnson's semifinal finished early I was asked to go out for a few minutes. I started by making a quip at Cliff Thorburn's expense, saying we didn't have time for me to do him. Cliff was in the audience and took it in good humour. What made it easier then was being able to wear a radio microphone so I could make it more of an act and tell jokes rather than have to rush back to my seat, as before, to pick up the mic.

The 1986 World Championship was notable for one other reason. The youngest player ever to qualify for the Crucible pushed Willie Thorne nearly all the way in the first round, losing narrowly 10–8 and putting up such a fight that Willie applauded him from the arena. The young player's name was Stephen Hendry.

Not only would the Scot with nerves of steel soon be competing for all of the game's major honours, but also his manager, Ian Doyle, would soon become a rival to Barry Hearn's dominance.

Hearn would have ended the season smarting that his star player, Steve Davis, had been beaten once more by the underdog in a world final. Steve would bounce back of course, but his days at the top of the sport were numbered.

Sadly, one player whose best days looked behind him was Kirk Stevens. He failed to turn up for the Benson & Hedges Masters in Ireland. Couple this with his well-documented problems off the table and it was obvious that Kirk was on a downward spiral.

To give an insight into Kirk's mindset at the time, when he was staying with us we travelled to Walton-on-Thames Snooker Club one day to practise. After one frame Kirk said he didn't want to play any more. So for the next two hours he sat and watched me play on my own. On the drive back home I tried to explain to him that he had an important tournament starting in a few days and should be practising.

With his ability, there was a lot of to be earned, money that he desperately needed and couldn't get anywhere else – or, at least, so I thought.

To my amazement he said, 'You don't understand. I don't have to play snooker. I could be a pop star.'

This from a man I didn't even know could sing. The same man who didn't like playing snooker exhibitions because he said it made him feel like a prostitute and had problems going out in front of the public. Now he wanted to sing on *Top of the Pops*. I wondered if Kirk's cocaine problem was affecting his judgement.

★ ★ ★

At the WPBSA board meetings ructions continued to dominate proceedings. The organisation, originally set up more as a players' union as well as a governing body, was seeing its role change to that of promoter and regulator, with a host of new issues with which to contend.

Mike Watterson, the promoter, was having a rough time. The board decided, rightly or wrongly, that all television contracts should be with the association, so that profits went back into the game. Mike wasn't happy with this arrangement. In the meetings I attended, it was still the intention to allow Mike to promote his existing tournaments, including the World Championship, but, unfortunately, it didn't work out and the WPBSA and Mike started to drift apart.

The main culprit for this was thought to be Del Simmons, who was hired as contracts negotiator, but I didn't believe that to be the case. The WPBSA were constantly criticised for paying Del £65,000 per year in wages, more, it was said, than the Prime Minister. Compared with other sports and industries, this was by no means excessive, but no mention was made of that. I felt Del did a lot for the game, and that's not just because we had a good working relationship. He believed that snooker should have a Rolls-Royce image, that it would help attract top sponsors and that the players should be well paid for their talents.

I feel the increases we saw in prize money had a lot to do with the game's growing appeal.

Yet, while Del Simmons was getting the flak, Barry Hearn was becoming stronger and stronger. In 1986 he tried to show his influence on the game by releasing the 'Snooker Loopy' single, featuring Chas & Dave and players Steve Davis, Tony Meo, Willie Thorne, Terry Griffiths and Dennis Taylor. Having signed up Jimmy White, he had a stable of eight players, giving him eight votes in an electorate of twenty-nine. Even he admitted it gave him an influential shout.

For the first time, top players were not playing in all the events. It led to a clash that resulted in the 1986 Belgian Classic not going ahead – the first time a tournament with a sponsor had been cancelled.

Snooker's incessant internal strife – to which I was a witness, being on the board – was getting worse. Hearn accused the WPBSA of 'Mickey Mouse decision making'. He joined the board and it seemed at every meeting there would be some argument as to who was doing more for the game, he or we.

In all my time on the board, this period had to be the worst. I always felt the strength of the association was that it was mainly players who made the decisions. Sometimes, I admit, I questioned their motives.

The cracks in the game widened when a row developed over Hearn's World Series event. Even since the game had become popular, the association had tried to protect the term 'world'. Using it too often lessened its impact. So, when agreeing a new contract with Embassy for the World Championship, the clause about using the word 'world' only for that tournament was never an issue. It became an issue with Barry Hearn's World Series.

Hearn insisted that all the tables used for his World Series event had to be Riley's. He had his players signed to the table manufacturer. This didn't go down well with BCE, Riley's competitor and the supplier of the World Championship tables. BCE had put a lot of money into the game, but for a quarter of that investment Riley's were getting their tables at every overseas event.

Instead of any criticism being aimed at Hearn's Matchroom, it was the WPBSA that got the flak for not itself running the events. The problem was that the constitution didn't allow for, what can only be described as, elitist events. Although the World Series was not being shown on British television, it seemed only a matter of time before our position was threatened once more. Hearn's tournament was eventually scrapped after three events. Within a month it was rumoured that Hearn, Rex Williams and boxing promoter Frank Warren were on the verge of setting up a rival body 'for leading players'. Initially, the idea was that it could coexist with the WPBSA as long as the association had worthwhile prize money to play for. What a cheek!

During this period, the chairman, Rex Williams, seemed to be getting increasingly involved with Hearn, causing a lot of unrest among the rest of the board. Matters came to a head in December 1987, when Rex resigned after eight years in the post. The straw that broke the camel's back was an argument

Rex had got into over a billiards match. They asked him to resign and he did.

I was vice-chairman at the time. Del Simmons said to me, 'You should take over. Are you prepared to stand?'

Without really thinking about what the implications might be, I said I would. That was it. I was voted in. All of a sudden I was the chairman of the World Professional Billiards and Snooker Association. I was forty-one, just passing my peak but still feeling I could make an impact at the major tournaments. Getting involved to this degree was the last thing I should have done, but that old socialist fire still burned inside. I felt that now I'd got involved with something I wanted to see it through.

The press immediately dubbed my chairmanship a renaissance period for the game, but I have no idea from where they got that.

Patrick Collins of the *Mail on Sunday* rang me and asked for an interview. The piece he wrote ended with calling me a 'a man with integrity' or something, but he added, 'One has to ask what does a man who's come from Salford have any idea about running a multi-million pound industry.'

Well, there you go, I thought. Maybe he was right, however. What did I know? I was just an office clerk. I had never chaired a meeting before. I'd been thinking on my feet my whole life and now I'm the chairman of a multimillion-pound company.

I wanted to make a difference but I spent most of my time fire fighting. The flak was coming from all directions. The WPBSA headquarters were in Bristol and, after driving through from Normandy for a 10 a.m. meeting, we would be there until 8 p.m. We were having discussions about the pettiest of things.

There was so much backstabbing going on that it was

frightening. A lot of it was down to the weakness of the players and the culture – there was still a drinking culture back then. We were making a rod for our own back. We were easy pickings for the press because the players were ordinary working-class people and all of a sudden snooker became this phenomenon.

Then there was the power struggle between Barry Hearn and Del Simmons. Del was using me as a buffer because he was frightened Barry Hearn was taking over the game. In my mind Del did a great job but his philosophy – that we had to spend money to show potential backers we were a serious operation – didn't sit well with some observers. Del was lunching people and, of course, to impress people he would go to good restaurants and they would enjoy champagne lunches. That was how the business world operated.

If you went to snooker tournaments back then you would have a good day. We would have a lovely VIP lounge, where we could invite potential sponsors. Whenever a tournament was on Del suggested the association book rooms in the best hotels, his idea being that my suite could be used for meetings. In Blackpool I was booked into the Imperial Hotel, the same place Prime Minister Margaret Thatcher stayed in when the Conservatives were having their conference there.

During this period, Rocky Taylor was effectively my driver. He had been unable to work after a horrendous on-set accident nearly killed him. Rocky had been filming *Death Wish 3* with Charles Bronson and was due to perform a stunt where he jumped through flames onto some boxes. The director, Michael Winner, demanded more flames to make the scene even more dramatic than it already was. The flames were so intense that, from where Rocky was, he was in danger of being burned alive. He had no option but to jump but couldn't see where he was supposed to land. He missed the boxes by a fraction. Instead of landing on his back, he landed on his hip and his pelvis finished up underneath his arm.

When I'd first met Rocky, Noel Miller-Cheevers had asked him what the hardest stunts were. He had said, 'Anything to do with fire, because you can't control it.' So it proved. He was in hospital for a long time. Michael Winner went to his hospital bed and said, 'I hear you're thinking of suing my boy. I wouldn't do that: you won't work in the business again.' That was probably the last thing you want to hear when you've got your pelvis put back into place and two eighteen-inch rods in your back holding it together. All the top stars he doubled for – the likes of Sean Connery, Roger Moore – got in touch, but the only one he didn't hear from was Charles Bronson, the man he was doing the film with.

Slowly but surely, Rocky recovered but for a long time he wasn't anywhere near fit enough to go back to work. To keep him active, I asked him to come to snooker tournaments with me. We were a bit like the odd couple.

When we went to Reading, I was booked into the Ramada hotel in a suite with a big Jacuzzi-style bath. 'John, come here,' Rocky shouted. I went in to find him lying in the bath, with foam up to his chin and, in his East End accent, he said, 'Do I look like Marilyn Monroe?'

There were some enjoyable moments. That was Del's thinking. Create the right image and you don't need to go cap in hand to sponsors. They will want to be involved and you get respect from people.

Not everyone saw it that way, however. This so-called extravagance was frowned upon as wasting money.

Clive Everton, the owner and editor of *Snooker Scene* and one of my co-commentators, was particularly scathing in his criticism. He was like a dog with a bone with Del, and seemed to be on a mission to expose what he saw as failings.

I set out with the hope that we could be all things to all people, but we couldn't. Despite your best efforts, you finish up with the tail wagging the dog. The people who sold the game were the big names; they had made the game for the people coming through.

In some ways we were victims of our own success. The game was expanding at such a rate that lots of players wanted to turn professional. Barry Hearn said everyone should be able to turn professional. It shouldn't be that you needed to be the amateur champion of your own country, which was how it was before I turned professional. Prior to the rule change, there used to be a qualifying school at the holiday camps, but we would get people complaining. Maybe someone got beaten in the final qualifying match and accused the other guy of being on drugs. It was mayhem. Those rules were relaxed and soon anyone with the money could turn up.

I used to look at some of them and think they should never have been professional. They were just making up the numbers.

Obviously, the constitution stated that we had to act for the benefit of all players. However, we also had to recognise that, without the top names, people weren't going to watch it. It was the viewing figures that attracted the sponsors.

My philosophy has always been that if a player was good enough he would make it. When Ronnie O'Sullivan turned professional he played seventy-six qualifying matches and won seventy-four of them. He was good enough and I felt that the game should be structured so that the players who do make it know they are going to be able to make a living once they get there. If you have too many players and too many tournaments the prize fund gets watered down. I thought we had to protect the top-end prize money because that was what was encouraging people to take up the game – and what motivated parents to get their kids to play. It was as I used to say: if you could get a million pounds for playing croquet, lots of people would play croquet.

Then there was the issue of Hearn and his Matchroom stable. They were doing their own little tournaments out in Thailand and China, which we couldn't do anything about, because we were concentrating on having the television rights for the UK. We didn't have much say on anything that happened abroad.

There were so many things to contend with. One day a fraud detective from Scotland Yard came to my house. He was investigating irregular betting patterns relating to a match at the 1988 Benson & Hedges Masters between Terry Griffiths and Silvino Francisco. He showed me slips from bets that had been placed all the way from Wembley Conference Centre, where the event was held, to the M1. Most of the bets were on Griffiths to win 5–1 in the best-of-nine match. The bookmakers had suspended payout because of the betting patterns. Terry went on to win the match 5–1. As far as the bookmakers were concerned, nothing came of the investigation because Scotland Yard couldn't prove that any attempt to influence the outcome of the match had been made. It was, however, a first glimpse into allegations of match fixing that would blight the name of the sport in years to come.

It was one thing after another.

I thought nothing could surprise me. Then, in the build-up to the 1988 World Championship, the ugly issue of drugs reared its head again.

Another scandal threatened to rock the game I loved. But this time I was the focus of the allegations!

CHAPTER 20

FACING THE FLAK

'**B**IG BOSS ADMITS TO TAKING DRUGS'.

That was the headline in the top corner of the *Sunday People* front page, the week before the World Championship began at the Crucible. To my horror, the 'big boss' was me.

What was shocking and disturbing was not only the circumstances that led to the story, but that in the weeks before the tournament the focus had not been on me at all, but on Barry Hearn's Matchroom stable and Cliff Thorburn. Cliff had joined Matchroom and in February 1988 the snooker world was stunned when he failed a drugs test.

Thanks to what was described as a battery of lawyers, Cliff's camp applied for an injunction, which allowed him to compete at Sheffield. The worry for the WPBSA was that the situation would overshadow the championship, where Steve Davis was aiming to win his fifth title. As it turned out, it wasn't Cliff dominating the headlines.

Two weeks before the tournament began, I had a phone call from a *Sunday People* journalist asking me if I'd offered a girl in Sheffield some cocaine the year before. I said I didn't know what he was talking about. He then asked me if I had ever taken drugs. Naïvely, I admitted the only time I'd ever taken anything was while we had been over in Canada in 1976, when I'd been offered cannabis at a party. He carried on asking questions and I tried to be as honest and open as I could. He apologised for troubling me and I thought that would be the end of it. How wrong I was! I'd been stitched up.

I played Steve Davis in the first round; but, with calls for me to resign coming from almost every quarter, it seemed, the match was the last thing on my mind and I lost 10–8. I refused to quit, feeling that, if I did, it would only be an admission of guilt.

Thankfully, one person who did support me was Stephen Hendry's manager Ian Doyle and, with his help, a lot of other people followed suit. I managed to ride out the storm but I couldn't help wondering what a coincidence it was that such allegations would surface about me at the time when one of the game's star players was embroiled in his own drugs scandal. Why were allegations of my historical dabbling publicised now? Whatever happened, I took the spotlight off Cliff.

Given the circumstances, Cliff didn't seem to let his own troubles affect him. He reached the semifinal, losing to Davis. As Steve said after the match, 'I don't think I would have put up as a good a performance that Cliff has in his circumstances.' Davis went on to beat Terry Griffiths in the final.

The Thorburn verdict was delivered after the championship. He was fined £10,000, docked two ranking points and barred from competing in the next season's first two ranking tournaments. The punishments were determined by Gavin Lightman QC, who had been appointed by the WPBSA as a one-man tribunal. It was thought an independent tribunal was fairer than players sitting judgement on other players. I didn't agree, but it was claimed that players might make decisions that could benefit themselves.

The association issued a strongly worded statement setting out its position. It said that we had taken a firm stance against drugs and that the matter was a serious one. But the statement pointed out that Cliff had not sought to use substances to gain an advantage and there was no evidence to suggest he had. He also had an unblemished record and now regretted his actions.

The newspapers were scathing. Snooker was accused of being 'limp-wristed' in its handling of Thorburn; the presence of a QC did not dispel the suspicion that an 'uneasy compromise' had been reached; and it was claimed our stance was no more than a 'token gesture' towards cleaning up the game. Snooker, it was also said, was a 'gravy train' – a game that was run by the players.

The criticism hurt. What more could we have done? We had taken a lead from the Sports Council and introduced drug testing. We hired a respected QC to be impartial, but still that wasn't enough. What got me was the claim that the game was being run by the players. That was far from the case. In fact, when the players had run the game we didn't have the same problems.

However, criticism also came from Alex Higgins's manager, Howard Kruger, who said he was upset that the punishment handed to Cliff was less than his client had received a year earlier.

On that occasion, Alex had refused to give a drug sample

during the UK Championship and when told to take it by tournament director Paul Hatherell Alex had headbutted him. As chairman, I had rushed down with John Spencer and Del Simmons to see Paul holding cotton wool to an eye injury. When I saw Alex he stormed past me and put his fist through the players' lounge door. As Del, John and I tried to calm him down Alex made a vicious, personal remark at John. Soon they were both rolling around the floor like cowboys in a barroom brawl. He was later charged with assault and criminal damage and fined for his misdemeanours.

The drug test Alex eventually took came back negative but he was fined £12,000 and banned from five tournaments. Alex said publicly, on the *Wogan* show, that he felt he'd been used and exploited by the game.

At a press conference, he asked, 'Could snooker live without me?' He added, 'Would the British public stand for me not being able to play snooker?'

His behaviour had been unacceptable but to my mind he had a point. Some believed that, if we had taken a harder line with him earlier, we could have helped him. But we didn't. The truth was that we wanted him in tournaments and the sponsors wanted him. I suppose that was exploitation in a way. The flipside was that Alex could be his own worst enemy. I recall once reading a quote from David Bowie: 'A lot of people crave adulation but when they get it they don't know how to return it.' That could be applied to Alex.

The upshot of all of this was that the WPBSA's credibility was under fire. Coupled with that was the threat from Barry Hearn. It always amazed me that somebody like Barry, who made no secret of the fact that he was there to make money, got so much support from the snooker press. It wasn't only the game's magazines that were knocking the association: a *Sunday Times* journalist poured scorn on Del Simmons and tournament director Paul Hatherell after a visit to the association's HQ, where he was plied with wine. His abiding impression was of the band playing on as the *Titanic* slowly sank. He would not be the first or last person to wax lyrical about the shortcomings of the WPBSA's paid employees.

The big problem was that we had a game that in the space of ten years had become the most popular sport on television. Along with that came the managers who saw earning potential for their clients, something that had never been thought of before. We had drug-testing problems, but to my mind we also suffered from that great British tradition of trying to knock something that was successful. The great success snooker was having wasn't the story the press wanted. What was going on behind the scenes, what the players were getting up to – that was more interesting. Snooker players were becoming celebrities, whether we liked it or not.

It was a fraught period and during it I felt we were damned if we did and damned if we didn't. The association seemed to be spending as much time trying to protect itself from the flak flying from all directions as it did running tournaments. Lots of people in the game had opinions, but when it came to offering real help were found wanting.

Barry Hearn, who had done very well out of the game, thanks to Steve Davis and his Matchroom players, didn't offer any help. He didn't need the association. The *Snooker Scene* magazine, which benefited from the game's growing popularity, didn't help. It would say that in its editorials it gave suggestions, but there was a big difference between making suggestions and helping to implement them.

One example of what I mean came not long after I became chairman. I had a meeting with Clive Everton, of *Snooker Scene*, and Ian Doyle. Both voiced their concerns about the way things were going with the association. They felt that to get back some credibility I should have a meeting with IMG, the production company who had taken over the overseas television coverage, to establish their support. Since Margaret Thatcher's government had ruled that 25 per cent of the BBC's outside broadcasts had to be done by independent companies, IMG were the company handling the overseas snooker tournaments. I met with the company and strengthened our relationship with them. Within four weeks Clive Everton rang me to tell me that signing up with IMG was a bad thing for the association. When I reminded him that he had thought it was a good idea only weeks earlier, he replied, 'I was wrong.' He gave no other reason and his criticism of the WPBSA continued unabated.

Some people have said over the years that what *Snooker Scene* had to say wasn't that important. However, despite having only a small circulation, it had a big impact. Certain figures, I believed, used it to put forward threats to the foundations of the game. Any outrageous suggestion, if it wasn't quashed immediately, could become policy.

The magazine gave column inches to Barry Hearn even in the light of comments he made saying he was interested only in the top sixteen players, not the 'also-rans', as he put it. No association could be run like that.

Against this backdrop was the threat of a breakaway faction. Despite my efforts with IMG, the media company looked set to be part of a consortium made up of Hearn, IMG and the boxing promoter Frank Warren, which questioned the authority of the WPBSA.

In his attempts to wrestle control of the staging of tournaments from the WPBSA, Barry used to say that he was not out to destroy the association. Then he would go on to add, 'But I do think that all the board should resign.' And this would be quoted in *Snooker Scene*.

The WPBSA's contract to supply five tournaments a year, including the World Championship at Sheffield, expired in 1990. The threat was that, if the new consortium didn't get their own way, they would withdraw their players from these events.

It was a threat that would never seriously be carried through because, after we held meetings with the BBC, the broadcaster confirmed that any contracts would be with the association. They were still not happy to deal with rival factions. Despite this, *Snooker Scene* carried a comment claiming the WPBSA looked likely to return to their original function as a players' union and that they had become a governing body only because at the time there was no viable alternative. I found that insulting and scaremongering.

Around this time ITV, it seemed, were becoming disillusioned with their product, particularly with the World Doubles. Instead of that tournament, Frank Warren had suggested they look at a World Matchplay. The idea was to have the top eight players based on a one-year ranking list.

Unlike the World Doubles, where every member had a chance of playing, this would benefit only the top eight. However, we agreed to most of their requests, but held out on a requirement to expand the tournament to take in twelve players. We were sanctioning a tournament for only twelve players, but, as it was based on rankings, theoretically every member had the chance of playing in it.

Although the tournament was the brainchild of the new consortium, by coming to an agreement with us and paying the association a sanction fee, they were acknowledging that we were the governing body. That was important.

★ ★ ★

That year, 1988, was probably my *annus horribilis*. Even apart from the threat of a breakaway, the issue of drugs refused to go away. Our drugs policy once again came under the spotlight. As we had declined to follow the IOC's guidelines on banned substances, the sports minister was withdrawing the subsidy it provided by the Sports Council to all sports to use the drug-testing centre at King's College London. The association's response was to say that we would find an alternative. I wasn't too involved with that decision, as we had employed our own drugs committee to oversee the issue.

Whatever the rights and wrongs of the situation, once again it seemed we had made a rod for our own back. The problem of beta blockers was escalating. More players were admitting to using them. It was inevitable that we had to ban them. Being a player and knowing the workings of a snooker player's mind, I don't believe that beta blockers enhanced performance. What *I* thought was irrelevant, however. They were a banned IOC substance. Players who had a medical condition requiring beta-blockers were forced to find an alternative or stopped taking them altogether. Unfortunately, Bill Werbeniuk decided to take on the association.

Bill had a hereditary tremor. At first he drank lager to help his problem. However, the more he drank, the more of it his system needed to have any effect. It was said that, in a best-of-nine match that went the distance, he consumed eighteen pints. Add that to the drinks he had before the match and some days he could drink up to thirty pints. He was prescribed beta blockers when a doctor became concerned for his health. In the wake of the ban he refused to stop taking them or find an alternative. He was told that, if he failed a drugs test, he would face a fine or suspension, as we had to follow the IOC guidelines. It was the end of Bill's career.

I felt very sad for him. When we introduced testing I assumed it was aimed at steroids or illegal drugs. This is not the case and, even if a player has a cold, he or she has to read the label to make sure there are no illegal substances contained within. To me, this went too far, but you cannot fight the antidrugs campaign. Of course, I agree that you cannot let young people think they can improve their performances by taking drugs, but, if a footballer has a pain-killing injection just before a match, is that right? The people who know say it is 'performance-enabling', not 'performance-enhancing'. For a player to have to give up the game because he couldn't take a medicine prescribed by a doctor sat uneasily with me. Sport was the only profession that could stop you earning a living this way.

There was the odd moment of light relief. One of my roles as chairman was to present the trophy and prizes at the World Billiard Championships, which in 1988 were held in Bolton. In the final, Eddie Charlton had a great chance to be a legitimate world champion at last. However, he was up against Norman Dagley, the reigning champ. After trailing early on, Charlton launched a determined fightback but Dagley held on to win. After the presentation of the coveted trophy, Dagley was handed the microphone to make the winner's speech. Once he'd dispensed with the usual thank-yous, he said how pleased he was to win the title again.

'When I was well in front, coming into the evening session, I thought I would win comfortably, but every credit to Eddie for making a tremendous fight of it.'

He carried on, 'They say that the best thing to come out of Australia is Foster's lager.' Then, looking at Charlton, he added, 'But to my mind it's a jumbo jet!'

Charlton's face was a picture. I thought he was going to punch Dagley but, fortunately, if he did he thought better of it. He stormed out of the arena with everybody, including me, trying not to laugh. Sadly Norman Dagley is no longer with us but if billiards had been a spectator game he would have been a star.

Those moments were few and far between, however. For the remainder of the year, whichever direction I looked, trouble was brewing. Rothmans, who had sponsored Barry Hearn's Rothmans Grand Prix, had decided to pull out. They were unhappy about Hearn's Norwich Union European Grand Prix event. Although Rothmans did not have copyright over the name 'Grand Prix' they were concerned that the new tournament would conflict with the Rothmans Grand Prix in Reading. A similarity of players and venues might have led to confusion.

Hearn was not pleased and thought Rothmans were being unreasonable. Battle lines were drawn. The association was caught in the middle.

As it was a ranking tournament, Hearn did not want to withdraw his players but instructed them not to cooperate in press or television interviews during the 'Grand Prix' at Reading. He felt he couldn't be suing Rothmans on one hand and helping promote their brand on another.

The association couldn't allow that to happen. Rothmans

were one of our major sponsors. We sent a letter, signed by me, to the players stating that no members could pick and choose, accepting the benefits but refusing the obligations of membership when it suited. The letter concluded by saying, 'If you feel you cannot support the WPBSA and comply with the rules the membership have made, then you should seriously consider whether you wish to continue your membership.'

The letter received great criticism from some who said it would do nothing to improve relations between the WPBSA and the Hearn camp. On this matter, I didn't care. I was friends with most of Hearn's players and I thought surely they couldn't hide behind him for ever.

Most snooker players I've met are mercenary. Give them someone else to blame and they will be more than happy to do so.

Regarding Rothmans, we owed a lot to the tobacco companies. And, after all, their dispute was with eight players. We had a responsibility to the other 128.

Immediately after the Grand Prix of 1988, the WPBSA held a disciplinary hearing. Gavin Lightman was in the chair. Two other board members, Gordon Ingham and Bill Oliver, plus me, were assessors.

Mr Lightman's fines were stiff but, as I explained to Barry years later, not as severe as he originally intended. We toned them down. Steve Davis was fined £12,000. He won a £65,00 first prize, plus a bonus of £40,000, for winning the Rothmans League the season before. Dennis Taylor was fined £8,000, Jimmy White and Terry Griffiths £4,000, Neal Foulds £3,000, £2,000 for Tony Meo and a £1,000 fine for Willie Thorne. All the players received prize money that outweighed their punishment.

Hearn was outraged, calling the decision to penalise Steve Davis – 'who has done more for snooker than anyone' – 'obscene'. He threatened to take the matter to the High Court.

Barry didn't realise the effect his players' boycott would have. Rothmans weren't the only losers. The BBC, press and indeed the WPBSA itself were all affected. Interviews could have been structured by prearrangement to 'match questions only', so there would have been no risk of Hearn's players prejudicing any case they might have against Rothmans. Gavin Lightman's view was that by agreeing to play in the tournament they must adhere to the rules. He didn't curry favour with the take-the-money-and-run attitude.

The next tournament was the UK Championship at Preston Guild Hall. Most of my time between matches was spent answering questions about recent events.

Juggling the role of chairman at the same time as being a player wasn't easy – and what happened at that tournament made me realise it was near impossible.

After I'd won the tournament in 1979, my performances in the UK were, to say the least, average. I went into it playing well, however, and fought my way through to the quarterfinal, where I met Doug Mountjoy. He raced into an 8–3 lead but I battled back to take it into a deciding frame. With the momentum I thought I had a chance of another semifinal. Doug, however, managed to regain his composure and closed out the frame to win the match.

He was obviously relieved to win and, after shaking my hand and the referee's, he shouted, 'Yes!' He left the arena and all the way through the practice room he shouted, 'Yes!' I was walking a few paces behind. All the way through the players' bar, he shouted, 'Yes!' By the time we got to the tournament office, where our cue cases were, I was getting a little hot under the collar. I knew he was pleased but to keep shouting, 'Yes!' It was getting on my nerves. When putting his cue away he shouted again. I snapped.

'What the fucking hell are you playing at?' I said as I grabbed hold of his shirt collar.

He looked at me. 'Mr Chairman.'

Slowly I let go of his shirt and apologised.

Doug went on to win the tournament, beating a rapidly improving Stephen Hendry in the final and upsetting the odds. At the press conference he was in tears, such was the emotion at winning the second-hardest tournament after the World Championship.

By contrast, I could only reflect on what had been a tumultuous year and contemplate what might have been.

While my contemporaries were enjoying a revival in fortunes, my twilight years at snooker's top table would be spent sitting in board meetings.

Above: Panto, my out from the game – I perform in *Dick Whittington* in Bristol with Scott Harvey (left) and Victor Spinetti (centre) – the evil King Rat has us under his spell.

Below: In *Cinderella*, at Southend-on-Sea's Cliffs Pavilion, with TV presenter Timmy Mallett, the original man with the mallet.

Left: (left to right) Walter Swinburn, who rode Shergar to win the 1981 Epsom Derby, Richard Lines, now a trainer, and his father Cliff, who was Shergar's work rider.

Right: 'Jo' for John, 'Ki' for Kirk and 'St' for Steve – my racehorse Jokist.

Left: My intense expression as I study the table.

Left: Jim Davidson, the crafty cockney Conservative-voting comedian, and myself, dour-faced Northern socialist, in a publicity shot for the BBC's snooker quiz show *Big Break*, but the chemistry worked.

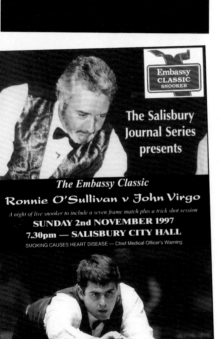

The Salisbury
Journal Series
presents

The Embassy Classic
Ronnie O'Sullivan v John Virgo
A night of live snooker to include a seven frame match plus a trick shot session
SUNDAY 2nd NOVEMBER 1997
7.30pm — SALISBURY CITY HALL
SMOKING CAUSES HEART DISEASE — Chief Medical Officer's Warning

Above: With great friend Rocky Taylor, a stuntman who stood in for two James Bonds in one year.

Left: The Embassy Classic programme for a match between Ronnie O'Sullivan and myself, at Salisbury City Hall in 1997. What an extraordinary talent.

Above left: At the Crucible, performing an impersonation of Terry Griffiths, complete with wig and bemused expression.

Above right: Firing up the audience as master of ceremonies for Alex Higgins and Jimmy White's tour, *Snooker Legends*.

Below: With Alex Higgins, one of many former snooker rivals, friends and family members to appear on my episode of *This Is Your Life*, aired in March 1996.

Above: With my pals from the commentary box: (left to right) Willie Thorne, Dennis Taylor, myself and John Parrot.

Below left: Snooker player? Commentator? Entertainer? We all have to juggle a bit in life.

Below right: With 'the voice of snooker' Ted Lowe, MBE, who died on 1 May 2011. I had gone to his house to celebrate his honour.

Above: Jimmy White helps with my bowtie before a *Snooker Legends* show. His son Tommy joins us backstage.

Below: Who could I be impersonating in these impressive specs? You guessed it – Dennis Taylor.

Above: The first-ever *Snooker Legends* show, at the Crucible, April 2010. From left: myself, Cliff Thorburn, Michaela Tabb, Jimmy White, and Alex Higgins, his one and only appearance on the tour. Sadly, he died three months later.

Left: With the legendary Ray Reardon when the six-times World Champion made a surprise visit to a *Snooker Legends* night in Plymouth.

With my wife Rosie, happily married twenty years after our first meeting. Lucky me to get a second chance.

CHAPTER 21

THE PEASANTS' REVOLT

I could see the writing on the wall. My days as chairman were numbered.

Our first overseas tournament, the European Open, was held in Deauville, France, in January 1989, in partnership with IMG, but the chances of its being a success were scuppered by the withdrawal of Steve Davis. His fine for missing a ranking event was £200. It was said that, had he done the same thing at the Rothmans Grand Prix ,it wouldn't have cost him the £12,000 fine. Perhaps, but then he wouldn't have had the chance to win £105,000 prize money.

Looking back, I don't think taking ranking tournaments overseas was a good idea. We needed to expand the game but the cost, not only to the association but the players, was too much. Snooker had taken off overseas initially through *Pot Black*, which had been sold all over the world. Perhaps, if everyone had been pulling together, it might have been a success, but it seemed so many different factions were springing up and everybody had their own agenda.

The renewal of the contract with the BBC was signed in Deauville. As I put pen to paper on the £11.5 million deal that secured the broadcaster the rights to the World Championship for the next four years, I did pause for a moment to take it in. There was I, a boy from Salford, whose first boss predicted he'd be selling shoelaces in the park, signing multimillion-pound deals with the BBC.

It was a significant moment – and there were others, too. When the French cable television broadcaster Canal+ were interested in showing some matches there, I played an exhibition match with Stephen Hendry under the Eiffel Tower. We held another exhibition in Monte Carlo on the same week as the Grand Prix. The Formula One cars were having practice laps while we were playing. 'Big bees you've got round here,' I said, referring to the persistent roaring outside.

The reality of the role, however, was that I was finding it hard to keep up with the day-to-day running of the company. I had to rely heavily on what was reported to me. In retrospect, I do feel that, in my time as chairman, I was used. I could understand Del Simmons's problems. He was fighting for his livelihood and I still believe that he had the best interests of the game at heart, certainly initially. However, I have to admit that by the end he was just trying to survive at all costs.

Clive Everton, through his *Snooker Scene*, was like a dog with a bone with Del Simmons. The strange thing was that Clive and I never had any problems. We worked well together when we commentated together and I never had any criticism from him personally.

With Del, however, it was a different story.

Simmons's contract was up for renewal and I agreed to give him a new deal because I thought he was good for the game and we were trying to build a legacy. I hadn't noticed that the date he signed was 1 April. Every month for three years there would be a footnote in the snooker magazine: 'Del Simmons, who signed his contract on 1st April has now got . . .' And they'd list the number of days before his contract was up.

Now I'm not a great believer that you can drive someone to make them really ill, but I do feel, having spoken to Del, that during that time the stress and the strain of the nonstop badgering completely got him in the end. It turned what I would describe as a man's man into someone who was looking over his shoulder all the time. A few years later he took ill and died long before his time.

The constant criticism of Del and how the game was run wasn't constructive. It just wore people down. As Willie Thorne's old pal Reg said, it was 'relentless'. It was coming from all directions. It was a nightmare.

The rush to expand the game gathered pace. Everybody, it seemed, wanted to turn professional. I received a letter from a father who said his son would like to be a member of the association. His highest break was thirty-four, he said, and to whom should he apply? It was an extreme case but it epitomised how attitudes had changed. It seemed that everybody who could hold a cue wanted to turn pro.

I was and still am a great believer in the amateur side of any sport. It's where players serve their apprenticeship and gives them a taste of what competition play is all about. It's also where players can discover whether they can handle the pressure.

To cope with the demand we introduced a qualifying

school. Each year eight new professionals would join the ranks, along with the amateur champions in the respective countries. Perhaps this was a little restrictive but at least those that qualified joined the main tour, and in any tournament, if they were to win a couple of matches, they would more often than not be at the main venue mixing it with the big boys. Those with talent ought to have been able to make it.

Some people thought anyone who could afford the membership fee should be able to join. Geoff Foulds, father of Neal, formed a group nicknamed 'the Peasants' Revolt'. I had known Geoff for many years, mainly as an amateur, but there didn't seem to be a meeting without a proposal from him about how the lower-ranked players were feeling and what we were doing about it.

The problem was that the cost of playing more qualifiers was getting out of control. Each match was costing in the region of £300 to stage. At the same time we were getting reports that, at the qualifiers in Blackpool, players who had arrived there were so short of money they couldn't afford to stay in hotels and were sleeping rough under piers and in bus shelters. To alleviate the problem, the association decided to pay first-round losers £250 and second-round losers £400. It wasn't a bad deal, but now we were accused of trying to bribe the rank and file to keep us in power.

Being chairman became increasingly difficult because the moves being made weren't necessarily for the good of the game. Snooker had come a long way in a short time. I had put myself in the firing line for the good of the game, even though it was to the detriment of my own.

I think most people, given the chance, would want to make a contribution. In my case that was true. Snooker had given me so much and taken me from Salford and around the world. Yet, no matter my good intentions, I couldn't be all things to all people. I became disillusioned.

Being on the board affected my playing career and my love for the game. I had turned professional with an ambition to be world champion and number one, to put my name in the record books. Now I was confronted by people who held no such ambitions. To me they were simply on an ego trip.

Rumours started flying around that the rank and file were so unhappy that they planned to overthrow the board. Word was that IMG were planning to take over the game and, if they did, every player would be guaranteed £1,000 first-round-loser money.

It was rumour-mongering, pure and simple, and just simply wasn't true. I had meetings with IMG and they assured me they wanted to work with the governing body, and supported us.

One of my old friends, Paul Medati, rang me up and said, 'John, I'm just warning you, if you don't pay first-round losers more, then you're going to get voted out.'

To me it just summed it up. For players who, with respect, shouldn't have been professional to be threatening the foundation of the game was frightening. However, that was the way it was. Players the public had never heard of and who you would never have thought were owed a living from the game were calling the shots.

We did listen to their concerns and made great strides to accommodate these players. We instigated a health scheme for the members and opened up a benevolent fund for players who had fallen on hard times. The bottom line, though, which had been forgotten, was that the association's main job was to supply tournaments to play in. I suppose, however, for some players, the top prize money was never going to be a consideration.

It got worse. Although we had signed the deal with the BBC, that year's accounts showed a loss, since the money hadn't come through yet. This was leaked to the press. For me it was the last nail in the coffin. I was the one left to explain the situation. I wasn't a businessman but my philosophy was to be as straight as possible. Yet I took the brunt of the criticism. Believe me when I say that, when they are after your blood, honesty is the last thing they want. Board members didn't want to know, and nor did the paid employees.

The role of chairman wasn't a salaried position. I received expenses and that was it. To put our side across, the association decided to put out a newsletter. We couldn't rely on *Snooker Scene* to conduct a debate, after all. Even that was to backfire. In one article, written with the full involvement of our lawyers, I criticised Hearn, Everton and Doyle. They threatened to sue. I had a meeting with the lawyers, who again assured me that what I had said was fair and there was no case to answer.

Ian Doyle resigned from the board. Like Barry Hearn before him, he cited concern over a conflict of interest. He was about to enter into partnership with Barry. With the number of players in their respective stables they could soon sabotage anything the WPBSA wanted to do.

In 1989 the UK Championship at the end of November was sponsored by Stormseal and promoted by Matchroom. Barry had brought the double-glazing company to the game and, if his company wanted to promote it, that was fine. In fact, to have a new sponsor was great news. Although I didn't make the last thirty-two, beaten by Kirk Stevens early on, it turned out to be a great tournament. Hendry, the beaten finalist twelve months earlier, made no mistake this year, defeating Steve Davis 16–12. It truly felt as though we were witnessing the dawn of a new era.

Interestingly, however, earlier on in the championship, one of the matches finished early. Had the event been promoted by the association, we would have made sure players were on standby to do an exhibition, to give the audience their money's worth. Not so here. Once the snooker was over it was thank you and goodnight. I know this only because at every tournament Janice Hale from *Snooker Scene* wrote a day-to-day diary. With the session over, she wrote that no one knew what to do with themselves, so she and Sharron Tokley, of Barry Hearn's Matchroom outfit, watched a video in the tournament office. I couldn't help but wonder what the magazine would have said had the WPBSA been the promoter.

The association's annual general meeting was held on 29 December. It was the day my two-year reign as chairman came to an end. All but one of the board were voted out. It was sad to be voted out by fellow professionals.

John Spencer was voted in as my replacement, which seemed odd, as in the previous eighteen months he had barely attended a board meeting, and had seemed to do so only if it coincided with a tournament he was commentating on for the BBC. When I asked Ray Edmonds why he elected Spencer, he said there was no one else with any credibility.

Also onto the board came, among others, Geoff Foulds and Gordon Ingham, a non-playing businessman from Halifax. It had been thought that having a non-player on the board would be an advantage but, in all the meetings, I never heard him contribute anything. He just seemed to claim the £1-a-mile travelling expenses from Halifax. He used to have two or three trips to Bristol per week – I'll let you do the maths.

I had been ten years on the board, two as chairman, and for what? I was still a player, but my performances had come at a cost to the political side. Could I get my career on track?

CHAPTER 22

NO POCKETS IN SHROUDS

My first tournaments as a nonmember were strange. I felt like a gunslinger walking into a saloon. Nobody, it seemed, wanted to look me straight in the eye. Were they feeling guilty?

In the Benson & Hedges Masters I drew Jimmy White. He won 5–3 but I was pleased with the way I played. Maybe I did still have what it took. Behind the scenes at the Wembley Conference Centre I couldn't help noticing the new chairman holding meetings with Geoff Foulds and new board members Barry Hearn and Ian Doyle.

Returning to the Crucible as simply a player for the first time in ten years was another odd experience. While I was on the board I could use the directors' lounge. That privilege had gone. Although over the years I'd continued to visit the players' lounge, entering it in 1990 I felt out of place. It seemed to be a much more family-oriented place than the room I remembered. Players invited their wives and there were kids running around. This used to be the room to entertain potential sponsors.

Peter Dyke, the promoter for Embassy, came in. 'What are you doing here?' he said. He invited me to the sponsors' lounge. I appreciated the gesture. It felt nice that at least I wasn't being dismissed by everybody.

In the championship itself I drew Jimmy again. My friend was in fine form. He defeated me 13–6 during a run that would take him to the final. In a gripping match he lost out to Stephen Hendry – sadly for Jimmy, an experience he would have to get used to. The young Scot had fulfilled his potential and captured his first world crown as his domination of the sport began in earnest.

That year was also the last we would see Alex Higgins at the Crucible. In his first-round match he was beaten 10–5 by Steve James. In the mid-session interval, instead of going back to his dressing room, Alex sat in his chair. Looking at him, I couldn't help but feel sorry for him. His game wasn't up to the incredible standard he had set for himself and yet more controversy had surrounded him coming into the championship. During the World Team Championship Ireland had reached the final but the event was mired by an outburst from Higgins when he threatened to have fellow countryman Dennis Taylor shot the next time he was in Northern Ireland.

Even after his defeat at the Crucible, Alex refused to go quietly, punching a press officer in the stomach on his way to the press conference where he announced his retirement and referred to snooker as the most corrupt game in the world.

I wasn't ready to quit the game but I was caught in my own tailspin. The period spent on the board and as chairman had masked some serious problems. I hadn't just been under pressure from those trying to transform the game, I was feeling it at home, too.

Since I'd dispensed with the services of Henry West as manager, my performances were impacting on my earning potential. It was a vicious circle. Yes, I was doing the commentary for the BBC and still had some exhibition work, but if you are not winning you are not earning as much from tournaments. Then, if you're not progressing, you don't appear on television, which impacts on the exhibitions. And, when the income dropped, the questions about why I wasn't earning as much as I had been began.

Perhaps, if things had worked out differently, I could have been part of Barry Hearn's Matchroom mob, going to China and Thailand. Instead, I'd been in board meetings in Bristol with flak flying from all sides. It didn't matter that I'd given some of the best years of my career to running the game. There's an additional pressure, too, when you're seen as a reasonably successful sportsman. Just because you appear on television, people assume you're earning a good living, so there's an expectation to keep up with the Joneses. Snooker was booming and the luxuries the top players were able to afford wasn't going unnoticed. Suddenly, there was pressure on me to have the newest car, a more expensive holiday. It was all about keeping up appearances. When you're used to a certain lifestyle, you want to preserve that at all costs. For some people that's certainly the case.

When the results weren't coming on the snooker table, I tried to supplement things by gambling on horses even more. My big weakness was that I had become what was known in the business as a 'Chase Me Charlie'. I was the type of gambler who has to be very careful with his first bet of the day. If I had £50 on the first race and my horse lost, then I'd spend the rest of the day trying to get it back. That could result in my having £500 on the last race just to get my £50 back.

That's how racing can get you. It's one of the many pitfalls of gambling and it's not something I'd recommend to anybody.

The more financial pressure I was under, the more I was getting into the gambling. But, as with everything, it's hard to win backing horses and that was one of the main reasons, if I'm being totally honest, why I was struggling financially.

I had seen people, such as Kirk Stevens, who had been addicted to cocaine, but I went through a period when I was addicted to gambling. It was something I could trace back to the early days in the billiard hall when I got that letter through the post with the tips. It was a compulsion that I struggled to get to grips with.

Gambling had got in the way of one of my best chances of winning the World Championship and by 1990 it was in danger of ruining my life. I had some great days and big wins, but that was the problem: it gave a false impression that I could win on a consistent basis.

To cover the shortfall, I was borrowing against the mortgage just to keep up the pretence that I was successful. Looking back, I see it was crazy. To give you an idea of how much I was spending at the bookmaker's, at one stage Des O'Connor, whose own gambling debts have been well documented, offered to be my bookie.

I wasn't the first or last snooker player to fall victim to gambling. Willie Thorne is another whose problems have been well documented. Willie was a great player but, like a lot us, me included, he went through difficult times. Snooker was a means whereby we were getting money to go out and live a certain lifestyle. Barry Hearn once said that he had Steve Davis in his stable, who won everything yet wouldn't spend a penny; and then he had Willie, who didn't win anything but spent everything. Like me, Willie was brought up in a snooker club and it was all about having a bet and gambling. We've learned the hard way the dangers of living beyond your means. Willie and I were born on the same day, although he's eight years younger. He's a dear friend but we were both victims of trying to keep pace with the leading lights in the game. You did that by either getting results on the table or utilising the money you were earning.

I had a gambling problem but I don't think I was in the same category as Willie. I remember at the start of the 1982 season that Cliff Lines told me Michael Stoute had a two-year-old filly called Widaad that was one of the best they'd had for a while. We went to Sandown Park and Willie came down from Leicester. I had £400 on the horse at 9–2. Willie would have had at least double that. The horse duly obliged and won at 9–2. It prompted the question as to why, then, at the end of the day, Willie was begging £50 off me for his petrol home. That was the type of gambler Willie was. He didn't stop having a bet until the money was gone. Widaad had been the third race that day. He'd won big and there were only three races to go. Yet he had blown the lot.

The thing about Willie was that his enthusiasm was infectious.

Not long after, we went to Royal Ascot and Widaad was running in the Queen Mary Stakes, ridden by Walter Swinburn. Coming inside the last furlong, Widaad went to the front and began to draw away. Willie and I were getting excitable and, with a good bet on, we were shouting, 'Go on, Walter, go on, Walter.'

Willie got a tap on the shoulder. A woman, done up in all her finest regalia, snipped, 'Do you mind? This is Royal Ascot.'

Quick as a flash, Willie said, 'Look, love, you've got yours; we're still trying to get ours. Go on, Walter!'

He was very quick, Willie, and always has been.

It may have looked to the outside world that snooker players were living the life. But, unless you were in the top sixteen, you were not earning a good living. You'd be lucky to be earning more than £25,000 a year. That's why the holiday camps and the exhibitions were so crucial. During the time when I was doing quite well from the exhibitions, thanks to the impersonations, I drove to an event in Middlesbrough. I was getting £1,000 for the appearance. On the way there I placed some bets over the phone. By the time I reached Middlesbrough I had done my fee in. I went all the way there and back for nothing.

What brought it home to me one day was when a bookmaker friend rang me up. I used to bet a lot with his company and after a good couple of weeks' results he owed me nearly £10,000. Over the phone he said, 'I'm just a bit tight at the moment, John. You don't mind if I pay you some now and pay you the rest on the next account?'

'Don't worry about it,' I said. That was the dangerous thing. Particularly over the phone and with a credit account it didn't feel as if it was your money. To me that money he had was like a float that I could use. He never sent me the cheque for £10,000. Two weeks later he sent me a bill for £200. Then it clicked. I'd done £10,200 in just two weeks.

That's when I realised. What a mug! But you can easily get caught up in it.

I used to look at the people at the dog track thinking, What a way to ruin your life! But I was doing the same thing. The only difference between those people and me was that I still had an earning capacity. Although I was still losing on the horses, I was still getting a bit back on the exhibitions. But it was a slippery slope. Very soon I was no different from the people I'd looked down at. The money was running out.

I needed a new manager so I spoke to Rocky Taylor, who was back working again after recovering from his horrendous injury. He had landed a part in the *Batman* remake. It was fantastic to see him up there on the big screen, albeit briefly before the Caped Crusader knocked him out. Rocky put me in touch with two former pop stars from the sixties who had gone into management: Dave Dee, who had a number-one hit as part of Dave Dee, Dozy, Beaky, Mick and Tich, and Troy Dante, of Troy Dante and the Infernos.

There were a few new managers on the block, attracted to snooker because of the amount of money in the game and the profile it had. Most managers had some involvement with the game, however. Having managers who knew nothing about snooker was strange, but they knew the entertainment industry, so I thought they could help broaden my appeal.

One of the first things they did was go through my finances. Their advice was to get rid of the racehorse Jokist. He had won eight races in total from about fifty outings but hadn't developed into a top-class horse. His fees were costly. The trouble with lower-grade horses is that they don't run consistently. Sometimes it can depend on which side of the stable they came out of as to how they're going to perform that day.

I was sad to see Jokist go. He wasn't worth anything in

the end. The days when we could have got £40,000 for him were long gone. He'd given me some incredible moments and, thanks to him, I had the wonderful memory of the Breeders' Cup weekend in New York, on Concorde. No one could take that away from me. I certainly didn't regret getting involved. I've got to think how lucky I was to have that opportunity. As a friend once said, there are no pockets in shrouds.

What I do regret was losing a lot of money on the horses and our reckless spending. When we moved into our house in Normandy it cost £72,000, on a mortgage of £35,000. By 1990 the mortgage was £240,000. It was another of the problems with being a sportsman. You have your accountant saying you only have to win your next tournament to clear your debts. Then you get another mortgage. This was at a time when banks were giving mortgages away.

The trouble was, whether I admitted it to myself at the time or not, I was nearing the end of my career. Once a player gets over forty it's hard to maintain the concentration. The hardest part is putting in the hours of practice that you need to do each day. When Fred Davis reached a semifinal at the age of sixty-four he was the exception. For the rest of us, we are on borrowed time.

★ ★ ★

The other thing coming to an end was my marriage. Due to the guilt I had felt over the collapse of my first marriage I tried to do everything to make my relationship with Avril work. In the end, though, it was futile.

I had no excuse for leaving my first wife – none whatsoever. Back then, it was just a case of having my head turned and seeing another side of life.

Maybe if we hadn't been in such a mess financially things would have been different but, as it was, we were broke, and there was no sign of things getting better.

When we split up for the last time I went to live in a house that Rocky lived in with his partner Pammy before they were married. It was a three-bedroom house and Rocky said I could have one of the spare rooms. By complete coincidence, one of Pammy's friends, Rosie, was also staying there. She had split from her husband.

The first time I'd met Rosie she'd thought I was a right misery, perhaps understandably because I was going through a bad time and my head was in a jar. It wasn't the best circumstances in which to meet.

Over the years we would sometimes make up a four to go out for dinner, but I still think Rosie continued to think of me as dour. It took me twenty-two years to ask her out for dinner. Only then did she see the other side of me. I must have impressed her with my charm and repartee because we were married six months later. That was seven years ago.

Back when we first met, however, we had no idea our futures would be intertwined.

She got an early glimpse of the downsides of being a reasonably well-known snooker player. One day, while we were staying at Rocky's, she came out of the house and a photographer jumped out and started taking her picture.

Rosie used to work as a journalist and recognised him from one of the tabloids.

'What are you doing?' she said.

'Oh, hello, Rosie,' the snapper said. 'We heard John Virgo was living here with a blonde.'

'Well, it's not me,' she said.

She was right, of course. Back then, the thought of our being a couple was a bit absurd.

Our happiness together would have to wait. In those early days of being on my own I really was in a bit of a state. With my marriage over and my finances in ruins, it seemed my life of doing what I loved was over.

Then one day I was summoned to the BBC studios at Shepherd's Bush for a meeting with some producers. Was I interested in doing a new quiz show based on snooker? The show was to be called *Big Break*.

Somebody up there was indeed smiling down on me. I had been given another chance.

CHAPTER 23

IT'S ONLY A GAME

When I was first shown an early pilot for *Big Break* I must admit I didn't have high hopes that it would be a success.

The idea to develop a snooker-themed quiz show had been around for a while. In fact, two years earlier Central Television, the producers of *Bullseye*, had approached me to help devise a snooker version of that hit darts-based game show. That idea was from Tony Green, who worked on *Bullseye*, and it followed the same format: an amateur player and their partner, one answering questions while the other tried to pot some balls. We filmed a pilot but Central decided it was too similar to *Bullseye*, so they gave it to Tyne Tees. For a variety of reasons Tyne Tees dropped it and two years later the BBC were developing their own snooker quiz show.

The pilot the BBC showed me had *EastEnders* actor Mike Reid as host, with Len Ganley, possibly the only referee people would recognise, as the officiator. Sadly, Len is no longer with us but I think he would have relished the chance for some greater television exposure. When we used to do exhibitions together he was often the first to sit down when it came to signing autographs and he used to say that sometimes when he was refereeing at the Crucible he was more interested in looking at the crowd and making sure he got his face on TV than looking at the table.

For whatever reason, the producers wanted a different line-up for the series proper and asked if I'd be interested in the Len Ganley role. At the time of watching the pilot they hadn't chosen who the main presenter would be, but Jim Davidson had recently ended his association with Thames Television and the fact that he was available may have got them thinking about a whole new line-up. Their idea was for me to present two trick shots every show. They were planning eight shows for the first series and in my head I was counting up how many trick shots I actually knew. I think I could do only fifteen at the time. I suggested having just one trick shot per show. They agreed, and plans were made to start filming at Elstree Studios.

In the years to come, notably after the show became a huge hit, a few people claimed responsibility for my involvement. Troy Dante said he had mentioned me, the producer said they had seen me doing my impersonations and thought I would be ideal, and Jim Davidson said he had seen me in an exhibition with Ray Reardon at the Crucible and thought it very funny. Perhaps it was a combination of all three. I didn't know and I wasn't complaining.

The show was my one chance to salvage something from my career. I think Jim saw it that way too. Apart from that meeting we had at Yarmouth, when he presented the trophy for Jokist's victory, I knew him only from his TV appearances. I was to discover that I'd be working with one of the most generous and professional entertainers in the business.

However, when we met on the set at Elstree Studios in Hertfordshire, it was obvious he knew little or nothing about snooker. I wasn't sure if he even liked the game. Certainly, he didn't know how to play it. I never asked him specifically, but I can imagine he was wondering where this show was going to go.

The star player for the first show was Alex Higgins. He was serving a tournament ban for his misdemeanours but we rang the association and they confirmed it didn't extend to light-entertainment appearances. I was glad. Having Alex on the first show practically guaranteed that people would tune in. Jim had never met Alex but knew of his reputation. Before Higgins arrived, Jim asked me, 'What's he like?'

'He can be awkward,' I said, trying to be diplomatic. 'But he's usually all right if he doesn't get upset.'

Jim assured me he would treat him with kid gloves and get the best out of him.

When the runner showed Alex to his dressing room he said, 'Bring me two bottles of champagne.'

Typical Alex. He didn't get them, though. This was the BBC, remember.

Filming was delayed because of heavy snow. Each show was filmed in front of a live audience and the coaches carrying them had been held up in the bad weather. Eventually, after a horrendous journey, they arrived. Jim decided to go out, welcome them and warm them up. He asked if anyone had seen Alex. There was a mumbled 'No'.

Jim carried on. 'Apparently he was last seen in the car park with a straw trying to sniff up the snow.'

Everybody fell about laughing. That was Jim's attempt to treat Alex with kid gloves. I'm sure Alex could hear everything backstage but he never mentioned it. The only message we got from him before filming was that he was wearing a waistcoat from Gilbey of Savile Row and, if he could give the store a mention, he would get to keep it for free.

After a glowing introduction, Jim welcomed Alex on stage and complemented him on his waistcoat.

'Yes, Gilbey's,' said Alex, 'and not the gin.'

Quick as a flash, Jim leaned over, took a sniff of Alex and said, 'Well, it smells of gin!'

That was Jim. I grew to learn that if he could shock people he would, and he shared my view that, if something was funny, it was funny.

Alex had got his plug and he didn't just get to keep his waistcoat. Both of us were treated to new ones from Gilbey. Thanks to Alex, the idea for the elaborately designed waistcoats was born.

After filming the second or third show the producer came up to me and said, 'Everything all right, John?'

'Yeah,' I said, 'everything's fine.'

'You don't look too happy,' he said.

'I always look like this,' I said.

'Oh, great,' he said. 'Keep it up. It looks good.'

People talk about chemistry and from the day we started filming many of the production crew said Jim and I had it. Where that chemistry comes from I don't know.

One bit of advice my manager gave me when we were doing *Big Break* was not to try to compete with Jim Davidson for who had the better gags. So, basically, I used to stand there with my deadpan expression talking about the snooker side. Eventually, after several shows, Jim started to bring me in and ask me things and I'd come back with a funny remark. Slowly but surely he involved me more with the show. I don't know why it worked. After all, he was the crafty cockney Conservative-voting comedian and I was the dour-faced Northern socialist. But it did.

★ ★ ★

The BBC scheduled the first series of *Big Break* to launch at the same time as the 1991 World Championship, which began in April as usual. I went into the tournament feeling fairly good about my game. In the first round at Sheffield I drew Tony Knowles. I started well and, by the mid-session interval, had opened up a 4–0 lead.

By then Dave Dee was busy touring Europe singing in sixties revival concerts, so Troy Dante was managing me on his own. I came back to my dressing room feeling good. You can imagine my shock, then, when Troy came in and said, 'Keep it going – you're boring him to death.'

As motivational speeches go, it wasn't up there with the best of all time. I couldn't believe this was coming from my own manager. I had always regarded myself as an attacking player. This type of comment was the last thing I needed to hear. When play resumed Tony mounted a comeback and I ended up losing the match. I didn't realise it then but, as I left the arena, I had walked through the famous Crucible curtains for the last time.

After the match Troy announced he had to get back to London and promptly left. I sat on my own having a drink until 2 a.m. I didn't want to go to bed. I felt as though I were staring into a black hole. My money worries were mounting, my marriage had failed and now I was facing up to the reality that my snooker career was coming to an end.

Fortunately, I had the commentary to focus on for the rest of the tournament, but my whole life felt in a state of flux.

Big Break aired on the Tuesday night of the second week. It was appearing in the slot normally reserved for *A Question of Sport*, the long-running and extremely popular quiz show featuring a host of top names. I had no idea how it was going to be received. I was desperately hoping it would be a success. If it flopped, what then?

The morning after the first show aired I went into the Embassy lounge for a coffee. The first person I saw was my fellow commentator Jack Karnehm. He told me there was a write-up of the show in the *Yorkshire Post*. I grabbed the paper and started looking for the review. Just then the TV director Mike Adley, who had worked on *A Question of Sport* for many years, came over and said, 'It's not a very good review.'

Curiosity got the better of me and I read the piece from the paper's television critic.

'The combination of Jim Davidson and snooker triggers the sort of cerebral meltdown previously achieved only by *Are You Being Served?*,' she wrote. Turning to my performance, she said I had 'the self-assurance of Frankie Howerd trying to split the atom'. She concluded that *Big Break* was 'The nadir of non-achievement – anyone who watched without weeping deserved a Purple Heart.'

I thought during my years as chairman that I had grown a thick skin but I have to admit it hurt. And this was a review Karnehm wanted me to read. Strange.

I tried to dismiss the review as someone just trying to make a name for herself. At least it hadn't appeared in a national newspaper. However, the criticism didn't stop there. Alexander Clyde, a columnist for the London *Evening Standard* – and, importantly to me, also a writer for the *Pot Black* snooker magazine – described our show as 'the worst thing that had ever happened to snooker'. He added that the show did nothing for the game and should be taken off air immediately.

There we were again – snooker having a prime slot on television and a snooker writer knocking it.

Fortunately, the viewing public obviously paid no heed to the reviewers. From the moment it aired *Big Break* was a success, going on to beat the audience figures for *A Question of Sport*. The blend of snooker and humour had struck a chord. We had a hit on our hands.

The BBC immediately commissioned a second series, but from eight shows they now wanted twenty-eight. We were to go back in the studio in November that year to film them.

Big Break looked set to be exactly that. As one door was closing, another was opening – and I intended to kick it open and grab whatever opportunity lay on the other side.

CHAPTER 24

FAME AT LAST

Not long after we began filming *Big Break* one of the researchers said to me, 'Are you ready for the fame?'

I wondered what they were on about. I couldn't see how a quiz show could make me that well known. Besides, I had been appearing on television for years playing sport. I knew what to expect. Or so I thought.

We had originally filmed two shows a day. We used to rehearse with the contestants in the afternoon and film the first show at 5 p.m. When I'd filmed for television before I'd found a half-hour programme could take three times as long to record. The duration of each *Big Break* show was twenty-seven minutes but filming took only forty-five. It helped not having any big set changes. The BBC twigged we could film them quickly so, when we went back into the studio, they wanted three shows a day.

Jim's opening monologue was scripted by Bryan Blackburn,

a scriptwriter for many top comedians and TV shows and possibly most famous for the Peters and Lee song 'Welcome Home'. After Jim's stint we would have a chat and from the moment he went off and met the contestants it was all ad-lib.

Although we rehearsed the run-through of the show, we couldn't predict what would happen on the snooker table. Whenever I tried the trick shots in rehearsals, invariably they worked and the director would come down and work out the best way to film it. When it came to filming, Sod's Law ensured that a few of them didn't work first time. One in particular I should never have done. After twelve attempts I still couldn't get it. The ones that didn't work were a gift for Terry Wogan and his *Auntie's Bloomers* blooper show. I seemed to be on there every other week!

Midway through the second series I was running out of trick shots. Luckily, I had mentioned to Ray Reardon the demands on me and, when he appeared on the show, he brought with him his book *Ray Reardon's 50 Best Trick Shots*. Noel Miller-Cheevers also bought me a book on 300 classic pool and billiard trick shots. Eventually, I had so many that after two years I brought out my own collection of 100 shots, *John Virgo's Book of Snooker Trick Shots*.

The fact that they weren't working first time was fun in itself. The cameramen used to have a sweep to see how many attempts I'd have at these trick shots. The worst series I had was thirty-four trick shots and seventy-two attempts.

In the end we did more than two hundred shows and by the end I repeated some of the shots because, as the contestants were doing them, we had to make them fairly easy.

We had one where you put a tube on the cushion, with the black ball on top of the tube. The idea was you hit the tube, the black hit the cushion and rolled across the table into the pocket opposite. Jim saw me setting it up and said, 'Can I have a shot?'

He took nine attempts and didn't hit the tube once! Over the years I've had kids out of the audience during exhibitions and they can manage it. So when people ask me if Jim was any good at the game, the only answer I can give is, 'No!'

Jim may not have been the greatest snooker player but as a host he could not have been more helpful. He used to have a couple of slugs of brandy before he went out to film. 'Do you never get nervous?' he asked me.

I didn't, mainly because the people on the show were all colleagues of mine and, when I was talking about what they were doing on the snooker table, it was what I had been doing in the commentary box for years. My only problem came once the producers saw that Jim and I were working well together and they started building up my part.

Being a professional, Jim was great with the autocue. I, on the other hand, was not. I was painfully aware that it looked as if I were reading a book. I used to get my lines just half an hour before we did each show. Usually, it was only a couple of lines but, even then, I struggled to memorise them in time. One day Bryan Blackburn handed me a sheet full of lines. Jim could see the trepidation on my face. 'Are you OK?' he said.

'It's all these lines,' I said.

'Don't worry about it,' he said. Too late. I was worried.

When the cameras started rolling he welcomed me out as usual and said, 'The problem is when you get a lot of dialogue they put it on the autocue.' Then he grabbed me and read the lines off the autocue screen. So he made a joke about it, rather than let me make an idiot of myself.

Aside from Jim, the players made the show. The good players, such as Steve Davis and Jimmy White, did well, but the format seemed to suit other players whose temperament perhaps let them down on the big stage. Tony Drago, the Maltese snooker and pool player, was ideal for the game.

Many of the top players didn't need the television exposure but they all wanted to be on it. For the others, it was a chance to enhance their profiles. And they threw themselves into it when they appeared. As *Big Break*'s popularity grew a junior version was developed that featured the likes of Mark Selby.

For some, the format wasn't suited to them. When the notoriously slow Cliff Thorburn was on the show he defied the odds and made the final. For anyone who can't remember, in the final round the contestant was asked five general-knowledge questions in ninety seconds. For every question the contestant got right we removed a red ball. Once all the questions were answered we stopped the clock and the player had the time remaining to clear up. Cliff's partner had got all five questions right, so Thorburn had a decent enough time to pot one red, followed by a colour, and then all the colours. Every colour potted meant a prize. If he managed to clear the table the top prize was usually a holiday to Walt Disney World or similar.

It was obvious by the time Cliff got to the yellow, with the six colours left on the table, that he wasn't going to get anywhere near winning the jackpot. With the time running out, as he potted the green I put the brown in, just to give the contestant another prize of a CD player or something. Jim got carried away. He put the blue, pink and black in the pocket. 'You've won the jackpot!' he said.

The producer stepped in. 'Hang on, Jim,' he said. 'You can't do this. If you do we'll have to do it every week. You're setting a precedent.'

'All right, then,' Jim said, 'we'll do it again and, if he doesn't get it, I'll pay for the holiday.'

I watched all this thinking, Jim, you don't know how slow Cliff Thorburn is.

So we did it again. Now, the guy knew the answers to the questions, so he did it in double-quick time. This time Cliff had one minute and twenty seconds to pot the last red and clear the table. He still didn't do it. Jim had to pay for the holiday. The story made the *Sun* tabloid before the programme was even aired. It was great publicity for the show.

At the end of filming for the second series Jim gave me a little package and said, 'Thank you for resurrecting my career.' I opened it up and there was a £10,000 Cartier watch. It was a remarkable gesture and a sign of how grateful Jim was that he was back on primetime TV. His wasn't the only resurrected career.

★ ★ ★

Big Break went from strength to strength. It was so successful the BBC moved it to Saturday night – the prime slot on the schedule. At its peak it attracted just under fourteen million viewers, the highest rating figures for a quiz show.

The more popular the show became the more I was reminded of the producer's words at the end of the first season. They had been right. Yet, despite the prediction, nothing prepared me for the reaction from the public to a primetime show.

When the show was at its peak I travelled to York races. I hadn't organised tickets but basically blagged my way in by claiming I had tickets for the owners' area left for me by a bookmaker contact. I needn't have bothered. I was recognised the moment I arrived, not only by the steward on the gate but, as I walked from the gate to the enclosure, a crowd of people who had been sitting by the racecourse seemed to rise as one. It was unbelievable.

In Blackpool, Troy and I were going to see Bobby Davro but nipped into a pub beforehand for a drink. We were mobbed.

When Jim first uttered the words, 'Say goodnight, JV,' to which I responded 'Goodnight, JV,' neither of us had any idea it would become a catchphrase. However, given the number of times people have shouted it to me in the street since *Big Break* first appeared, I can testify that it certainly has. Hardly a day went by when someone wouldn't call, 'Say goodnight, JV,' or 'How's Jim?' to me. Another phrase that caught on was my advice to 'pot as many balls as you can' to players when they attempted the final clearance.

How well known Jim and I had become was brought home to me when I took my daughter to Thorpe Park theme park in Surrey. No sooner had we walked through the entrance gate than a bus arrived packed with children. As soon as they saw me they all ran towards us. 'It's John Virgo!'

They were all shouting, 'Say goodnight, JV' and 'Pot as many balls as you can.'

We couldn't move. My daughter was hiding behind me. Eventually, we had to give up and go straight out again. In a small way I was finding out what it must be like for film stars.

Along with the catchphrases, my waistcoats were also the subject of much interest. A waistcoat manufacturer called Piscador approached me about developing my own line, inspired by the designs I modelled on the show. After taking advantage of Alex Higgins's agreement with Gilbey's, the next thing I knew I was walking down a catwalk at a fashion show with two models with waistcoats on and not much else. Soon after, I had my own line of waistcoats on sale in John Lewis. I still get people coming up to me today saying, 'Recognise the waistcoat, John?' One year we had different-coloured snooker balls, another we had triangles for buttons.

Whichever contestant performed the trick shot was presented with a waistcoat as a souvenir. I had a few of my own but I gave a lot to charity. One of my favourites from Gilbey was inspired by a Goya artwork. It was beautiful. I put it up for auction at a golf day in La Manga and the racing driver Nigel Mansell bought it for £1,000. He was involved with a golf club near Exeter and somebody told me that on the wall, next to photos of all his racing cars, is the waistcoat with a photo of Nigel from me.

The reach of the show never ceased to astound me.

Jim told me about an event he had been to where he had been speaking to Margaret Thatcher, who had only recently been forced to resign as Prime Minister. She was there with her husband, Denis.

She said, 'Oh, we love that show you do – *Big Break*. We really love it, Denis, don't we?'

Denis said, 'Yes, we love it.'

'And we particularly like that John Virgo, don't we, Denis?' Thatcher went on.

I didn't have much time for Thatcher, given the Conservative policies that brought pain to the North of England, so Jim found this hilarious. 'If only she knew what you think of her,' he said.

Just two weeks later Jim and I were invited to an evening at Brinsworth House, a Royal Variety Charity-run nursing home near Twickenham for 'old pros' from the entertainment world.

A fireworks display was held that night and, just before it kicked off, Jim grabbed me and said, 'Come and have a word with Maggie.'

I really didn't want to but Jim was insistent. 'She'd like to meet you. She likes you on the show.'

Reluctantly I agreed.

'Lovely to meet you,' she said.

Just then the firework display started and – I am not joking – she gripped hold of my hand. I don't know if the first bang gave her a fright but she gripped my hand for the entire twenty minutes while the display went on.

All I kept thinking was, If people in the North could see me now!

With the success of *Big Break* we were frequently invited to appear on other shows. One such programme was *Kelly*, a Belfast-based chat show hosted by Gerry Kelly. It had been my first return to Belfast since the exhibition I'd played there years ago. I couldn't believe the transformation in the city. From seeing sandbags around the hotel on my last visit here, now was a place on the up. It was wonderful to see.

Appearing on the show with me were the magician Paul Daniels, the hugely successful lyricist Tim Rice and Carol Thatcher, daughter of the former PM. I couldn't resist telling Carol about my meeting with her mother and the fireworks display.

She looked rather put out. 'Well, it wasn't because she was frightened of fireworks,' she said haughtily. 'My mother was frightened of nothing!'

While we had a drink after the show I tried to engage

Tim Rice in conversation. I told him I'd just seen *The Rocky Horror Picture Show*. 'Absolutely marvellous,' I said, thinking he might appreciate the compliment.

He looked at me rather vacantly. 'Yes, it is a good show,' he said stiffly.

Only later did I twig. I'd confused him with Tim Curry, the star of the film. Rice? Curry? It was an easy mistake to make!

Recalling my run-ins with the Thatchers reminds me of the time when Jim, who was very active with the British Forces Foundation, was looking for a figurehead for the charity that provides entertainment to boost morale of our troops.

After getting on well with Margaret Thatcher he asked her if she would be interested. She told him she'd be delighted. Shortly afterwards, however, Jim was at a function where Prince Charles was also in attendance. The prince told Jim he had heard about his work with the foundation and added that, if there was anything he could do to help, Jim only had to ask. That got Jim thinking. Margaret Thatcher would have made an excellent patron – but compared with Prince Charles? Well, there was no contest. He had the unenviable task of contacting Mrs Thatcher and telling her he had found someone better.

The benefit of having Prince Charles involved was instant. I went with Jim to a function for the foundation at the prince's Highgrove home. When the prince put on an event people flocked to it. On this occasion, I kept in the background, mindful of the mayhem caused the last time I'd rubbed shoulders with royalty.

That had been at Sandown Park, where, for me, the Eclipse Stakes for three-year-olds and upwards is the highlight of the summer there. One year I was invited by Coral to their box, courtesy of winning the UK Championship, which they had sponsored. To get the best out of a day like that, though, you have to go and see the horses in the paddock. If there is a better sight than seeing a thoroughbred with the summer sun glistening on its back I have yet to see it.

Trying to get near the paddock that day was well nigh impossible. So, peering over the heads of the crowd, I was suddenly knocked sideways. From the power of the blow it felt like a hit rather than a push and I only just managed to stop myself falling. Instinctively, I made to lash out in case there was another blow coming but thankfully stopped at the last moment.

When I fully turned round I realised I was face to face with the Queen Mother.

One of her security guards had obviously been clearing a path for her to get through to the paddock. I shudder to think what would have happened had I carried through my swing. They'd have locked me in the tower!

Every time I go to Sandown I glance at the bust they have there of her and think how close I came to clocking her one. Not even the popularity of *Big Break* would have saved me then!

Thanks to Jim, I got a chance to do something for our armed forces when he asked me to step in for him after he was invited to visit one of our submarines in the Mediterranean. This was just after the Kosovan conflict. The crew had been underwater for a hundred days and they were fans of *Big Break*.

I got a private jet from Farnborough Airport, where I met Sir Donald Gosling, a great benefactor to naval charities and who made his money from NCP car parks. We flew to Bari in Italy to join his yacht. Jim had joked that I'd be experiencing five-star luxury on board the submarine. I didn't know about that but the yacht was something else. It had its own sixteen-strong crew and a helipad. Prior to that the most luxury ship I had been on was the Isle of Wight ferry.

I don't think Sir Donald knew who I was, but he told me the supply ship was in dock and we had been invited to the officers' mess. In the build-up to the trip I had been through security vetting and sworn to secrecy about the submarine we would be visiting the following day.

When we arrived on the supply ship, an officer came up to me. 'Nice to see you. What are you doing out here?'

'I'm visiting a submarine tomorrow.'

'Oh, splendid,' he said.

Wow, I thought, they do talk posh in the navy.

Then another chap came up and asked me the same question. I told him I was visiting the submarine.

'Splendid,' he said.

It was only when a third officer responded in the same way that I asked someone why they all said, 'Splendid.'

'That's the name of the submarine,' I was told. That explained it!

On our return to the yacht I went to bed and when I looked out one of the portholes in the morning we were in the middle of the ocean. After breakfast we met up with the submarine and all of a sudden it came out of the water. It was an amazing sight. Once everything had been sorted out we had a barbecue on the casing. The crew of submariners presented me with a custom-made waistcoat, which I was incredibly touched to receive. I proudly wore it on *Big Break*.

They gave me a tour and I couldn't believe the cramped space they lived in.

I asked one crewman how they did it. He said, 'We get more money than the ordinary navy!'

Later, when we were back on the yacht, we watched the submarine submerge – another impressive sight to behold. Splendid indeed!

★★★

Big Break ran for twelve years from 1991 until 2002 and sadly became a victim of its own success. After ten years we were recording four shows a day, which really was too much, especially as we were ad-libbing. We couldn't remember what we had said in the first show of the day. It became quite wearing but we were happy to continue as long as the viewers loved it.

We used to record in the studio next door to *The Generation Game*, which Bruce Forsyth was presenting. One day Bruce was ill and couldn't record that particular week's show. The producers asked Jim to step in, which he did and not surprisingly made a great success of it. A year later when Bruce announced he was quitting, the BBC asked Jim if he would fill his shoes.

For a year Jim was appearing on two primetime Saturday shows, but there was no way it could continue. It soon became obvious the one that was going to be dropped was *Big Break*.

Over the years our show was moved around the schedules but series after series was commissioned. Sometimes we would be on midweek. Once, they moved us to a Friday night. The viewing figures were going up and down but the producer told me it was a great compliment to the show that they can put it in any slot and it will still attract a good audience.

When we had the after-show party for the twelfth series we didn't know it was going to be our last. Only after it aired did we learn there wouldn't be another.

Even though the show has been off air for years, it's amazing how fondly it is remembered. People still come up to me quoting the catchphrases and recalling the waistcoats.

I can't overstate how much *Big Break* transformed my life. Before landing that series I was in a black hole, wondering where my future lay. Thanks to it, I got back on my feet financially and was able to forge a little niche for myself that continues to this day. When I perform exhibitions I still come out to its theme 'The Snooker Song', originally written by Mike Batt, of Wombles fame, for the West End musical *The Hunting of the Snark*, where it was first performed by Kenny Everett before being recorded by Captain Sensible.

Due to the success of the show, the commercial arm of the WPBSA, the World Snooker Association, asked me to help promote tournaments in a sort of goodwill role. Clearly, all the previous politics had been long forgotten. In the week before a tournament started I'd visit the town and conduct radio interviews to try to drum up publicity.

In Plymouth I got to drive a Chieftain tank, the British Army's main battle tank from the 1960s through to the 1980s.

One of the most startling visits was when I went to Derby, where I got a tour of the Rolls-Royce factory, where, besides cars, they also build engines for aircraft. There, I learned that, as part of the process to test the durability of the aircraft engines to withstand a bird strike, they fire real birds into the machinery. That took me a little by surprise. I had visions of some poor pigeons minding their own business and then suddenly being catapulted into an engine.

I did another promotion in Bournemouth where a snooker table was put on the beach for me to do some of the trick shots I did on *Big Break*. That was a novelty, particularly when I was trying to do one of my favourites that involved a basket and it kept blowing off the table.

Prior to the Welsh Open I visited the Driver and Vehicle Licensing Agency headquarters in Swansea. My guide for the day happened to mention that a number plate was soon coming available that I might be interested in: V1RGO. I thought that would look great on my car. However, when she told me the auction had started, I was amazed to hear the bidding had reached £28,000. I said, 'I'll change my name!'

Big Break led to a host of opportunities I wouldn't otherwise have had. It was strange becoming a 'TV personality' in my own right. Noel Edmonds successfully did me with a 'Gotcha Oscar'. The ruse was that the band Right Said Fred wanted to record a new version of their famous hit 'I'm Too Sexy' with me. My manager had convinced me it was serious and was going to be a big Christmas hit. I was singing lines such as, 'I'm too sexy with my beard on / I'm too sexy for Ray Reardon.' Naturally, it was all a wind-up, but I didn't mind. It was great for my profile.

When I got a phone call that a contestant on *The Generation Game* was a big fan of mine and wanted to meet me, I thought nothing of it. I drove to the studios and walked onto the set as asked. Jim Davidson, my former co-host on *Big Break*, was the host. He was talking to the contestant about how much she liked me when all of a sudden I burst through a sheet of paper and onto the set. She was screaming and I gave her a cuddle. The next thing I know Michael Aspel is walking on set with his famous red book. I never thought it was anything to do with me. For a start, I was always of the belief that once you had been divorced twice it would not work practically to build a show around you. How on earth could they? I thought. But, sure enough, he walked up and said, 'John Virgo, this is your life!' It was such a shock.

They drove me to the studios in Teddington and I actually felt not unlike the Bob Hoskins character at the end of the gangster film *The Long Good Friday*. The IRA have got him in the back of the car and they are taking him away against his will. I felt much the same. All these thoughts were going through my head about who might turn up in the show, who would be sitting next to me in the studio.

Once I got to the *This Is Your Life* studios they handed me a glass of champagne and I felt a bit better. Finally, the time came for us to do the show. My daughter and son came out, then my siblings and other relatives and friends came in one by one. Next up some of my snooker friends joined us. Alex Higgins was one of them. When he walked on we had a big hug but as he shook my hand he whispered into my ear, 'You're still a cunt.'

Nobody else could hear him say it, thank God! But that is what he said. Outrageous. But typical Alex.

I did wonder whether I was worthy of the attention, after growing up watching war heroes on the show, men who had saved people's lives. However, some time later I was talking to Michael Aspel and it turned out that my show had the highest viewing figures for the entire series. This was partly because the moment when he first walked up to me had been shown live on *The Generation Game*. I was still very proud of that rating, though. It was amazing, really. Once again it illustrated the reach of snooker.

Showbiz was taking over from my professional snooker career, but, when the two worlds collided, which life would I choose?

CHAPTER 25

THE MAN WITH
THE MALLETT

For most of my adult life I'd been used to performing in front of an audience. As I've always said, snooker is theatre – the formal dress code, the hushed, reverential atmosphere, the fact that success owes as much, if not more, to mental strength and strategy as it does to potting skill on the table.

But when I stepped out on to the stage at the Cliffs Pavilion, Southend-on-Sea, Essex, in December 1993 I may have been in front of an audience, but I was as far away from the green baize as I could possibly imagine.

I wasn't appearing in a ranking snooker event, or even an exhibition. I was dressed in a ruffled shirt, large overcoat, stockings and buckled shoes, playing Baron Hardup in a pantomime of *Cinderella*.

And I was about to be whacked by a large foam mallet!

Making the decision to turn my back on snooker in favour of appearing in panto wasn't actually a hard one.

Since my last appearance at the Crucible, when I'd lost to Tony Knowles, I'd suffered defeats in the qualifiers. After all the tremendous memories I had on snooker's biggest stage it was soul-destroying not to have the game to get me there once more.

Big Break had opened up a host of opportunities – and one was an offer to appear in Southend-on-Sea in *Cinderella*. The star of the show was children's TV personality Timmy Mallett as Buttons. I was playing the dad to Anne Nolan's Cinders.

The schedule for the panto clashed with the qualifiers for the World Championship. I might have had another stab at it but one match four months earlier had made my mind up.

On the afternoon of Wednesday, 18 August 1993, I travelled to Blackpool for a UK Championship qualifier. The tournament that had given me my greatest triumph was still several rounds away. To progress I had to beat a player called Spencer Dunn, who, with the greatest respect, I had never heard of. I knew, going into the match, that if I lost it would probably be my last as a professional. I was finding it almost impossible to put the hours of practice in because of my commitment to *Big Break*. When I did practise I was missing easy blacks off the spot. It was debilitating. I hoped the high-stakes situation might inspire me. It wasn't to be. Reputations count for nothing on the snooker table and Spencer deservedly beat me 5–2.

I didn't wallow in self-pity. Far from it. The defeat had made my decision to miss the World Championship qualifiers in January much easier.

★ ★ ★

That was it. Seventeen years as a professional snooker player over. There was no announcement, no highlight clip reel on the BBC. I didn't have to notify anyone to formally quit, other than to say I wasn't going to enter any more tournaments.

Doing pantomime would not only be more lucrative, but it sounded much more fun than trying to get motivated for a qualifier I was likely to lose. Panto was the out I had been looking for.

Plus, that night was Manchester United's first home game of the season and their first at Old Trafford since they'd been crowned Premier League champions – their first top-flight title in twenty-six years.

Not only was I getting the chance to salute the new champions, but also I had been invited by league sponsors Carlsberg to take to the pitch at half-time to take penalties at the Stretford End. Angus Deayton, who I was always convinced was an Arsenal supporter despite his claims to be a United fan, was also taking them. Strips were provided for us. I insisted on the home strip, leaving Angus with the away kit. As I strapped on the boots and prepared to walk out of the famous tunnel, I had to pinch myself. Thoughts returned to my first trip to Old Trafford as an eight-year-old, sitting on the barrier on the terracing. The club was renovating the ground in 1993 so the capacity was reduced but there were still 42,000 fans inside Old Trafford and to hear them chant my name was beyond my wildest dreams.

Everyone asks me how many I scored. I got two out of five and, with each one I scored, I thrust an arm up in Denis Law fashion. Rocky and Rodney Hutton, a former professional golfer who is my daughter's godfather, were in the crowd. After the match, which we won 2–0 against Sheffield United, I chatted to Bryan Robson and some of the other players. Rocky sourced out Alex Ferguson's room and told him I was there. 'Bring him down,' he said.

Rodney's from Downpatrick in Northern Ireland and loves to wind people up. His first line to Ferguson – he wasn't yet Sir Alex – was, 'Before you offer me a drink I should let you know I'm a Liverpool fan.' Alex just laughed.

It was a night I'll never forget – one of the great thrills of my life – and it was the perfect antidote to the reality that my professional snooker career had ended not with a bang but a whimper.

I had no time to reflect on what might have been. My *Big Break* schedule, coupled with panto rehearsals, meant that I was working flat out.

By the time I took to the stage for the first time I could see instantly why people fall in love with the theatre. The 1,600 people crammed into the Cliffs Pavilion loved Timmy's antics and the madcap show.

I've often joked to friends that at times in my life it has seemed as if, just when everything was falling into place, there was always a man with a mallet lurking around the next corner waiting to bash me over the head and ruin everything. I don't know where he came from or why it always seemed to happen but it was incredible how often he struck – and always with impeccable timing to screw things up just when life was looking up.

Now, here I was, being chased around the stage by a real-life man with a mallet!

And what happened?

We'd had a press night so the local papers and trade magazines could review the show. Despite our having a director who seemed more suited to television than stage productions, I'd enjoyed my first outing treading the boards.

Then I read the review. The critic was a little fella in a pork-pie hat (his photo was in the paper). He went on about Timmy Mallett, giving him a good write-up. Then it came to me. 'What is this man doing in a pantomime? His jokes are going completely over the heads of the children in the audience.'

I knew I was taking a gamble doing the pantomime with no acting experience but I have to admit those words put me on a bit of a downer.

Just as we began our run I was chatting to my old friend Tony Hayhurst. 'You must be using that line,' he said. What line? He was talking about my *Big Break* catchphrase, 'Pot as many balls as you can.'

'Are you using that every night?' he said.

I had no idea what he meant.

'When Cinderella says, "Daddy, can I go to the ball?" aren't you saying, "Go to as many balls as you can"?'

I hadn't even thought about it. I didn't even realise it was a catchphrase. So I started using it and it went down well and I started feeling a bit better.

It helped that we had Timmy Mallett. He was an amazing character. The crowds loved him. We did this scene where I was hitting potatoes with a broomstick and he was catching them. It was absolutely wonderful. We also had these super-soaker water guns that could reach row five of the audience. Every night we ran into the crowd squirting them with water.

By the end of the run, however, word had got out and soon the kids were packing water pistols of their own. We got absolutely drenched. It was great fun.

My first pantomime experience was a steep learning curve. I learned a lot about the differences between television and the stage. On TV a close-up of a deadpan expression worked wonders but in the theatre the raising of an eyebrow was completely lost on the audience. You've got to be as big as you can be and project right up to the top and not just perform for the people in the stalls.

I must have done something right, though, because in 1994 I was invited back, this time to star as a Chinese policeman, PC 147, in a production of *Aladdin* at the Ashcroft Theatre in Croydon, south London. This was more of a traditional pantomime, with Chris Ellington, who used to be in *The Bill*, playing the villain.

When the run began I vowed not to look at the reviews but one day I was in Wardrobe and noticed in *The Stage* that there was a review of my mate Bobby Davro, who was appearing in Southend that year. Bobby came out of it well but the reviewer homed in on newspaper television columnist Garry Bushell, who was also in the show, for criticism. However, he said, he's still not as bad as that snooker player from last year! I couldn't believe it. A year on and the fella in the pork-pie hat was still having a go at me.

I was in a real state for two or three days. People were coming up to me saying, 'Are you all right, John?'

I was trying to do my best but that criticism really touched a nerve.

Thankfully, a chance encounter with one of my heroes helped lift my spirits. I was putting on my makeup one night when there was a knock on my dressing room door. One of the backstage crew had a message. George Best was appearing at the next-door venue in an 'evening with' slot with Alan Mullery. He was in the green room. Did I fancy a drink before I went on?

I wasn't due on stage for twenty minutes.

'Tell him I'll be down in two minutes,' I said.

As I closed the door I caught sight of myself in the full-length mirror. What a sight! With my comic policeman's uniform, rosy cheeks and hat, I looked a right state. I didn't have time to change, so decided to improvise. I walked casually into the green room, twirling my plastic truncheon.

'John, what's happened?' George greeted me with a look of utter bemusement on his face.

'Steve Davis took all the money!' I replied.

He laughed and we had a quick drink before I was due on stage. Sadly, it was the last time I'd see him before his health deteriorated and he eventually succumbed to alcohol-related problems.

George's demise was a tragic loss. He, like his fellow countryman Alex Higgins, was a flawed genius. They were similar in so many ways.

A story that always makes me laugh, however, was the time when Alex paid a visit to Ken Doherty's snooker room. Ken has lots of pictures on the wall. Being a United fan, he has as his prized possession a picture of himself with George Best.

Alex was looking at the pictures when he came to the one of Ken and George. Looking at the picture and sighing, he said, 'George Best. What a waste!'

Pot calling kettle, or what?

From *Aladdin* it was on to *Dick Whittington*, which the following year was being held in Hastings. I played Alderman Fitzwarren. My opening line was, 'Rover! Rover!' and my daughter Alice would appear saying, 'My name's Alice.' My joke was, 'Yes, that was your mother's idea – I wanted a dog.'

By now I really wasn't caring what the critics had to say as, by then, *Big Break* was a huge success, in spite of all the early comments it had had. I had to laugh, though, when one reviewer accused me of making 'the Woodentops look mobile'.

★ ★ ★

My pantomime experience changed completely when Jim Davidson told me he was putting his own production of *Dick Whittington* together and said he wanted me to be in it. He spent a million pounds of his own money devising the sets, suitable for only the biggest venues. We would be playing to audiences of two thousand people.

Even before we worked on the pantomime together, people told me what a great stage performer Jim was. His portrayal of Buttons was up there with the best. For his own show he was taking the lead role.

I was playing Captain Creep and my bosun was played by Barbara Windsor's husband Scott Mitchell. On the opening night we came out to the 'Camptown Races' tune. The first person I saw in the front row was the legendary actor Sir John Mills. That made me shake a little in my boots. Then, up in the gods, when we were doing the 'Row Your Boat Ashore' song, there was Mick Jagger and his kids all doing it along with us.

We did the pantomime for eight years, taking it to a different venue each year. The great thing about sticking to the same script was that after the first year we hardly had to rehearse. We just revised the script and took out the things that didn't work.

The only time it made a loss was when Jim couldn't find a theatre. We'd been at Bristol, Manchester, Northampton, Southampton, but one year he couldn't find a venue and he decided at the last minute to do it at the Hammersmith Apollo. Unfortunately, it wasn't really a pantomime theatre: it was a stage built for a band or orchestra. However, we had committed, so we did it.

One of the highlights for me was getting the chance to work with the great Victor Spinetti, whom I loved watching in the Beatles movies back in the sixties.

Vic and I used to sit on two barrels while they got ready for the second half and while we were there he used to tell me some wonderful showbiz stories. He knew Marlene Dietrich very well and told how he had lunch with her one day when she was in London doing a one-woman show. During the run, her agent had called to say Noël Coward wanted to watch the show.

When Vic asked how she'd found Noël, Marlene said, 'I don't like him. I hate the man.'

Victor said he thought she was quite friendly with him, but Marlene replied, 'I was, but when I did my last number, "Falling in Love Again", I sang it to Noël. I looked him straight in the eye. I sang it for Noël. And do you know what he did? He came into my dressing room after the show and he said, "Lovely show Marlene. The last song – wonderful . . . but the yellow teeth killed it."'

Victor was endlessly fascinating and he told me how his life had changed at the outbreak of World War Two. His father was Italian and made his home in Cwm in South Wales, where the snooker player Mark Williams comes from. Victor went to school on the day that war broke out and got beaten up by some lads in an attack that left him deaf in his left ear. Overnight he'd become a target because of Mussolini's support for Hitler. His father was arrested and put in an internment camp for six months.

His life changed again with Beatlemania. I'd thought the Beatles were huge here but it was nothing compared with how massive they were in America. The fans loved Vic because of his association with the band. Victor sadly died in 2012. Paul McCartney spoke at his memorial service.

Of all the things I've really enjoyed apart from playing snooker, treading the boards was the most wonderful experience. Having had a taste of it, I can understand why people get addicted to the stage. There's nothing quite like it.

To have had more than ten years in pantomime was something I never expected. Not bad for someone with no acting training and who made the Woodentops look mobile!

* * *

To say *Big Break* had changed my life would be an understatement. Becoming a well-known TV personality had opened doors I didn't think were possible. Going on morning television shows, where they would put in a snooker table (I would wear one of my fancy waistcoats and display my array of trick shots). Going on chat shows and guesting on shows such as *Noel's House Party*.

All these opportunities had one thing in common. Snooker.

That had all changed when I was asked to do pantomime. If getting nervous had been a problem in playing snooker, it was nothing compared with how I had felt the first time I'd trodden the those boards alongside Timmy Mallet.

My main problem was learning my lines. On *Big Break* there had always been an autocue to fall back on. For the first week of a show, though, I would run back to my dressing room to read the script. One night I was so busy running backwards and forwards I finished up on the stage on my own only to be overrun by the dancers coming on both sides. I hadn't noticed that it said 'chorus' on the script.

I just shrugged my shoulders, and exited stage right. Just as an example, I started my performance chasing a pantomime horse onto the stage. When we stopped my opening line was, 'This is my horseradish.' It got a bit of a titter, which didn't bother me because I didn't get the joke for a week.

When Jim Davidson asked me to play Captain Creep in his *Dick Whittington*, pantomime became a lot more interesting for me.. It also gave me the opportunity to work with 'proper actors'. Most pantos are made up of television stars; soap stars in particular are used more than most. Not only British stars, but some of cast from the likes of *Home and Away* and *Neighbours*. The influx from overseas didn't sit too well with a lot of people, but, as they say, 'if it puts bums on seats' why not?

One of the many highlights of doing a panto with Jim was how much you were allowed to express yourself.

In one of the scenes, as Captain Creep I would come onto a stage that resembled a ship. I went up to Jim and asked him who he was. The question was, 'You're not one of my crew?' After a week into the second year, I decided to change my line to, 'You're not one of my seamen.' I hadn't spoken to Jim about the change nor, to be honest, considered the connotation of the word. But Jim saw it at once, and went into a five-minute routine that had the audience in fits.

Then there was the joy of working with Spinetti. He played the part of King Rat, the villain of the piece. I learned lots from Vic. One thing that always sticks out from his advice was always to listen to your fellow actors. This might sound simple but sometimes you're so busy with what your next line will be that you don't.

Working with these people was a delight, but now and again I would let myself down. Funny things happen on and off the stage in a show. Occasionally, for some reason, I would get a fit of the giggles so bad that I couldn't speak. As Roy Barrowclough, star of *Coronation Street* and his comedy routines with Les Dawson, said after coming to see the show at the Palace Theatre, Manchester, 'It might be funny to you and the rest of the cast, but if the audience don't know the joke it's unprofessional.'

He was right, but certain things conspire that throw you completely.

At the start of the second half of *Dick Whittington* my ship sinks. This is followed by an underwater ballet. As is the way of these things, I would exit stage left. As I walked under the stage, Mark the ballet dancer would be coming out of his dressing room. There was a question that I had been meaning to ask him. I had read that in the film *White Nights* – which was about a Russian ballet dancer who had defected – the dancer Michael Baryshnikov, who played the part in the film using no camera tricks, did twelve pirouettes. I asked him how many he could do; his reply was, given a good floor, about six or seven. By the time I had got the answer, we were by the side of the stage. In earshot of us was Les, our stage manager. Les was from Liverpool, lovely guy, nothing was too much trouble.

'What that you're talking about?' I relayed the story about the pirouettes, and that Mark on a good floor could do six or seven.

'I worked with Nureyev' was his reply.

'Oh, how many could *he* do?'

In his best Liverpool accent, he said, 'Fucking thousands.'

Try walking on stage with a straight face after that.

★ ★ ★

But back to television, and all things come to an end, as they say. *Big Break* ran for ten years, in which we did over 200 shows. Many people to this day ask me if the BBC will ever bring it back. I think the show would still work, but if they did I don't think it would be Jim and I doing it.

It's funny how people to this day come out with the catchphrases, 'Pot as many balls as you can', and of course 'Say goodnight JV' being the most memorable.

One of the sad things that came out of this is that we don't get to see Jim Davidson too often on television. The last time he was on for any length of time was on *Big Brother*. To prove his popularity, he went on to win it. It was during that show that he demonstrated what a funny man he is. He was constantly having arguments with Linda Nolan, sister of Ann, whom I worked with on my first pantomime.

Linda and Jim went way back and were forever bickering. Also on the show was a girl called named Louise, who had been runner-up in the popular TV show *The Apprentice*. She decided to take the side of Linda, so Jim had two women making his stay in the house hard work.

It all came to a head when Jim was called into the Diary Room. He was asked how he was feeling, and they asked him, if he had to go to bed with Linda or Louise, which one he would pick.

Jim's reply was that, being a happily married man, he had not thought about it. Then he added, 'But, if you put a gun to my head, I would have to pull the trigger'.

He still tours the theatres with his one-man show, and I am sure has them rolling in the aisles.

★ ★ ★

No *Big Break* or pantomime now, so what did the future hold? My snooker commentary was still there, and my profile from *Big Break* helped my exhibition work.

My next venture was purely down to Alex Higgins and Jimmy White.

A promoter named Jason Francis was putting together a tour for Alex and Jimmy, calling it *Snooker Legends*.

Jimmy had suggested that I be the master of ceremonies. Jason liked the idea but what he also wanted me to do was commentate on the match. I didn't think that would work. The players could hear me, surely it would put them off. He persuaded me to give it a try. It worked better than I could ever have imagined.

In a way it was what I had been doing on *Big Break* for ten years. But, as we know, sometimes you can't see the wood for the trees. *Snooker Legends* has proved a great success, and brought some of the iconic names back to the table. It's still going strong, thanks to Jason. So much so he gave up his pantomime appearances to concentrate on it full time.

What do they say? One door closes another one opens. Result!

CHAPTER 26

MINE'S A TREBLE

The broadness of snooker's appeal in the wider sporting and celebrity world never ceases to amaze me. So many people love the game.

One huge snooker fan is Sir Alex Ferguson. Funnily enough, he's never been to the World Championship but a lot of his Manchester United players have come to the snooker over the years, including Roy Keane and Paul Ince, plus the former Liverpool captain Steven Gerrard. Paul Ince used to have challenge matches with Ferguson in his house.

For any United fan, our greatest achievement came in the 1998–9 season, when a historic treble of league, cup and Champions League was on. The Premier League title had been won on the last day of the season against Tottenham Hotspur, and the FA Cup had probably been won in the semifinal when – after Roy Keane had been sent off and Peter Schmeichel saved Dennis Bergkamp's last-minute penalty – Ryan Giggs scored the greatest goal I have ever seen to beat Arsenal and take United to Wembley to face Newcastle.

A friend of mine, Frank, had come down from Salford to do some work in the house and, as we watched that semifinal game unfold, we thought our only chance was somehow to hold on for penalties. As Giggs set off on his mazy run I was aware, out of the corner of my eye, of the cat coming into the room. Ryan went on and on, dribbling past two players and blasting it high past David Seaman into the goal. Frank and I jumped into the air and the cat's hair stood on end and the animal looked just something from a cartoon before it bolted from the room. I didn't see it for two days. Sometime later, when I was speaking at a dinner to honour Giggs and Bryan Robson, which Alex was at, I told Ryan that story. He thought it was funny.

With the double in the bag, United faced Bayern Munich in Barcelona – the last hurdle to overcome to secure the treble. Geoff Lomas managed to get tickets for the game. Our only problem was, we didn't have a hotel. 'We'll get one easy over there' were Geoff's words when we left for Barcelona. What we didn't know was that it was the week of the Spanish Grand Prix. The city was crammed.

As we were walking out of the airport I saw a guy from Ford, one of the Champions League sponsors. He had a clipboard and was ticking off people for their hotels.

'Hello, John, where are you staying?' he said.

I told him we didn't have one. He gave me his card and said if we got stuck to give him a call. The first place we tried was the best hotel in Barcelona. The porters came out and took the bags upstairs, but, when we tried to check in, the hotel was full, so we had to bring them back out again. Our taxi driver drove us all around the city.

I then remembered the card. When I called the chap from Ford he said he'd just had two clients who hadn't arrived. We were in luck! His hotel was in Sitges, twenty minutes outside the city. When we arrived we couldn't believe it. Who was staying there? The Manchester United football team! Unbelievable!

Geoff had got word that the team bus was going to leave the hotel at about 4.45 p.m. He'd also got T-shirts that said 'FERGIE'S FIVE TIMES CHAMPIONS' as we'd won the league only five times back then. So, come the time, Geoff and I were standing outside with the T-shirts on. All the players came out. The last to emerge from the hotel was Alex Ferguson. When he saw me he came over and gave me a big hug.

'This is the big one now,' I said. 'The treble.'

'Yeah,' he said. 'Fingers crossed.'

As he got on the bus he gave me a wave. David Beckham was on the bus, looking out of the window, pointing, waving and mouthing, 'There's John Virgo there.'

People have said afterwards that it was a bit of a liberty they didn't give us a lift to the ground. That was the furthest thing from my mind.

History will tell you what a night it was. One–nil down with a minute to go. From nowhere we got the two goals.

As we were walking out of the Nou Camp, Geoff said to me, 'It'll never get any better than that.'

He was right. We went back to Sitges and drank the night away in a feeling of euphoria I'd never had before.

Manchester United's success gave Salford credibility throughout the world and to be there in our finest hour and to have known and met Alex Ferguson was something very special.

I've been fortunate to discover what a real gentleman he

was. I remember before that treble success when United were playing Wimbledon at Selhurst Park and I was going to take my son Gary to the game. It had rained all day and there was a rumour the match wasn't going to be on. Rocky rang me to say the match was definitely on and that he had spoken to Alex's secretary and two tickets were waiting for me at the players' entrance. I'd never been to the ground before and, as I drove up, a security guard put his hand up to stop me. Then he said, 'Oh, hello, John. Come with me.'

We parked right outside the players' entrance and asked about the tickets. Who should come down with them in his hand but Alex. I introduced him to my son and we talked a bit about the game at the weekend when we'd struggled against Everton, who were a bit of a bogey team. We were going on about the old days when Albert Dunlop used to play in goal for Everton in the fifties.

Alex said, 'I've got to go. I've got to have a word with the lads in the dressing room before the game.' Then, turning to my son, he added, 'Lovely to meet you, Gary.'

To remember his name when he'd only just met him spoke volumes. When we went into the ground we were sitting in the directors' seats. Alex watched the first half from there before going down to the touchline for the second. He could not have made us feel more welcome. And what a manager! He gave us back our identity and put Manchester United back where we thought we belonged.

Another unexpected fan of snooker was the actor Peter O'Toole. I learned of his interest – and that he knew of my existence – through Rocky Taylor. Rocky had spent five years out of the business while he was recovering from the injuries sustained on *Death Wish 3*, but, when he was fit enough to resume his stunt work, he was on a film with O'Toole in Ireland. When Peter asked him what he'd been doing with himself Rocky said he'd been going round with a snooker player pal.

'Which player?' asked Peter. 'I like snooker.'

'John Virgo,' Rocky replied.

'Oh, I love him,' Peter said. 'I'm his biggest fan. I bet he likes a bet.'

Rocky was amazed. 'He does,' he said, 'but how did you know that?'

'I can tell by the way he commentates,' Peter said.

Rocky was regularly involved with the Stunt Ball, held annually at the Grosvenor Hotel in London. That year he invited Peter O'Toole to join him on his table. However, by the time we'd started the meal, Peter hadn't arrived. Rocky, not wanting to have empty seats at his table, asked two people – a film producer he would ordinarily have invited and his wife – to move to his. No sooner had they sat down than Peter arrived, so Rocky had to move them back off again.

Peter O'Toole was a Hollywood legend, thanks to roles like Lawrence of Arabia, but all he wanted to talk about was what Dennis Taylor and Steve Davis were like and was asking me about all the other snooker players. He was like any other snooker fan. Despite his hellraiser reputation, he didn't have a drink and was a lovely man. It was a pleasure to meet him, and to have Peter O'Toole as a fan was a big feather in my cap.

That night Rocky had also invited former Yes keyboard player Rick Wakeman along. He agreed to do a spot on the piano. There was a big build-up from the DJ Mike Read, and I'm not sure whether the people there thought he was providing incidental music but you can imagine that, with 650 guests there, a 22-piece orchestra and all that was going on, no one was really listening. He finished to practically nothing and Mike Read said, 'OK, well that's the end of that. Let's carry on.' He didn't even give him a big send-off.

Rick came off pointing at Rocky. 'Don't ever invite me to come to any one of your dos again.' He stormed off with his wife.

There was another night that Dame Vera Lynn was the guest of honour. The forces' sweetheart – that's how she was introduced. Once again, there was a big twenty-two-piece orchestra on the stage. All the tables encircled the dance floor and at the bottom of the dance floor was the top table. When Vera was introduced and the orchestra started playing 'We'll Meet Again' everybody gave her a standing ovation. She did this slow walk down the middle of the dance floor – to do the raffle!

As with all raffles, it took about forty minutes to get through all the prizes. By the time it was over it was as if the audience had lost interest. It happens. If you're not winning a prize you don't pay much attention to who is. When it was all done and dusted, Vera had the slow walk back to her table, but this time there was near silence. Rocky spotted this and didn't like it, so he jumped out of his seat, ran up to the stage, grabbed the microphone and said, 'Come on, lads, let's hear it – for Dame Edna.'

The whole place fell about.

When he came down off the stage he came up to me and said, 'All right, what have I said now?' He hadn't even realised he'd said it.

Another story that typifies Rocky is the time during the movie memorabilia auction at the ball. I had been speaking to someone and returned to the table to hear someone say of Rocky, 'You're not going to believe what he's just done. You know that replica John Wayne gun they're auctioning off? He's only gone and paid £3,500 for it.'

'You're kidding,' I said.

Rocky came back to the table and he said, 'What do you think, John? I've always been a big fan of John Wayne. It's something I've always wanted. I've not done anything wrong, have I?'

I said, 'Rock, if you want it, you want it.'

All his stunt pals were saying what an idiot he was but I was trying to put a different slant on it.

By this time he'd opened his karaoke bar in Surrey. Jimmy White actually got him the gear cheap from Hong Kong. I assumed Rocky would get the gun framed and put behind the bar. 'Where are you going to put the gun, Rock?' I said.

'Oh I threw it in the bin,' he said. 'I can't bear to look at it any more.'

It cost him so much. But that was Rocky!

I discovered another unexpected snooker fan in Glasgow when I was up there doing an exhibition. I bumped into Billy Connolly in the hotel. He said how much he enjoyed the snooker. As I was walking away he said, 'And I really admire your work.' To which I invoked the spirit of Patrick Swayze from *Ghost* and replied, 'Ditto.'

It was nice to be recognised by people I admired because I had always assumed I operated under the radar as far as having respectability in the game was concerned.

Rolling Stone Ronnie Wood is another who always comes along to the Masters and spends three or four days taking in the action. Ronnie's always had a snooker table in his house and loves playing the game, too. Even now, Ronnie is still very rock'n'roll but one night I accompanied Jimmy White and Ronnie to a club. This was back when you could smoke indoors, but Ronnie and Jimmy had decided to quit. They were telling me that the patches they wore on their arms really worked. I was still smoking and having the occasional cigarette. After I lit my second they both looked at one another, took the patches off their arms and asked me for a cigarette. I duly obliged and watched as they smoked their fags and when they were done put the patches back on their arms! So much for willpower.

Not every celebrity I met was a snooker fan, however.

I was in Cyprus playing in a golf day, which my good friend Kenny Lynch had put his name to. A few celebrities were there: Robert Powell, best known for his performance as Jesus; P. H. Moriarty, who played Razors alongside Bob Hoskins in that great film *The Long Good Friday*; an actor from *The Bill*; myself and Rocky.

One night we were all sitting watching a football match when a couple who were there to be married came in. The woman instantly recognised me and got a bit excitable, trying to clamber over the other celebrities to get to me so she could sit and get a picture. As she clambered over Robert Powell, he said quite disdainfully, 'Go on, then, get your picture taken with the snooker player.'

Rocky leaped to my defence: 'Don't talk about John's profession like that.'

You wouldn't think it by hearing us both speak but Robert was also a Salford lad. However, after that little episode I didn't have a lot to say to him for the duration of the trip. When we were flying back he was across the aisle from me. I wasn't talking to him, he wasn't talking to me. Just as we were coming in to land at Heathrow, an air stewardess said, 'Do you mind if I get a picture taken.'

I was a bit dishevelled but I said, 'No problem.'

She didn't ask for a picture with Robert Powell. Virgo 2, Powell nil.

★ ★ ★

Big Break opened doors I'd never think possible – but there were some people who didn't have a clue who I was.

Each year after Wimbledon a charity celebrity tennis event is held at Queen's Club in west London. You could count the number of times I'd played tennis on one hand, but one year I was invited to take part. I was partnering former Wimbledon champion Virginia Wade against her fellow tennis star Annabel Croft and the jockey John Francome. The court was pristine – the grass was like a snooker table. I went down to hit a ball and collapsed on the court. Virginia stood over me. Obviously she wasn't a watcher of Saturday night television. 'These people really think you're funny, don't they?' she said.

When we had been warming up, John Francome had asked me if I played much tennis. I told him this was about the fifth time. 'You're a natural,' he said. You never know, maybe I could have been a tennis player had I not given my life to snooker. I haven't played since but I'm sure to this day Virginia still hasn't a clue who I was.

The opportunities presented thanks to *Big Break* seemed endless at times – but not all were as memorable as playing centre court at Queen's with a Wimbledon champion.

My managers, Dave Dee and Troy Dante – because they had experience in the music industry – thought it would be a great idea if I cashed in on the success of *Big Break* by releasing a record. After the Noel Edmonds experience I was wary but they found a writer who penned a song called 'Oh What a Game' and booked me into a studio in Liverpool to record it.

As Rocky and I drove there I felt a bit in awe. It wasn't as if the Beatles had ever recorded in the same studio but the fact that I was going to make a record in Liverpool, the city from which so much great music originated, was daunting.

We walked in and met the producer. As I was chatting to the writer I could hear in the background Rocky saying to the producer, 'If he gets through this pretty quick any chance of me recording "Green, Green Grass of Home" for my mother?' That was typical Rocky.

My family were all big singers, but whenever I'd sung before I always mimicked the original singer. If it was an Elvis song I'd sing it like Elvis. Now, to be given some words to sing without any idea of how anyone would sing them left me stumped. So I thought I'd do a Buddy Holly impression. After we recorded it, the writer said to me – and I'll never forget it – 'I wrote the words, you've made it into a masterpiece.'

I didn't know about that but I did have a surreal moment when I played an exhibition at a working men's club in Preston and my song was blasted out. To see all these guys in flat caps listening to me trying to do an impression of Buddy Holly was a bit strange, to say the least.

When you sing a song, the producer gets 50 per cent, the writer gets 50 per cent, so even with my basic grasp of maths that doesn't leave a lot. However, as the singer you get about 40p every time a song is played on the radio. Rocky was all for having a hundred singles printed. They would cost 50p each to make and we could have sold them for £2, but, with the

310

prospect of having all these records in the boot of my car, with the golf clubs being thrown in, I didn't think they would last that long. I looked at the cost of having the record produced and, when I realised I was going to have to pay but was getting only 40p per play, unlike Elvis in 'Jailhouse Rock', I reneged.

One opportunity I couldn't pass up, though, was the chance to be president of my local golf club, Hersham Village. I took over from Kenny Lynch but I had an auspicious start when the club first opened as an eighteen-hole course.

I had just bought a new lob wedge, which somebody said would improve my short game. My ball landed near a sign for the next tee but, with my new club, I thought it posed no obstacle. I hit the ball but thinned it and smashed the sign so hard my ball became embedded in it. Rodney Hutton, the director of golf, put the sign on the wall with a caption: 'VIRGO'S LATEST TRICK SHOT.'

Very funny! What I also found funny was that in two days someone nicked the ball!

Hersham is a great club and every year I host a charity golf day for the local hospice, which gets well supported. Rocky and I have a good evening on the karaoke. We get a few complaints because they can't get us off! My single may not have materialised but at the club they know all about my biggest hit!

CHAPTER 27

CALLING THE SHOTS

S nooker, I've had cause to think over the years, is at times its own worst enemy. Some things that happen in the game are strange. And one moment I found very strange indeed was when my mentor in the commentary box, Ted Lowe, was due to retire after fifty years as the 'voice of snooker'.

A lot was made about his retirement. Ted was presented with a set of crystal glasses and viewers were left in no doubt that the 1996 World Championship would be his last.

The final that year saw Stephen Hendry take on Peter Ebdon. The commentators' schedule had Ted Lowe down to cover the final frames after the last session break. Clive Everton was in the commentary box for the penultimate session. That was fair enough but no provision had been made in case the match finished early. As the match developed, Hendry was racing into a commanding 17–10 lead and needed just one more frame for victory. If Stephen won the next frame there would be no final

313

session and Ted Lowe wouldn't finish the match. I watched this unfold and told the producer there was a real danger Ted might miss out on the chance to take viewers through the final frame. The producer's response was that he didn't want to upset Clive Everton by asking him to step aside.

I was absolutely aghast. All this fuss about Ted Lowe's final year and yet here we had a very real situation that the 'voice of snooker', 'whispering Ted Lowe', whose hushed tones viewers had loved for half a century, would be silent after all he had done for the game.

I have to say I don't think this would have happened had the BBC been doing the broadcast, but this was a legacy of the Margaret Thatcher government's decision to outsource 25 per cent of the corporation's outside broadcast. It was an independent company in charge and once again we had a situation where no one wanted to upset Clive Everton, whose *Snooker Scene* already wielded an undue influence on the sport. To be fair to Clive, I'm sure if he had any idea of the fuss he would have happily stood aside.

Poor Ted was in such a state. His wife Jean was upset. It was mayhem.

Fortunately, the snooker gods came to the rescue and the unthinkable was avoided. Peter Ebdon won the next frame to take the final beyond the break. Ted was able to say his goodbyes to the British public, which he did in his customary immaculate fashion.

To think, though, that he might have been sitting in the Embassy suite listening to somebody else end that match would have been unforgivable – but that's snooker. Some of the decisions made by people are beyond belief.

I'd admired Ted a lot and have so much to thank him

for. He taught me so much about commentating. Something I've never mentioned before now is that I like to think I was instrumental in getting him an award. After those fifty years and his retirement, I took it upon myself to write a letter to the then Prime Minister Tony Blair suggesting that, after all his services to snooker, Ted deserved some sort of recognition. I got a letter back from the Prime Minister's secretary and to my great surprise and joy, while I was doing a pantomime in Hastings and was looking at a paper on New Year's Day, I saw that Ted had been honoured with an OBE. Hastings was only fifteen miles from where Ted lived, so I rang him up and congratulated him.

He said, 'Oh, John, I can't believe it. People from all over the world have been sending me congratulations. Why don't you come round and have a glass of champagne?'

The first chance I got I went to see him. He got a local newspaper photographer to take a picture of us. I never mentioned that I'd written to the Prime Minister. I was just happy to see the joy on his face. He had lost touch with people in Australia and New Zealand and other countries and the great thing about receiving an honour like that was that many of his old friends got in contact. They were all sending telegrams and ringing him up to congratulate him. Whether it was my letter or not I don't know, but it was joyful to see how happy he was.

I invited Ted and Jean to watch the pantomime in Hastings. They sat in the house seats and, when the time came for us to drench the audience with our super-squirters, I didn't have the heart to soak him. I'm sure he'd have loved it but I didn't want to spoil the illusion of Ted Lowe the man.

I learned a lot from Ted. The commentary catchphrase

that everyone shouts at me in the street 'Where's the cue ball going?' I give Ted Lowe credit for that. I heard him saying it in his hushed tones. I raised it up a notch and I've used it ever since. It keeps the watching audience alert and if they're falling asleep it wakes them up and makes them focus on the table.

I don't mean to do Ted down because I consider him the best commentator snooker has had, but I think the one thing that he had in his favour was that he didn't know a great deal about the technical side of the game. He wouldn't start calling and describing shots; he'd leave that to someone else. That was a good way to commentate.

Now most of the commentators are experts and sometimes we are guilty of going into a bit too much detail and maybe Ted had it just right. He gave it atmosphere.

He started off as a marker, when Joe Davis used to play the Leicester Square Hall. Then, when they brought cameras in he began commentating, but because the players were in the same hall he whispered so he wouldn't be heard. He didn't profess to know much about snooker but he made up for any deep knowledge of the game by being interested in the players and the sense of theatre. He didn't rely on the pages of notes we have today. He spoke to the players and built his knowledge naturally.

Ted was good company and he had an impish sense of humour, but he thought snooker should be played in a certain way – a gentleman's way. Someone once said to him there were some good players in a club nearby in Sheffield. He went to have a look and when he came back he said, 'All I saw were people running around bashing balls all over the place. That's not snooker.'

That's probably why he didn't much like Alex Higgins and

his style of play. He liked this more genteel way of walking around the table. Like all the people from that era, he loved Joe Davis. He always said that Davis was twenty-one points better than any other player. No matter what happened in the era of Steve Davis and Stephen Hendry, he still wouldn't change his tune.

After his retirement, Ted and Jean came to Sheffield to watch the snooker but sadly his health deteriorated and after a while he became too ill to visit. On the morning of the first session of the 2011 World Championship final we received the heartbreaking news that he had passed away at the age of ninety. As was appropriate, his passing was announced to the audience, the players who were still there and the commentators, but then, to my horror, they decided to have a minute's applause in his honour. I couldn't believe that for a man who helped create such a reverential atmosphere we couldn't have a moment's silence to reflect.

I can see why they have a minute's applause at some football matches in case the silence is disrupted but, in a theatre of 950, people no one would have said a word.

I was the only person who didn't applaud.

Afterwards some people rang up. Why wasn't John Virgo clapping like everyone else? I felt it totally inappropriate and I refused to join in and I think Ted would have agreed with me. I wanted to stand there quietly and have Ted in my thoughts.

I had lots of good memories to draw upon. One of my favourites was then I bumped into Ted at Newmarket. My friend Geoff Baxter had got up early one morning to watch the horses on the gallops and we went back to the hotel for breakfast to find Ted in the restaurant looking the worse for wear. He'd been a guest speaker at an event the night before.

'Heavy night last night,' he said. 'Feeling really rough.'

'I've got just the thing for you,' I said and I went upstairs and got some Alka-Seltzer. While I was gone he'd ordered a bottle of champagne. A hair of the dog, as he would have put it. I have a lovely vision, as I left the breakfast room, of Ted sitting there with a glass of champagne in one hand and an Alka-Seltzer chaser in the other. What a pro!

★ ★ ★

Ted taught me lots of things during our time in the commentary box but one thing he couldn't counsel was how to avoid those moments when you can't help upsetting people.

When I moved into commentary I soon learned that you have to be careful because, although the players can't hear what you're saying, they have plenty of people backstage who can.

I remember one young lad, Anthony Davies, from Wales, who was playing at the Crucible for the first time. He played a shot and was a bit short on the pink but he had a straight blue to the top pocket. This was in my early days of commentating and I said Anthony had a bit of pressure on the blue but he had to take it on. He decided to play safe and I said, 'Well he's not going to win a World Championship if he's refusing shots like that.'

When I got back into the players' room his mentor came at me.

'You shouldn't be saying things like that,' he fired. 'Do you know that lad's out there playing for his life?'

I said, 'Listen, I've been out there playing for *my* life and I'm telling you: if he's going to turn shots like that down he ain't ever going to be world champion.'

Sometimes the mentors tell young players not to go for risky shots. He was a lovely lad, Anthony, but he didn't fulfil his early potential. You've got to give your ability a chance and go for your shots. There's a fine line between an honest opinion and a sympathetic opinion. I don't go out of my way to criticise a player because I've been there. If I say a player will be disappointed with a shot, he will be disappointed. If I say it's a bad shot, he doesn't need me to say it. He'll know, and I'm not having a go at him personally: I'm explaining how he will be thinking. My belief is that a good commentator should try to explain what is going on in a player's head.

The other lesson I've learned all too painfully is the question of bias. I've had occasions when producers have come up to me when Jimmy White's been playing saying, 'We've had a couple of complaints that you're sounding biased in your comments towards Jimmy.'

My reply is always, 'Yeah, because I want him to win! I can't help it.'

They've gone, 'OK, but try and calm it down a bit.'

The worst occasion didn't involve Jimmy, however. Prior to the World Championship in Sheffield I'm asked by a newspaper to give my predictions for the tournament. The first year I was asked to do it, in 2001, my selection was O'Sullivan – 'the Rocket'. He hadn't yet won a world title and there was still a question mark over his temperament, but he was playing well and it looked as if this could be his year. That was what I said publicly. Privately, I told my pals I thought John Higgins was the bet. The 1998 world champion was drawn in the opposite half to Ronnie and at 14–1 was surely the value option.

Higgins had a smooth run to the final, but so too had the

Rocket. It was a no-brainer. As it was too close to call, best to lay off and save their stake, which my pals did.

The final of the World Championship is played over two days. Although my pals had laid their bets off they still had a chance of a decent return if Higgins could overcome Ronnie. After the first two sessions of Day One, the match was close.

Come the final session on Day Two, though, it was obvious that Ronnie had his game face on. When he plays at his top level it is a joy to watch. My appreciation of his talent must have slipped into my commentary. During the interval before the final frames of the last session the executive producer, Graham Fry, informed me that they had received phone calls accusing me of being biased towards O'Sullivan.

Biased? If anything I wanted Higgins to win. As the one who encouraged others to place a bet, I had a vested interest.

Ronnie went on to beat Higgins 18–14.

Afterwards, however, I still asked myself whether some viewers would think I was favouring Ronnie. Maybe I got carried away. The Rocket had put on a masterclass, a performance worth eulogising over.

It's a mistake that can be easily made. I remember when Jimmy White led Stephen Hendry 14–8 in the 1992 final. Commentating on the last two frames of that third session and thinking it was all over, Ted Lowe was calling home Jimmy as the winner. Stephen won the next ten frames in one of the greatest comebacks the game had seen.

I thought no more about my own criticism.

However, two days after the O'Sullivan–Higgins final, I was at Celtic Manor for the World Snooker golf day. The first player I saw was John Higgins. I hadn't seen him after the final. I went over to give him my sympathies. Before I had a chance to say a word his wife approached me and slapped me across the face!

John held her back and apologised profusely for her actions. Maybe I had found the source of the complaints about my commentary, or maybe it was one of her friends.

I didn't ask for an explanation. Perhaps I deserved it.

A couple of years later I tipped John again for the title – and was delighted when he indeed went on to win. No financial gain for me, though.

It's hard to be neutral when you have a bet on!

During the World Championship I can sometimes be found outside the back door, among the trucks. It's the only place you can go to have a quiet smoke these days. I was out there in 2013 during my break after commentating on one of the first morning sessions, when the then reigning world champion Ronnie O'Sullivan appeared.

'Give us a fag, JV.'

Just seeing him at the tournament that year was something, given this was the first event he had chosen to play, never mind that he was out the back trying to score a cigarette. He tries his best not to smoke, but old habits die hard.

'No problem,' I said, handing him one.

There we were, blowing smoke into the clear blue sky.

Ordinarily, Ronnie would been favourite to retain his crown but, being out for a year and with his track record of personal issues and mercurial temperament, it was a brave man who would back him to become only the third person in history to regain the title at the Crucible, after Steve Davis and Stephen Hendry.

Nobody, including me, knew what to expect from the Rocket this year. Ronnie had got through his first-round match against the Scot Marcus Campbell comfortably, 10–4. In his post-match interview afterwards, however, he had said he wasn't comfortable with his tip. That type of comment from Ronnie would have set off alarm bells for those who backed him at 8–1 to lift his fifth world title.

'How's the tip?' I asked him.

'The best I have had for years,' he said, then, with a smile, he added, 'Get on.'

Talk about hearing it from the horse's mouth. The best price my pals got, after I passed on the good news, was 6–1. As a commentator for the BBC, it wouldn't be wise to have a bet but, as I said, old habits die hard and I was pleased to pass on how confident he was feeling about the tournament.

I was also pleased to see him go on to win at a canter, easing through the tournament without ever being behind, before beating Barry Hawkins 18–12 in the final.

It's difficult to mix business with pleasure. Commentating is my business, gambling is a guilty pleasure at best. Yet without the Rocket's guilty pleasure – that sneaky fag – I would never have known.

Nowadays the commentary box is filled with players I've spent a life with – Willie Thorne, Dennis Taylor, as well as Ken Doherty and Stephen Hendry. We all have a laugh and there's a great camaraderie between us.

I remember being in the box with Willie Thorne talking about 147 breaks. Willie, after our duel back in the early days, was nicknamed 'Mr Maximum', because of how many he made.

As we were speaking, Stephen Hendry came into the box. He was trying out the commentating to see if he fancied doing it on a regular basis.

'How many maximums is it you've made in your career, Willie?' I asked him.

'Oh, a hundred and ninety-eight,' he replied, 'but I'll never make another one.'

We switched off our mics and I turned to Stephen and asked him the same question. The most successful player the game has ever known shrugged. 'I stopped counting at four hundred,' he said.

The following day I was back in the commentary box and another player looked on for a 147. I recalled my conversation the previous day.

'Yesterday I was asking Willie Thorne, who was known as "Mr Maximum", how many hundred and forty-sevens he made and he said a hundred and ninety-eight, but wouldn't make any more,' I told viewers. 'Stephen Hendry was with us and I asked him how many he'd made . . .'

As I was speaking I could see my mobile phone light up. It was a message from Willie. 'You twat!'

I've been privileged to witness some magical moments in the commentary box. I was with Dennis Taylor at the Crucible in 1997 when Ronnie made his maximum in just five minutes, twenty seconds. It was unbelievable, an absolute blur. After I congratulated him, he said, 'John, I don't know how I potted the brown – I was shaking like a leaf.' He must have been on autopilot. It's a record that will never be beaten.

Commentators might have their detractors but I do believe that by giving our opinions we can help players and provide an insight. Look at the breadth of knowledge in the commentary box these days: Willie Thorne was a great break builder; Stephen Hendry is a seven-times world champion. I hope I do the same and bring some knowledge and experience.

Players like Ronnie, Jimmy and Stephen, when I'm doing the commentary, respect my opinion. It may be from another era and I may not have the World Championship on my CV but they respect the fact that I could play at the very highest level.

But we don't take ourselves too seriously. Jimmy White told me he was talking to a guy who had a snooker-commentary drinking game with his three mates. If Ken, with his Irish lilt, says 'tirty-tree' they knock back a shot of tequila. If Willie says, 'It's a frame winning opportunity' it's another shot, likewise if Dennis mentions the 1985 final. For me, they knock back one if I say, 'Where's the cue ball going?'

Listening to the four of us, they won't be sober for long!

CHAPTER 28

GETTING A RESULT

When I look back on my career, I find it incredible how much snooker has changed. I was lucky enough to be there just as the game was opening up further – after John Spencer and Ray Reardon had broken down the barriers for other players to turn professional.

From its origins as a parlour game, through the temperance clubs for the working class to a multibillion-dollar sport, the culture of snooker has undergone a dramatic transformation.

The likes of Joe and Fred Davis and John Pulman dominated the scene before the professional era but their lifestyle was so much different from what it is for players today. I remember going to the opening of a club where John Pulman was signing a bottle of whisky he had just drunk – and he was about to open another one. That was the culture back then, one of late nights and hard drinking – and there were many legendary drinkers. It was a different culture from the one that exists today. Now there are so many tournaments, it's more serious.

The drinking culture wasn't limited to the players. When we had the early starts at the Crucible, at eleven o'clock David Vine would look at his runner and say, 'I think it's time.' The next thing you knew she came back with a glass of red wine. Now, if you saw someone drinking alcohol you'd wonder what was going on.

Steve Davis changed the culture completely. He was, to me, the first real dedicated professional snooker player. He was very single-minded. Before Steve's domination of the eighties, the bread and butter for the rest of us was the exhibitions. There we honed our skills – but it could affect your match play. John Spencer once admitted to me that, during an exhibition, he often deliberately left himself straight on with pots so he would have to perform a deep screw to get into position, which earned a round of applause from the audience. But he said he could tell some elements of his exhibition game were creeping into his match play. He got into the habit of playing crowd pleasers and, because we weren't playing that many tournaments, we weren't always match sharp. In those early days we didn't have practice tables. Now they complain that there are so many players and only a few tables and they have to put their names on a list. We never had that problem because we didn't have any tables!

We found that for the first couple of frames we were getting our cue out and trying to get going. People like Spencer – and me at times – were slow starters, but you have to remember we would have to drive to wherever we were playing and go straight out onto the table. Now, the players are always on practice tables, getting into their stride, which is how it should be.

An interviewer once asked me, nearing the end of the 1980s, whether I had any new impersonations. I replied that Steve Davis had been so successful with a winning formula that the majority of the players coming through then were copying his style. So, I said, if you do Steve Davis you're doing 90 per cent of the modern players. That led to the headline, 'DAVIS IS RUINING THE GAME, SAYS VIRGO'. I never said that at all. What I meant was he was ruining my act!

Before Davis and the television revolution, snooker players had to develop their own styles and characteristics.

Then, after Davis, we had Stephen Hendry, whose long, drawn cuing action was mimicked by many. Television allowed up-and-coming players to study the styles of the top names. And the widespread coverage of snooker led to changes that viewers – well, some of them, anyway – may not have realised.

One year at the World Championship, the producer Nick Hunter told Mike Watterson he'd had a phone call from a woman saying she'd watched someone play a ball towards the middle pocket. It wasn't going in but she watched it turn and slip into the pocket. Mike explained that this was due to the nap of the cloth. It was brushed and ironed one way so, when a ball went up against the nap, it had a tendency to turn slightly.

Nick frowned. 'That doesn't look good, you know.'

The next thing we knew, the tables were covered in new superfine cloth and nothing turned. The balls all ran straight. And this was all because of one woman's call. All our lives we had been playing to allow for this drift; all of a sudden, there's no drift. Everybody tells me that the middle-pocket potting of the players today is unbelievable. But they don't have a thought in their head that it's going to drift, they are just aiming for the pocket.

The balls have evolved, too, over the years. They used to be a lot heavier. Now, every player carries a cue extension, meaning there's less call for the extended cue and rest that used to sit by the side of the table.

A lot of people have made snooker – which came on leaps and bounds from the early days – so watchable. One of the main people responsible for that was David Vine, who was a consummate professional. When he was presenting it was very much the David Vine show. We also had David Icke, who presented for a while, and Eamonn Holmes had a run at it, but they weren't, shall I say, exactly welcomed by David. He was in command and he set the standards. Even today, I never see the presenters use an autocue, so Hazel Irvine has carried on David's traditions and does a tremendous job.

The broadcasters have a difficult job putting together a live programme, so obviously the length of time a frame takes becomes an issue when you are broadcasting live. This came to a head when Peter Ebdon was playing reigning champion Ronnie O'Sullivan in the 2005 World Championship. The majority of people watching, including the people in the production team, were rooting for Ronnie because they wanted the biggest stars to stay in. Although Ronnie was well in front, Peter made this great comeback to win 13–11. In the studio during the match they were making the point about how long Peter was taking for each shot. At one stage he took five minutes for a break of twelve, the same time Ronnie had taken to complete a maximum. John Parrott, in the studio giving the expert analysis, was saying it wasn't right he was taking so long. Ronnie was standing on his chair, scratching his head and it was a little bit of mayhem, but, fair play to Peter, he found a way to beat probably the most talented player ever.

Peter told me that, after he had won the match, he went into the studio absolutely elated, only to be greeted by the interviewer, asking, 'Do you think it's fair to win a match like that?' He didn't understand what they meant. He said he couldn't believe it. He felt as though they were almost accusing him of cheating when in his mind he'd just pulled off the greatest victory of his life.

Sometimes in sport the tournament demands the best players at the business end. We were perhaps guilty of that with Higgins. But any sport needs it. The viewing figures for golf have dropped since Tiger Woods has not been competing. Snooker can't afford a similar drop-off in interest.

It's not just the players to whom the game owes thanks. Peter Dyke, the Embassy PR man, fought snooker's corner with the sponsors and upped the prize money. He really had the benefit of the game at heart. You can understand his disappointment, therefore, when celebrations were held to mark the twenty-fifth anniversary of the World Championship at the Crucible and the players who had won more than half the prize money during those years – Steve Davis, six times, and Stephen Hendry, seven times – were the only two past winners who were invited but didn't attend. One other champion wasn't present – Alex Higgins – but he wasn't invited. I wonder why.

Some people say that, as the game has become more professional, the standard has improved. I don't think that's necessarily true. I think we just have more good players now. I don't think there are any shots they play today that I couldn't play.

To compare eras is difficult, because of how the game and the culture have changed, but for me several players stand out, for different reasons. I think the key to being considered a great is longevity. All true greats keep returning year after year. Steve Davis and Stephen Hendry made the breakthrough in their teens and were able to dominate for years. Ray Reardon and John Spencer also managed to enjoy long careers. For Ronnie O'Sullivan, who at the time of writing is in his forties, to be still producing is remarkable.

I used to think comparing different eras in some sports was straightforward. For example, with running, if someone can post a quicker time, then surely they must be faster. However, in the 800 metres, although Sebastian Coe had broken the world record in 1981, the coach of New Zealand athlete Peter Snell, the 1964 double Olympic gold medallist, said that, although on the face of it Coe had run a much quicker time than Snell, if Peter was in front with 100 yards to go no one could catch him. So time isn't everything and, similarly with snooker, records aren't everything and therefore it is hard to compare the three greats: Davis, Hendry and O'Sullivan.

If only I had a penny for the number of times I have been asked who was the best player I have seen. Not an easy question, as all the great players have won multiple tournaments.

When snooker came to the notice of the general public, in the early days it was Joe Davis who was the dominant figure.

Joe was the man who introduced professional snooker. It was mainly thought this was due to the fact he couldn't beat the Australian Walter Lindrum at billiards. He decided that snooker gave him a better chance of becoming a world champion, and so it turned out, as he retired unbeaten.

After Joe came his brother Fred. He too had multiple World

Championships to his name. The last name from that era, when a championship was played on a challenge basis, was John Pullman.

I am a firm believer that, if you have a great talent, you would be able to compete in any era. John Spencer was to me the forerunner of the modern game. He and Ray Reardon were responsible for the game opening up.

Alex Higgins's lifestyle would have not been conductive with the modern game, but I am sure he would have to change. Steve Davis was the ultimate professional, and set the standard for those who followed.

When I mention Alex changing his lifestyle, that would also apply to Jimmy White. I know that Jimmy loved Alex, particularly the way he played. But emulating the Hurricane was probably why he has never won a world championship; it's certainly not through lack of ability.

Stephen Hendry, seven times champion of the world, started a new wave of snooker players from north of the border, John Higgins being the most notable. At the same time John Higgins turned professional, so did Welshman Mark Williams, as well as a certain Ronnie O'Sullivan. Ronnie is without doubt the most naturally gifted player I have ever seen. The fact that he can play with either hand makes him even more remarkable.

That said, however, if I was to mark them out of ten, for safety I'd give Steve Davis ten out of ten, which would mark him higher than Stephen, maybe, not Ronnie. Temperament? I'd put Hendry ten. Potting ability? Hendry ten. Cue-ball control? I'd put Ronnie ahead of the other two, but only just. It's the touch they have and the way they get down to the shot; it is one of the most important facets of snooker. Lots of people can pot balls but controlling that cue ball to make the next shot just as easy is an art in itself. When you look at the top players, with very few exceptions it's clear that you won't be a true great unless you have good cue-ball control. Those young lads had it in spades.

When you talk about natural ability, it has to be Ronnie. Putting all the required skills together and the fact that O'Sullivan can play with either hand, I would give him the edge over those two.

I once told Ronnie, while watching him play an exhibition match in Scotland with Hendry, 'You're the best there's ever been.'

'Really, JV?' he said. 'Better than Davis and Hendry?'

'Better than Higgins,' I said.

'Higgins?' Ronnie looked incredulous. 'Over those two?'

'Alex Higgins,' I told him, 'thought of the table as his stage.' He was the player people came to see. And Ronnie has that quality that elevates him above the rest.

It's all a matter of opinion, though. When Steve Davis was regarded the best ever, before Hendry and O'Sullivan came along, Ted Lowe was convinced Joe Davis would have beaten them.

Whenever people talk about the best players who have ever lived, invariably the one who doesn't get quoted among the true greats, because of the absence of a world title, is Jimmy White. But, for me, Jimmy had just about everything. As a young player he had the temperament. His safety wasn't as good as Davis's or O'Sullivan's, but his break building was there; his cue-ball control was there.

Jimmy's been around a long time but he will always be remembered for not winning the World Championship. What people forget is that it is a very tough competition. I can't think of any other individual sporting tournament that lasts seventeen days. Before the game was opened up, remember, it was played over a week and on a challenge basis.

For someone like Jimmy, seventeen days was a long time. He got to six finals, an incredible achievement in itself, but by each time, mentally, I think he was tired. I've heard people tell stories about Jimmy being his own worst enemy, staying out late and not coming back to his hotel until 6 a.m. However, when we first went there, we used to start at 10.30 a.m. and we were players who didn't use to get up until that time. It was totally foreign to us. Jimmy was probably just getting up, going for a walk and trying to wake himself up.

When he made the 147 at the Crucible he rang me at eleven o'clock that night and said, 'I've just won £147,000. Do you want to go out for a drink?' It was understandable that he couldn't sleep: he was on a natural high after an incredible achievement. I couldn't have slept had I been in his shoes, either. I couldn't have imagined Steve or Stephen wanting to go out, though. We had a drink but we didn't overdo it and we weren't out late. But, then, the rumours start circulating about Jimmy being out all night and returning to his hotel room at 3 a.m.

There was a lot for Jimmy to contend with and often, by the end of the tournament, he was spent. I can remember in one final it went to the deciding frame against Stephen Hendry and Jimmy missed a black off the spot. To me that was mental tiredness. That cost him a couple of opportunities to win the title he coveted most. But he won every other tournament the game had to offer.

Jimmy once made a shot that I defy any snooker player to try to play it. It was in Kingston Snooker Club. He put a red ball over one of the corner pockets and the cue ball in the jaws of the corner pocket diagonally across. He potted the red and without hitting a cushion screwed the cue ball back into the pocket from where it had left. I was so amazed I didn't even try it myself but later I put it into my book of trick shots. Technically, it's not one but I included it as a token of respect for Jimmy White's cue power.

I remember with these players that, from the first moment I saw them play, I knew they were special.

I first saw Ronnie O'Sullivan when he was up against a player Troy Dante had signed. I was among only three or four people watching but I could see then the boy was class.

Players such as Ray Reardon, Steve Davis and Stephen Hendry were great champions, while others, such as Dennis, Taylor provided shocks that offered memorable moments. But snooker owes the likes of Alex Higgins, Jimmy White and Ronnie O'Sullivan a huge debt of gratitude for giving the game its star appeal.

I think the game is now sold. It has got its viewing figures but it still needs that type of player that can excite an audience. As I've said, I've always thought of snooker as theatre and, when you have the blend of the unpredictable raw talent against the pure professionalism, that's when snooker is at its best. The standards the game is famous for, set by Joe Davis and his era, remain today and it makes me proud to be part of a game where sportsmanship is so very important.

From those early days, when we struggled to find the tournaments, to the modern game, with record prize money and opportunities, there is still the issue of a few players getting a large slice of the cake, while other players are struggling to make a living – but that is the nature of sport.

I remember in 2000 when Mark Williams beat Matthew Stevens in the final of the World Championship and they both drove up in yellow Ferraris to the reception that Embassy put on. What a difference from my Morris Marina!

Only a select few will get the chance to enjoy luxuries like that, but the game continues to evolve with more tournaments and more professionals. I only hope that, with the continual drive to modernise the game, the governing body doesn't lose sight of what makes it unique and popular. Barry Hearn – who left the game temporarily to focus on boxing and other sports, but has since returned to become chairman of the WPBSA's commercial arm, the World Snooker Association – has said that when people come along to watch snooker they like to see a finish. In the World Championship they don't necessarily get that because of the length of the matches.

There's a trend in sport to develop short-form versions of the main game. They can have the quick-fire tournaments and shootouts if they think it will attract a new audience but if you start diluting the World Championship, as has been mooted, you are on a slippery slope, because there's a danger every tournament will just blend into one. The World Championship has to be protected. Every sport has to preserve its history.

When I won the UK Championship, the final was the best of twenty-seven, played over three sessions. Now, in the earlier rounds, which used to be best of seventeen, they play best of eleven, like the Masters and everything else. Some of the players have said that the UK has been spoiled by the reduction of frames. It's nice to compare how people won their finals and it's a measure over two days who the best player is. The UK has been diluted, but that's as far as you want to go. If you start to reduce the frames in the World Championship all the history of matches gone by will have no bearing on what's happening today. We have forty years of history at the Crucible and people can hark back and know exactly what type of match it was just by looking at the frame score.

Barry was originally in favour of making every tournament consist of longer matches. Now his views seem to have changed.

I like Barry and, overall, he has been a force of good in the game, but not everything has to be a quick fix. You can't make changes to suit television if it is to the detriment of the game. Ted Lowe used to say that money would be the ruination of snooker. Was he right? I don't think the likes of Steve Davis, Stephen Hendry and Ronnie O'Sullivan would agree. If you're a player you're not going to argue with any increases in prize money. I don't agree, either, because the only way you are going to get youngsters taking up the game is by dangling that carrot that you can be a millionaire if you're successful.

If I have one worry, it's that, when the game took off at the end of the seventies, there were snooker clubs opening up everywhere. There are not many clubs opening today. Where are the future British champions going to come from? I don't know. In China, where the game is taking off, there are clubs with 350 tables inside. We have nothing like that.

You could argue that it's never been easier for young players to come through and make an impact because the short-match format makes shocks more likely. In a best-of-seven match a top-ranking player might still be getting warmed up and suddenly they're out. It's cutthroat and I'm envious of the young players today and the number of tournaments they can play. When I first turned professional, when you were knocked out of one tournament you had to wait four months for the next one. Now the players move from one tournament to the next. It may be cutthroat but I do think the top players need some protection. It's OK putting on these ranking events but I think they should be able to pick and choose the events. I know they can but if they miss some they can soon slip down the rankings. That would be a shame if the top players aren't going to be there in the latter stages. They are the household names and we're losing them.

Perhaps the money is unsustainable. There are more opportunities for players but has it benefited the game?

My old friend from my amateur days, Paul Medati, found that, when he opened a snooker club in Stockport, there were so many players turning professional – and consequently getting to practise for free – that they were doing his money in. He had to restrict the number who could use the club. That illustrates an imbalance we have today.

Me? I had ambitions to be the best in the world, but a combination of turning professional late, giving too many of my best years to the politics of the game and being at the mercy of my own unpredictable temperament saw me fall just short of the game's biggest honours.

But I have no regrets. Snooker has taken me all around the world and given me opportunities I could never have dreamed of when I was an amateur.

For as long as the BBC want me I will continue to commentate and with the live commentary I have found another little niche, which I hope can continue.

As snooker has evolved, so too have I managed to adapt to keep pace.

When I look back to those early days in the backstreets of Salford through some wonderful memories on the green baize I can only consider myself lucky.

SAY GOODNIGHT, JV

As I say to Jimmy White when we reminisce about what we've achieved, we got a result.

We got a result!

EPILOGUE

I never had any intention of writing my autobiography, but Richard Johnson, the CEO of Bonnier Publishing, along with my publisher wife, Rosie, insisted it had to be done.

Who would be interested in my life story, I asked?

But the more I wrote the more I learnt about myself – Rosie was right, it did prove to be cathartic.

However, I didn't see any necessity to go into my private life too much – I feel I made such a mess of it. We all make mistakes and the key is to learn from them.

On 9 February 2010 Rosie and I – after a twenty-year acquaintance – were married. Given my track record she made a brave decision, and this time I was determined there would be no messing up.

The daughter of a Royal Marine brigadier and the granddaughter of a Royal Marine Commandant-General, Rosie is organised, disciplined, charming and bloody funny.

Who would have thought it? But they do say that opposites attract, and I can be bloody funny as well. Unfortunately, both her father and grandfather had passed away many years before we got together – what they would have made of me is anyone's guess!

However, I did get to meet her mother. When we first went to visit I was full of trepidation. I need not have worried – gracious, cultured, and with a mischievous sense of humour, she immediately put me at ease and we hit it off right from the start. It wasn't long before we realised that we had a few things in common. She loved sport and especially horse racing, which was right up my street. Although she passed a couple of years after our marriage, I still look back on those few years with great fondness. The knowledge that Rosie and I were together made her very happy.

Whenever we can take a break from our busy schedules we love to go on holiday. Before Rosie, holidays for me consisted of golf trips – I never went anywhere without my clubs. All that has changed. I have been to places I would never have dreamt of, eaten food I would never have touched. Life with Rosie is an endless, exciting adventure – I am lucky to be married to her and I think the world of her.

My two children live close by, and to be part of their lives and watch them make their way in the world is a true blessing. My daughter, Brook-Leah, is happily married and my son, Gary, is also in a good place. Although – like me – he loves the horse racing... I just hope he has learnt from my mistakes!

Lessons I have learnt over the years will stand me in good stead. Lucky me to get another chance.